D0801890

Refinding
the Object
and
Reclaiming
the Self

Refinding
the Object
and
Reclaiming
the Self

David E. Scharff, M.D.

JASON ARONSON INC.
Northvale, New Jersey
London

Production Editors: Judith D. Cohen and Adelle Krauser

This book was set in 11/13 point Palacio by Lind Graphics of Upper Saddle River, New Jersey, and printed and bound by Haddon Craftsmen of Scranton, Pennsylvania.

The author gratefully acknowledges permission to reprint or adapt from the following:

"Painful Memories" in *Medical Aspects of Human Sexuality*, June 1985. Adapted by permission of *Medical Aspects of Human Sexuality*.

Excerpts from *The Oedipus Rex of Sophocles: An English Version*, by Dudley Fitts and Robert Fitzgerald, copyright © 1949 by Harcourt Brace Jovanovich, Inc. and renewed 1977 by Cornelia Fitts and Robert Fitzgerald. Reprinted by permission of the publisher. CAUTION: All rights, including professional, amateur, motion picture, recitation, lecturing, public reading, radio broadcasting, and television are strictly reserved. Inquiries on all rights should be addressed to Harcourt Brace Jovanovich, Inc., Orlando, FL 32887.

Figures 1 and 3 in Chapter 3 from *The Sexual Relationship: An Object Relations View of Sex and the Family*, by David E. Scharff, Routledge & Kegan Paul, 1982. Reprinted by permission of Routledge, Chapman Hall.

Portions of "In Memory of Sigmund Freud" by W. H. Auden from *W. H. Auden: Collected Poems* by W. H. Auden, ed. by Edward Mendelson. Copyright © 1940 and renewed 1968 by W. H. Auden. Reprinted by permission of Random House, Inc. and Faber and Faber Ltd.

Library of Congress Cataloging-in-Publication Data

Scharff, David E., 1941–
    Refinding the object and reclaiming the self / by David E. Scharff.
        p. cm.
    Includes bibliographical references and index.
    ISBN 0-87668-458-4
    1. Object relations. 2. Psychotherapy. I. Title.
    [DNLM: 1. Ego. 2. Object Attachment. 3. Psychoanalysis Therapy.
WM 460.5.02 S311r]
RC489.025S32 1992
150.2'2 – dc20
DNLM/DLC
for Library of Congress   91-45257

Manufactured in the United States of America. Jason Aronson Inc. offers books and cassettes. For information and catalog write to Jason Aronson Inc., 230 Livingston Street, Northvale, New Jersey 07647.

To my patients
whose trust and generosity
fill these pages

. . . the theory has not yet properly conceptualized Buber's "I–Thou" relation, two persons being both ego and object to each other at the same time, and in such a way that their reality as persons becomes, as it develops in the relationship, what neither of them would have become apart from the relationship. This is what happens in good marriages and friendships. Winnicott describes its beginnings in the evolving pattern of a good mother–infant relationship. This raises the fundamental question: how far can we know and be known by one another? It is what psychotherapy seeks to make possible for the patient who cannot achieve it in normal living. It raises the question Winnicott . . . says psychoanalysis has not yet faced: "What is life about, apart from illness?"

—Harry Guntrip, *Schizoid Phenomena,*
Object Relations, and the Self (1969)

Contents

Preface   xv

PART ONE
SELF AND OBJECT IN PSYCHOTHERAPY

1. Adam   3
   The Dream as Transference 4 • The
   Dream's Communication about the Analyst 6

2. **Self and Object Intertwined**   9
The Inextricability of Self and Object *14* • The Self
within the Object *16* • The Self and the
Object *23* • The Object within the Self *25* • Self
and Object Mutually Held *26*

3. **Contextual and Focused Transference and
Countertransference**   29
Fairbairn's Contributions to an Object Relations
Theory of the Personality *30* • Melanie Klein's
Contributions *37* • Winnicott's Mother
and Child *44* • Winnicott's True and False
Self *45* • Reconciling Winnicott's Transitional
Phenomena and Bion's Container/
Contained *47* • The Therapeutic
Process *49* • Transference and
Countertransference *50* • A Current View of
Transference and Countertransference *53* •
Contextual and Focused Transference *54* • The
Relationship between Patient and Therapist *57* •
Transference and Countertransference in Conjoint
Therapy *58* • Adam's Evolving Treatment *59*

PART TWO
THERAPY OF THE SELF IN RELATION TO OBJECTS

4. **Using Transference and Countertransference
to Understand Projective and Introjective
Identification in a Couple**   69
The Initial Countertransference *71* • Enacting
Co-therapy Countertransference *75* • Working
through Countertransference *78* • Clarifying the
Couple's Envy and Sexual Relationship *84* • Co-
therapy and Countertransference *93*

5. **Changing Internal Object Relations in the
Psychotherapy of an Adolescent**   95
Tammy's Treatment as a Young Child *96* • The
Course of Adolescent Treatment *102* • Tammy

Refinds Her Father   *109*   •   A New Self and a New
Relationship to Her Mother   *112*   •   Termination   *116*

6. **The Therapeutic Transformation of Screen Memories**   121
    Earliest Memories   *123*   •   Memories of Later
    Childhood   *127*   •   Adolescent Memories   *129*   •
    Distortion of Adult Memories   *130*

7. **The Birth of the Self in Therapy**   135
    Delivering the Self: The Case of Fernando
    Gonzales   *137*   •   Building a Resilient
    Self   *149*   •   Refinding the Therapist's Self   *152*

PART THREE
THE OBJECT RELATIONS OF DREAMS

8. **The Dream as Communication between Self and Others**   157
    Fairbairn's Discovery that Dreams Depict the Structure
    of Self and Object   *161*   •   The Dream as
    Interpersonal Communication   *163*   •   The Family's
    Object Relations   *164*   •   Projective Identification and
    Unconscious Communication   *165*   •   The
    Transference Meaning of the Dream   *166*   •   The
    Dream as Interpersonal Communication in Individual
    Therapy   *166*   •   Dreams in Couple
    Assessment   *172*   •   Dreams in Group and
    Institutional Settings   *176*   •   The Dream in Social
    and Cultural Communication   *180*

9. **Dreams in Marital Therapy**   183
    Clive and Lila: Decreasing Distance   *184*   •   Shirley
    and Sam: Examining Interlocking
    Dreams   *196*   •   Don and Maggie: Interlocking
    Dreams of a Couple Ready for Termination   *203*

10. **Dreams in Therapy of Families with Adolescents**   207
    The Reluctant Drag-In   *209*   •   "My Parents Weren't
    Looking while I Grew Up!"   *217*   •   The Dream in
    Sally's Individual Session   *223*

PART FOUR
SELF AND OBJECT FROM THE VANTAGE OF THE FAMILY

11. **Oedipus Revisited in His Family**   233
    The Infant's Invention of the Family *234* • The
    Internal Couple *238* • Oedipus'
    Family *239* • The Wheeler Family *249*

12. **Role Relationships of Children and Adults
    in the Family**   263
    Partners-of-the-Moment *267* • The Child as an
    Incomplete Entity *269* • The Parent as the
    Leader *270* • Children and Adults: Similarities and
    Differences *271* • The Child as Container instead
    of Contained *274* • The Simpson
    Family *277* • Reparation Leads to Growth and
    Differentiation *286* • The Differentiating
    Elements *288* • Child and Adult Differences in the
    Internal Family *290* • The Role and Emotional
    Position of the Therapist *291*

13. **The Interlocking of Self and Object during
    Life Development**   295
    Violette La France *298* • The Holmes
    Family *299* • Adolescent Echoes of Parental
    Blocked Development *305*

PART FIVE
REFINDING THE SELF THROUGH REFOUND OBJECTS

14. **The Object Relations of the Therapist**   309
    Mrs. Mills and the Smith Family *310* • The Role of
    the Therapist's Unique History *314* • Vulnerability
    and Learning *317*

15. **The Object Refound and the Self Reclaimed**   319
    Sandra *319* • The Goals of Therapy *328* • Eve
    Faces Termination *329*

16. Epilogue: Refinding Our Selves through
    Our Patients   337

References   341

Index   355

Preface

This book investigates the way each of us is dependent
on others throughout life, and the way our self-image is
drawn from others—always relying on our relationship
to others while being at the same time our own unique
creation. In this study, the works of Fairbairn, Klein,
and Winnicott are the foundations of my theoretical
views. I also build on what I have learned from many
people, some from their writings, some from the
teaching and supervision they have given me, and some

from the privilege of colleagueship and mutual facilitation. Here, I list some of those to whom I feel the most obvious indebtedness.

I have learned at first from the prolonged tutelage of my psychiatric training at Massachusetts Mental Health Center and the Beth Israel Hospital in Boston as well as Children's Hospital National Medical Center in Washington, DC. The year of study that had the most impact on my early career was spent at the Tavistock Centre in London. Many of my teachers and colleagues there have continued to influence and support me in the ensuing years. I am also grateful to my teachers and colleagues at the Washington Psychoanalytic Institute for the support and teaching during my training in child and adult psychoanalysis. And for the last fifteen years, my colleagues and students at the Washington School of Psychiatry have contributed enormously to my work. Particularly, Mauricio Cortina, Justin Frank, Macario Giraldo, Joseph Lichtenberg, Gerald Perman, Charles Privitera, Kent Ravenscroft, Charles Schwarzbeck, Roger Shapiro, Robert Winer, and John Zinner have shared various aspects of theoretical and clinical interests over many years.

In exploring many facets of the relationship of self to other, I draw on the work of many writers and clinicians whose influence on my ideas and work is far more pervasive than can be credited by reference to specific spoken or written comments. They include A. H. Williams, who has remained a mentor since my days at the Tavistock, and the late John Sutherland, whose love for analysis and dedication to its application coupled with his personal knowledge of Fairbairn is an enduring model. There are many whose influence has come from a combination of personal contact and writing: Henry Dicks and John Bowlby of the Tavistock Clinic, Harold Searles, Joyce McDougall, Thomas Ogden, Vamık Volkan, and Christopher Bollas. All of them have written in ways that extend various aspects of theory while enriching the subjective experience of the therapist. Robert Stolorow and his colleagues have explored intersubjectivity from a Self psychology point of view. The theoretical advances and explorations of Stephen Mitchell

(1988) have a particular interplay with the ideas I am trying to explore. And certainly, the rich lode of infant research stemming from the tradition of John Bowlby, including T. B. Brazelton, Robert Emde, and Daniel Stern. Recently I have drawn particular stimulation from the guests to the program I chair in Object Relations Theory and Therapy at the Washington School of Psychiatry. Through that program, my colleagues and I have taught and studied with a number of British guests whose influence pervades this work: Christopher Bollas, Nina Coltart, Dennis Duncan, Earl Hopper, Isabel Menzies Lyth, Anton Obholzer, Adam Phillips, Hanna Segal, Elizabeth Spillius, John Steiner, John Sutherland, and Arthur Hyatt Williams. They have provided collegial inspiration to our faculty and students and have been an important current influence. Finally, and most of all, I acknowledge the help of my wife and sometime co-author, Jill Savege Scharff—my chief colleague, whose support, critical reading and editing, and patience not only made this book possible, but contributed immeasurably to its final form. Without her, it would not be what it is.

I am grateful to the Board of Trustees of the Washington School of Psychiatry for their support, and especially to Joe Oppenheimer, an old friend who has served as chairman of the board for the last years, and to the vice-chair, Dr. Christopher Bever, for their warm support of my writing, to the administrative staff of the school whose competence kept things going during my writing, and to Debby Ziff, my assistant, and Jo Parker for their help in support of this project. Gloria Parloff helped by wise editing of Chapter 11. Pearl Green kept our family going, and Zoe, Xanthe, and Daniel put up with my preoccupation and periods of fatherly negligence. Fran Langley did the wonderful figures depicting theory.

Jason Aronson has been, once again, an enthusiastic backer of my efforts without whose steady support this volume would have been difficult to manage. I am grateful to Adelle Krauser and Judith D. Cohen for their editorial guidance and assistance.

Finally, I am grateful to my patients, whose contribution

to this volume and to my life will be apparent on every page. I have made every effort to disguise their identities while conveying what I have learned from them. In the event some may read and recognize their words, I hope they will feel that the essence of our experience has been faithfully conveyed despite the need to fictionalize and combine experiences in order to protect their anonymity. And I hope that they can tolerate the revelation of my experience not revealed to them during treatment, given here in the interests of a scholarly and an educational endeavor.

What I hope to add to the rich tradition of object relations thinking and writing stems from my saturation in child and family therapy, group relations consultation, and marital and sex therapy, all of which have given me a view of ourselves in constant interaction with our others, in life as in therapy. The perspective of the interactional world needs not only to enliven family, marital, and group therapy, but to be incorporated into individual psychotherapy and psychoanalysis. Interaction with others forms the basic building blocks of our personalities. We are constructed of dynamic internalized relationships between self and object. In turn, we externalize our inner worlds onto our outside relationships, which turn again to influence our inner organization throughout our development as children and adults. This endless cycle of mutual shaping and renewal creates the richness of everyday life and the travails of the consulting room. It is such stuff as dreams are made of!

PART ONE

SELF AND OBJECT IN PSYCHOTHERAPY

1

Adam

In the middle of his first session, Adam reported a dream from the night before:

> The Los Angeles Dodgers asked me to play right field because they were a player short. What would the pitchers think of me? How should I bat against them? I tried to keep from dreaming what I would do when at the plate. I said, "Why not wait

until you're up at bat?" I worried that I'd drop the ball in right field.

Adam had come to me for treatment because he found himself still out of work a year after finishing graduate school in engineering, and because he was alarmed to find himself completely dependent on his fiancée for financial support, as he had been previously on the wife he had recently divorced.

During the session, Adam told me about the resentment he felt toward his father, who taught him to play baseball from the age of 4. He said his father's impatient criticism was the reason he had worried about his sexual performance since he was a teen-ager. Then he thought of Thomas Mann's *The Magic Mountain*. Adam said that although the relationship in that book between the patient and the doctor was homosexually consuming, it did not produce a cure.

THE DREAM AS TRANSFERENCE

I found Adam's dream arresting. I was drawn to his vivid baseball imagery and his boyishly grand role. I liked the dream, and thought it conveyed his fears about beginning psychoanalysis, about facing me as he had faced his father, wanting help but fearing a contest between us. I thought of his father, trying to teach him something but being seen as threatening and disapproving. And I thought of a father, proud of his son, wanting to help him. I said to Adam, "You're worried about how well you'll perform here in treatment."

"Yes," he said. "I'm not sure that I'm going to be able to do what I should in here. There are so many places right now I don't feel I can."

"There's something else in the dream," I said. "You may be worried about what I'll think about you. Will analysis be like things with your dad? Did you feel you never lived up to his expectations?"

"He would watch at practice or Little League games and I'd just feel I never did play well enough. I remember dropping the ball once in right field to lose a game, and I couldn't face him. I was so mad at him for wanting me to do well."

"You were mad at him for wanting you to do well when you felt you couldn't measure up," I said. "But you also were afraid you didn't play as well. Here you're afraid of that, too. I'm like the pitchers; you're worried what I'll think of you, but you are also playing against me, throwing balls you have to hit."

"I think you'll be trying to get me out. Or that you'll be a much better player than I am. After all, this is your sport. You're the one who is supposed to know how to play."

"So you're trying not to worry about it, to see if you can hit the ball. But you're worried that even if I hit it to you, you'll drop the ball."

"Yeah, then there's nothing you could do to help me."

"Then it would be like the relationship between the doctor and patient in *The Magic Mountain*. Consuming but it won't cure."

I noticed something more in this hour, something that felt threateningly close in to me: the homosexual allusion to the relationship between the doctor and patient, and the question of whether I would exploit him. Consciously, I decided to comment on his anxiety about starting treatment, but I was aware of the question of "what sort of balls I would throw at him." I decided that it would be too much, too intense, too soon to comment on the aspects of his worries that involved fears of a homosexual relationship. I filed them away for future consideration. Once I had addressed his concerns about beginning the work, he settled down and began to tell me about himself, focusing often on his relationship with his father, a doctor to whom he had looked for help but from whom he feared quackery.

THE DREAM'S COMMUNICATION ABOUT
THE ANALYST

Consciously, I took Adam's dream to be about him as he faced me. I assigned myself the role of the transferential father and helped him to understand his fear of facing me, wishing to please me and himself, but in the context of wanting to compete with me. Considering my own discomfort, it was a pretty reasonable effort for me, a good at bat for my first time at the plate.

I did not recognize it at the time, but the dream could just as easily have been mine. Adam was, for all practical purposes, my first analytic patient. A lot was riding on my efforts with Adam, and I was easily as worried as he was. As my first patient in psychoanalysis, Adam offered me my own chance to play with the Dodgers, the big leagues, to realize the ambitions of my own adolescence. He was my pitcher! What would he and the other pitchers—my teachers and supervisors—think of me? Would I drop the ball? Would I be able to interpret with the right speed, flick of the wrists, over the heads of the waiting resistance arrayed around the infield? I certainly worried I'd drop the ball. An earlier attempt at getting a patient going in analysis had failed. The patient had left after a month, feeling that analysis would impose too much and delve too deeply.

My supervisor was the late kind and wise Lucie Jessner, who did all she could to make me comfortable and to reinforce the understanding I brought from my previous experience conducting psychotherapy and my own analysis to my encounter with Adam. I have no doubt that she understood the worries I brought to the situation and to my own training. But looking back, I see that the material of my own anxieties was specifically in the field of interplay of this first hour. I was more identified with Adam than with his physician-father. I was never a good athlete myself, so I could understand his dream anxiety about performance all too well. How would I do, pitching, catching, and batting? Would my efforts be any better than Thomas Mann's description of the all-consuming relationship that did not cure? Would I drop the ball or strike out again? What would Dr. Jessner—and the patient—think of me?!

And in that denied homosexual reference? That business that I rationally decided was too hot to handle in that first session?

I can see now that I was not sure Adam was safe with me. He was too important to me and my training. I needed him too much, as every trainee does. And alongside my need was my fear that it would not work out, for him, for me. I could not face the way I needed him and that my need held the dangers of the doctor in *The Magic Mountain,* empty promises about an incurable disease. I worried, at that stage of my inexperience, that homosexual issues were beyond the scope of any help I could offer, that they were themselves the "incurable disease." And if they were treatable, I was worried that I lacked the skill to make it in the Big Leagues in which they might be treatable. And as for Adam's being out of work even after prolonged graduate training, who was I to talk while just embarking, at the age of 37, on a long and perhaps endless training in analysis?

As I look back, Adam's dream not only told us about him. It could have told us about both of us, if I had but known. In other places I could talk about my own anxieties—in my own analysis, in supervision with Dr. Jessner, with my wife, and with colleagues. But I could not use them and my identification with Adam to make sense of his dilemma, to use the resonance between us fully to explore the depth of his concerns and difficulties. Did Adam know about my own anxieties? Only vaguely, I think. But what he sensed and the resonance between us gradually did take form as an undercurrent for the duration of our work.

The field of interaction between Adam and me was a rich one from which we both learned a great deal. But, as I look back, the field was richer than I knew, one in which the resonance between us offered more than we could use. It was a field in which the depth of both our personalities was fully involved, not only the depth of his unconscious as understood by analytic or therapeutic technique. This interplay between two human beings in the therapeutic situation, or between several people and a fully involved therapist in family and couple therapy, is the subject of this book.

2

Self and Object

Intertwined

Our patients, who have lost parts of themselves and their objects, come to us to find them. In working with them, we, in turn, lose ourselves in each of our patients. If things go well—and with their help—we eventually find ourselves in them.

Although the infant is born constitutionally ready to be in a reciprocal relationship, it is only through the experience of relating to a devoted parent that the infant's self is born. Only within relationships does the self grow through being validated, responded to, and loved by others. From the beginning we need to be recognized and understood. We each need to love and be loved.

Object relations psychotherapy and psychoanalysis have as their purview the problems in loving and relating that stem from our fundamental need for relationships. The relationship between patient and therapist is at the center of the therapeutic field, just as the relationship between the growing child and parents is at the center of development. For therapists who work from an object relations point of view, it is axiomatic that the need for relationships motivates development. We are all organized by the way we have taken in the satisfactions and disappointments of our primary relationships. Internal reflections of experience with others structure a person's experience of himself or herself. These "internal objects" of our psychological structure carry the experience of the past relationships with the people most important to us, our "external objects." Each individual struggles to maintain a self within these primary relationships.

Fundamentally, patients seek psychotherapy because of troubles in relating. Such diverse therapies as individual psychotherapy, group therapy, family and marital therapy, sex therapy, and psychoanalysis are about difficulties in relating. These psychotherapies are therefore most usefully constructed out of theories that put relationships at the center, theories that help us to understand the encounter between patient and therapist, which is the crucible of change and growth.

Psychoanalysis began both as a theory and as a therapy in the most intense of encounters, the kind in which a patient got truly inside the therapist. Freud's early experience with hysterical patients, the work through which he invented dynamic psychotherapy and psychoanalysis, left him uncomfortably exposed, altogether too close to his patients. His collaborator, Josef Breuer, fled from his first patient, Anna O., when she attempted to live out her erotic transference with him. The theory that Freud subsequently elaborated helped him to keep an intellectual and emotional distance from such patients. It gave him a way of "knowing" what was happening that kept him at a safe distance, for the patients he saw were frequently of a kind who, we now know, have the capacity to get under a therapist's skin.

Thus the strengths of psychoanalysis also led to a weakness. Freud eschewed the surface of relationships in order to plumb the depths, and psychoanalysis became the premiere depth psychology of our time. In a corrective theoretical contribution, family therapy has focused on the surface of relationships, the interactions between family members and between therapist and patients, in order to mine the richness at the surface that analysts had treated with relative neglect. The result was that psychoanalysis and family therapy each ignored half the picture.

Object relations theory, through the psychotherapy, psychoanalysis, and family therapy that characterize its practice, corrects both of these omissions. It values surface and depth equally, and in so doing adds the resonance that comes from understanding how the depth mirrors the surface and the surface reflects the depth. I can make an analogy to the situation with modern poetry. When the poetry loses its capacity to make surface sense, to tell a story, it loses part of its capacity to lead the reader into contact with the depth. On the other hand, older forms of poetry could elaborate the surface without representing the in-depth richness. The "poetry" I would promote here would make sense at the surface—it would tell a story or convey a readily understandable experience—and would at the same time resonate deeply with human truths and complexity. It is through the surface that we can be led to understand the deepest and most hidden of our experiences. The theory and therapeutic tasks of the object relations approach look for stories we can all understand, and aim at the same time to resonate with the deepest of human enigmas and conflicts. They do so in terms of our fundamental need to relate and in terms of the unending difficulties relating always brings. It is this paradox that brings the complexity of the therapeutic relationship to the center of our study.

Patients and therapists are in it together, as I was with Adam, the patient presented in Chapter 1. Freud's theory, as fundamental as it has been to psychotherapy and psychoanalysis, built a picture of a therapist who was a trusted scout for a patient's expedition of discovery in the wilderness of the patient's unconscious world. It was the scout's job, wrote Freud, to understand that he was not himself or herself on such a journey, and to understand the patient's use of the therapist as transference from the patient's past. This was the understanding of analytic therapists for approximately the first 50 years of our field.

The second 50 years have brought many shifts. The contributions of Klein (1961, 1975a,b), Fairbairn (1952, 1954, 1958), Winnicott (1958, 1965, 1971a), Bion (1961, 1967, 1970), Balint (1952, 1957, 1968), Guntrip (1961, 1969), and others, who were loosely grouped as the school of British Object Relations (Sutherland 1980), along with the allied contribution of Bowlby (1969, 1973, 1980), from the vantage of ethology were among the first to recognize that relationships were at the center of human development, and therefore also at the center of psychotherapy. In the United States, Sullivan's (1953a,b, 1962) interpersonal theory of psychiatry represented a similar point of view. In more recent years, Kohut (1977) and other Self psychologists (Stolorow et al. 1987) have posited the centrality of each person's use of objects as the fundamental feature of development and the maintenance of the self. Among modern and current contributors, Khan (1974, 1979), Loewald (1960, 1980), Money-Kyrle (1978), Shapiro (1979), Zinner and Shapiro (1972), Mitchell (1988), Stern (1985), Emde (1988a,b), Stolorow and co-authors (1987), Beebe and Lachmann (1988), Modell (1984), Kernberg (1975, 1976), Gill (1984), Bollas (1987, 1989), Lichtenberg (1989), Ogden (1982, 1986, 1989), Searles (1965, 1979, 1986), Sutherland (1989), Hamilton (1988), Box and colleagues (1981), Wright (1991), and many others have offered fundamental contributions toward the theoretical ways in which the self forms and is maintained by the presence and action of the other, which in object relations terminology we call the "external object."

In this vision of the human, each of us exists not as a single unit, but within the context of our relationships. Our desires and fears, our sexuality and our aggression acquire meaning within relationships and are expressed in relationships. Our minds are organized in "relational configurations" (Mitchell 1988), and we can understand each other and ourselves fully only through understanding these relational patterns of each individual and the way they constantly interact with an individual's external relationships. Kohut's "self–self-object relationship" (1984), Atwood and Stolorow's (1984) "intersubjective context," and Mitchell's "relational matrix" (1988) are varying expressions of this central point.

To date, however, no theory has been fully able to keep an eye on *both* subject and object, on the self and other in constant interplay. Self psychology has focused on the self-seeking growth and cohesion through use of the object. Object relations theory has focused on the vicissitudes of the object while leaving the growth of the self in relative shadow. It is difficult to keep both self and object simultaneously in focus. Because they form a figure-and-ground relationship to each other, focusing on one necessarily tends to put the other into the role of forming the background. Yet both are crucial to theory and therapy.

This book is an exploration of the inextricable relationship between self and object. It begins with the thesis that there is no self without an object, and at the same time, there is no object without a self. Whereas both self and object are functions of an overarching self, the self is not the comprehensive unit of consideration. Rather it is a graduated and interlocking series of relationships. Perhaps the series begins with the mother and infant. This pair relates to their larger family, including a father or grandparents, which in turn relates fundamentally and inescapably to larger social units. In turn, all of these external relationships are taken into the internal world of each individual as his or her psychic organization, in forms that guide the individual in future relationships with others.

We each have selves organized in this way, and we are each the "others" to whom other selves relate, guided not only by our self-organizations, but by our own lifelong need to be another's object as an integral part of being our selves. The vicissitudes of this endless ebb and flow organize our lives from birth to death.

THE INEXTRICABILITY OF SELF AND OBJECT

The object relations view of the personality took root from the work of Ronald Fairbairn and Melanie Klein. This chapter introduces some of the general directions offered by major contributions, saving the theoretical details and my own elaborations on them for Chapter 3. The reader who is new to this material may wish to read Chapter 3 before this one for an introduction to object relations theory.

Fairbairn (1952) began the path we are following by disagreeing with Freud about the center of human development (Jones 1952). Where Freud put the unfolding of the drives as the engine of personal development, Fairbairn put the fundamental need in each of us for relationships. It is only within the context of this need for relationships that the unfolding of drives — of desire and aggression — and the gradual structuring of our psyches have meaning. From this beginning, Fairbairn (1952) elaborated a theory of the relationship between self and object. In his model, psychic structure is built from the experience each person has with the people most important to him or her. The operations of splitting and repression are fundamental to the handling of object relations as well as to the progressive structuring of the ego. And in Fairbairn's view, the self and object are always in intimate contact. The relationship between an internal object and a corresponding part of the ego that is attached to it constitutes the basic building block of psychological structure. Although Fairbairn used the term "ego" in referring to the part of the self that was in intimate relationship with the internal object, he accepted Guntrip's amendment that "self" was a better term (Sutherland 1989).

Fairbairn's clinical and theoretical writing focused equally on the relations of the self and the object, leading to the idea that they were, finally, inextricably intertwined and interdependent. We are always dependent on our objects, but development leads us from infantile dependency to a mature form of dependency. Guntrip (1969) extended Fairbairn's work, pointing to the problems of the self. He explored what he called the "repressed libidinal ego," a withdrawn part of the self that has great difficulty finding any object to which it can relate.

Klein's work began with closer links to Freud's drive theory. Although Klein is also credited with originating an object relations approach, in her view the infants relate to their mothers and other external objects based on their own needs and impulses, governed by their instinctual tensions and constitutional drives. Fairbairn saw a child influenced by the actual treatment of the primary objects. This experience was then incorporated as psychic structure. In contrast, Klein saw a child who was driven by its own conflicts to impose them on the primary external objects, fear the consequences, and react further to those fears. Klein's theory held relatively little regard for what the external object actually did in relating to the child. Her work was later elaborated by Bion (1967) whose model of the mother as the container for the infant's unmanageable primitive anxieties introduced the role of the actual psychological functioning of the mother as a factor.

It is when we put these views together that we can construct a model that captures the reciprocal influence of primary objects on the developing child, and the influence of children on the family and on their own psychological growth. Winnicott (1971a) and, more recently, such writers as Kohut (1984), Stern (1985), Mitchell (1988), and Wright (1991) helped us to have a richer idea of the complexity of the situation and have moved us toward a growing understanding of the relationship of self and object, both as they are lived out between people and as they provide the seeds of psychological structure for each of us.

THE SELF WITHIN THE OBJECT

The internal object relationship is born into the relationship with the external object. In therapy, it is born into the relationship provided by the therapist. Patient and therapist working together provide the holding for each other's work in support of a potential space that becomes the therapeutic space. In this process, the therapist takes the lead with the patient's cooperation.

The model for this activity is that of the mother or the father with their baby. Each of them—separately if one is a single parent—provides for the infant and its growth, offering to secure the environment, to enfold the infant in their arms, and to be receptive to the infant's efforts to return their concern with the first minute signs of encouragement that let the parents proceed with a sense of validation.

A series of concentric circles holds an infant. At first unable to hold themselves, infants rely on the parents, both one at a time and together, to hold them in their arms, to look into their eyes, touch and comfort them, clean and feed them. But an infant's responses also strengthen and hold the parents to their task—and even more, hold them in their relationship with the infant. In the widening circle, the mother holds the infant who holds her attention by returning her concern. As the two of them hold each other, a father holds the two of them by his concern for the baby, the mother, and for the two of them as a pair. In a reciprocal way, the mother holds the father and infant as they reach and hold each other. Then the parents as a pair provide a holding for the infant, for the three of them as a family, and for the larger family of the other children or extended kin.

Within this series of concentric circles that hold the infant and the family, the parents offer something else. They become the objects of the infant's desires and hopes, fears and aggression, love and hate. The parents are the first objects for the infant in the original sense of the term *object*, used by Freud (1905b) to denote the person who was the *object* of the child's sexual desire or aggressive impulses. Winnicott (1963b) called this aspect of the mother the *object mother*. Now that we are more aware of the father's importance to the infant and growing child, we know that both parents become the infant's earliest objects of love and aggression. Fathers and mothers are similar and have different intrinsic qualities in relationship to children—mothers offering a biological propensity for steadiness, and fathers for enhanced stimulation. (Scharff and Scharff 1987, Yogman 1982). Here, I simply want to introduce the term *the object parent* (adapted from Winnicott 1963b) and to distinguish this aspect of the child's experience from that with the *holding parent*.

In the relationship with the parents, the infant finds its objects, explores ways of relating with them, internalizes them, and lives with them both as real external people and as internalizations. I have previously described (Scharff and Scharff 1987) the way in which the infant forms a direct relationship with each parent as an object of desire and aggression, and have called this the focused or eye-to-eye (I-to-I) relationship, emphasizing the importance of gaze interactions in this process and the way it occurs as an intimate relationship between self and other. This eye-to-eye or "centered relationship" provides the experience of objects out of which the infant's internal world is built.

But it is in the arms-around envelope, created by the parents' readiness to be relatively in the background as providers and guards, that infants find themselves (Scharff and Scharff 1987). In this safe harbor, or in the ravages of rough or violent holding, the self is born and nurtured, and then gradually takes over the activities of providing, guarding, and navigating from the parents.

So, too, in therapy. The therapist takes the lead in the provision of the therapeutic space, but is encouraged by the patient's reciprocation. For therapy to go well, there must be this reciprocation, although it does not have to be conscious or rational. The universal desire to relate, to love, and be loved for ourselves must eventually nurture the therapeutic relationship.

The therapeutic relationship has these similarities to the parent–infant one, but it also has differences. The single parent family has to carry the entire potential of human development despite the lack of a central male–female couple. Similarly, the therapeutic relationship carries a larger potential than that of a two-person relationship. Each male therapist must be able to represent the female element in relation to his own maleness, and each woman therapist the male connection. Therapists can do so because of their own internal object relations, which include themselves in relation to others, male and female, and which provide an internal universe receptive to the patient's experience.

Therapists are also like parents in offering both arms-around and focused experiences to their patients. Like parents, they provide a background of holding like the parental arms-around experience, which allows patients to venture forth and deliver aspects of their internal worlds into the therapeutic space. And, on the other hand, in the I-to-I relationship, therapists offer themselves as objects of the patient's desires and hates, longings and fears—emotions that focus on therapists and convey the dynamics of the patient's internal object relations.

Both these aspects of relationships are relevant to therapy. Patients come with a lifelong experience with both from every previous primary relationship, and therefore with transferences both to the therapeutic space provided—the contextual transference—and to the person of the therapist—the focused transference. Each aspect is present in every intimate relationship, intertwined almost inextricably. We explore these aspects of transference in Chapter 3.

Mr. and Mrs. D.

Mr. and Mrs. D. managed their couple therapy
sessions by giving long speeches that could not be interrupted. When Mr. D. launched into his, Mrs. D. would
occasionally laugh at him in such a way as to make it clear
that she not only disagreed with him but was ridiculing
him. If Mr. D. had started, he would resist interruption,
often saying, "Let me finish." However, her pattern was
much the same. She would launch into a tirade about his
unreasonable and demeaning treatment of her, and if he
eventually protested, it was her turn to erupt by saying,
"Let *me* finish." If, however, I tried to intervene with a
comment about their shared pattern, an observation about
their interaction, or even a question about aspects of an
incident, whoever currently had the floor would berate me
for interrupting while the other spouse was apt to feel that
I was unfair in failing to intervene. Mr. D. especially felt
that I was unfair in interrupting him because he thought I
was unwilling to be even-handed and stop her tirades.

For my part, I felt brought to a stalemate, rendered
ineffective and silenced, forced to become an open vessel
into which they could both pour their anger and disappointment without protest. Occasionally I could tell them
that they were joining together to treat me this way. I
guessed that their fights must feel as though each was
trying to treat the other in a similar way. Their agreement
with this point did not alter the pattern of the discussions
in our sessions.

As the marriage and the couple therapy broke down,
I began to see Mr. D. individually. There I experienced the
same thing, although with a greater degree of relaxation
when I was free to become the kind of container he longed
for. In one hour, Mr. D. spent the first 40 minutes "filling
me in" on the events since his previous session, including
a weekend with his wife in which she had decided to take

him back. He talked nonstop. After 40 minutes he suddenly stopped, laughed, and said, "Do you have anything to say?" As I opened my mouth to reply, Mr. D. resumed speaking.

Later in the session, Mr. D. accused me of failing to stop his wife from taking the decision to initiate a trial separation. He blamed me for failing to confront her self-satisfied determination that had led to the decision and for failing to be even-handed in defending his wishes.

In this hour I was able to formulate the frustration that had remained wordless in the couple setting. I felt like a container strained to bursting with discharge, a balloon thinned by the force of its contents that had been pumped into me under pressure. Rather than feeling like a tolerant container of anxiety (Bion 1967), with walls capable of absorbing and processing unmanageable infantile anxiety, I felt filled to the point where the cellular architecture of my balloon walls had broken down. I hung on in exhaustion. I felt lucky to have survived the hour, yet relieved that I had barely been called on to respond—and further that the patient was more satisfied that I could be a compliant mouth open to receive what he poured in, rather than his anxious wife who would spit his projections back at him.

It was easier being with Mr. D. alone, where I felt free to be the inflated, stretched envelope, thinned to the point where I lost all tone. I could even relax and enjoy the feeling of being powerless to resist being stuffed even fuller. His checking with me late in the session seemed not so much to represent his concern whether I could survive, as it was to see if a baby wanted to burp before a parent resumed the overfeeding.

In this situation with Mr. D., I felt like a parent accused of providing inadequate holding. I felt attacked when Mr. D. blamed me for leaving him alone to survive without my protection and without the object of his love. Had I been a better parent, he contended, a more practiced protector, he would not have been abandoned and would not have faced such terrible loss and humiliation. I had let him down. And in the transference, when I felt attacked, it was clear that the threat of loss and humiliation had changed his image of me. I began the hour feeling I could function like a parent who was needed to absorb all that he could pour into me. Now I felt I had become nothing more than a failed container for the couple's love and hate. As he felt attacked and threatened by her, so he turned the attack on me rather than face loss. Feeling now the sting of his attack provided some life to my overstretched elastic walls, which had felt so lifeless. The attack thus revived me. Springing back to life, I could ask him about the loss and the humiliation. He was able to agree that it was these that triggered his attack on me. But I was puzzled why I had felt somehow freed by the attack on my therapeutic role, more relaxed and able to respond than when he had relentlessly pumped more into me.

Only later did I realize that when I felt more organized by his attack, my feeling echoed the way the couple treated each other. Their fights vented the excess pressure, allowing them often to resume a more intimate relationship. The fights often led to lovemaking. With me, the attack seemed to vent the disabling inflation of my containing capacity and led to relief and reorganization of my thoughts. This led to my being able to rejoin him in the therapy, no longer disabled by his evacuation into me.

The little I knew of Mr. D.'s history fit with my experience of being used as a necessary object. He now told me more. He viewed his mother as crazy. She would demand that he stand in place listening to her ravings. Usually she insisted that he not move. He blamed his father for failing to shield him from her demands that extended to taking him into her bed, holding him clutched to her anxious, scantily clad body. In therapy hours, he put me into the place he had so often occupied, while he became his mother. He forced me to absorb his anxieties without moving as he had been forced to become the container for his mother. Having stood my ground without flinching until he asked if I wanted to speak, he then moved to a later part of the enactment in which an angry exchange would puncture the stalemate and bring both him and his mother back to life. I was able to respond to his blame, now in his place as a young boy who wished to defend himself. He and I both felt vented and relieved. In defending myself, I spoke for him. He became more responsive, and later more self-reflective. The frozen scene was mobilized. He could begin to absorb the losses inherent in his position and to see me again as the sympathetic and containing parent he longed for.

Mr. D. longed for a mother who would take in his desperation without spitting it back or turning the tables so that he had to become the parent. From my experience of his internal object relationship, I thought more about his relationship with his wife. I began to see that they both felt threatened by the other's demands and accusations. They were like two cobras in reverse. Each put venom into the other not to devour, but in order to paralyze the victim into becoming a frozen, open mouth with a compliant, passive receptiveness. The mutual demands naturally broke down at home. There, when both spouses felt overstuffed, they acted like an overstretched bladder, closing down quickly and evacuating a venomous urine back into the other. At times, their fights helped them to reorganize by venting unmetabolized projections and thereby recovering the resilience of their boundaries.

In therapy, Mr. and Mrs. D. joined forces to pour their anger and sorrow into me, taking turns at pumping me full, then accusing me of failing to contain themselves and each other. Now they agreed I was failing in my arms-around function and that it was my failure that accounted for their inability to find loving objects in each other. As a couple, they hoped to find themselves within each other. In a similar way, the husband hoped in his individual therapy that I could take him in so that he could then find himself in me. And while the couple was together with me, each of them feared that if I was "taken in" by one of them, I would no longer be there to take in the other.

This vignette describes the use that a man and his wife made of me. His transference and their shared transference refer to a particular parental function and its failure. Mr. D. felt that his mother had failed to contain his anxieties and, moreover, that she reversed the ordinary situation by filling him full of her madness, demanding that *he* stand still lest *she* burst. The arms-around holding of the mother for the child was reversed until he could no longer stand it. He then blamed his father for building a family based on the assumption that his mother had to be tolerated and pampered, and for failing to protect him from her filling him with madness. He blamed his father, as he now blamed me, for never standing up to her and thereby forcing my patient to have to take it, too.

In this therapeutic situation, we can see the use and abuse of the object as a container. In the couple, the shared reenactment became mutually reinforcing of a static, frozen repetition. If it was difficult to stand the anxious evacuation of my single patient, it was downright paralyzing when he was joined by his wife.

THE SELF AND THE OBJECT

The self is inextricable from the object. It is always defined by its relationship with the object. Fairbairn's description (1951) of *techniques of relating to objects* as methods of compensation for unsatisfying relationships was an early effort to define the particular use of objects by the self. Thus Mr. D. attempted to define himself by controlling his objects in a particular way. He hoped to control me into containing his anxieties as a substitute for his own deficient tolerance. Approaching the problem differently, Kohut (1977, 1984) coined the term *selfobject* to capture this use of an object—the attempt to get another person, including a therapist, to fill a function for the self, to get a sense of self-cohesion through ridding the self of the fragmenting effects of aggression. Fairbairn's term (1952) *object relationship* emphasizes the *mutual relation* between self and object rather than the *fused use of the object* conveyed by Kohut's term.

Wright (1991) has elaborated a theme earlier stated by Searles (1963) in studying the therapy of schizophrenia. In the developmental situation, Wright notes, "The mother's face is the child's first emotional mirror, and that it is through her responsiveness (her reflections) that the child is able to come to know his own emotions" (p. 5).

The parallel situation applies to the therapeutic situation. Searles (1986) writes: ". . . in the therapeutically symbiotic, core phase of the work with any one patient, each of the two participants' facial expressions belong, in a sense, as much to the other as to oneself" (p. 379).

The self is always defined in relationship to its objects. By the same token, internal objects have no meaning except in relationship to the self. Fairbairn's early description (1952) of the internal object emphasized that it was organized inevitably in relationship to a part of the self, bound together by the set of affects that characterized the repressed relationship. It has been less recognized in this description, partly because it was less emphasized by Fairbairn himself that internalization includes not merely an object (an image of a part of a primary person) but a relationship, with a part of the self in an emotional relation to the crucial other (Ogden 1986, Sutherland 1989). This is so because there is no other without a self, and in a reciprocal way, there is no self without an other, any more than there can be a baby without a mother (Winnicott 1971a). So in the inner world, we cannot conceive of our selves without invoking and relying on our objects. We see ourselves in the reflection of the other's eyes, gaze, expression, mirroring body responses, and echoing sounds.

Just as we are a self defined by our bodies—that is, we cannot be a disembodied self—so we cannot be a dis-othered self. Our relationships to others in the external world and to the traces of these in our internal worlds continue to define our selves.

THE OBJECT WITHIN THE SELF

But the object is also defined by the self. Winnicott's (1971a) paradigm is that there is no baby without a mother. The other half of this paradigm must be that *there is no mother without a baby*. No one can be an other without someone to whom they belong, by whom their otherness is defined and validated. Fairbairn placed at the center of life that we each long to love and be loved for ourselves (Sutherland 1989). Love and development form a reverberating circuit in a relationship of reciprocity. We each need the parent to love, and we need the parent to love us. And then, later as parents, husbands, wives, or lovers ourselves, we need to feel we can care for others with love—that they will grow in our holding. But it is not only later that we need this. From the beginning, the baby needs to feel that the parent grows in the light of the child's love and care.

There is a further wrinkle. Within us, we also need to have taken in an image of the object of our love that is also felt to be loving to us in return. Internal objects—the loving, hating, beckoning, accepting, and rejecting objects—are embedded within us as cornerstones of our psyches. They are part of our selves. But they are embedded in us in a particular way: Deep within us, they must also have us inside them. The image of the object we carry must have room for us within it—that is, it must be an object capable of relating to us, whether kindly or cruelly, lest it be felt to have abandoned us altogether. The image I am trying to draw is one of parallel mirrors facing each other, each containing the image of the other with its own image inside. A series of these mutually contained images extends back to an infinite beginning and forward to the infinity of the future.

In a simpler vein, we can see that what is carried inside is an ongoing object relationship, one either characterized by aspects of mutual concern and caring, or by antagonism, rejection, and rage. Where mutuality and concern are insufficient, the internal object relationships become static, skewed, and distorted. When internal and external relationships go well, the individual is operating closer to what Klein (1935, 1945) called the depressive position—one in which there is concern for the well-being of the object as a whole person. When they go badly, the individual operates in what Klein (1935, 1940) called the paranoid-schizoid position where part object relationships predominate in relation to a fragmented experience of the self.

Ogden's (1989) addition of an autistic-contiguous position to Klein's paranoid-schizoid and depressive positions extends our understanding of the lifelong resonance between self and object. The autistic-contiguous position concerns the person's struggles to form and maintain a self. The depressive position involves the person's concern for and relationship to objects. And coming between them, the paranoid-schizoid position reflects splitting and repression in response to problems of integration during life's continual movement between concern for one's self and concern for objects.

AUTISTIC/CONTIGUOUS POSITION ⇄ PARANOID/SCHIZOID POSITION ⇄ DEPRESSIVE POSITION

The balance among the three positions alters during different developmental stages and various psychological tasks, while movement also occurs among them along the continuum from health to pathology.

The vitality of the self and its relationships with significant others rest on, and are expressed by, the degree to which relations between self and object are gratifying.

SELF AND OBJECT MUTUALLY HELD

Since there is no self without an object, the well-being of the object is of central concern to the self. Therefore, an object relations approach always considers the concern of one person for another's well-being. Actually, the term *object relations* is itself problematic in that it obscures the problems and centrality of the self. In contrast, the term *self psychology* obscures the centrality of the object, not only as an object to be of service *to* the self, but as a structure in intimate and mutually defining interaction *with* the self. A complete study has to take into consideration the mutual influence and concern of self and object, of what we might call personal relations (Sutherland 1989). This study can be informed not only by psychoanalysis, object relations, and Self psychology, but by the fields of infant research and of family and marital studies as well. Children and parents in interaction, or wives and husbands in marriages of frustration and repair lead us from the galaxy of external interaction to the universe of our inner worlds, to those regions where our blocked paths of mutual concern lead to the narcissistic disorders of an arrogant, empty triumph of self over object, to the despairing loss of self at the hands of the inner object, and to the brutal substitution of aggression for caring in attempts to keep alive relationships between self and object.

This book deals with the way our internal worlds are daily given birth through our external interactions, while at the same time these internal object relations spawn meaning and enrich the interpersonal realm. Born originally in the cradle of our primary relationships, our inner worlds seek meaning from and give meaning to our everyday interactions. In our professional world, they give life to the transferences and countertransferences of our psychotherapeutic relationships.

3

Contextual and Focused Transference and Countertransference

Before launching into new areas of exploration in object relations, we need to establish the foundation on which the work in this book is built. This chapter describes the building blocks of a theoretical foundation and, to that extent, repeats material for the reader who is already familiar with British object relations, especially with the work of Fairbairn, Klein, Winnicott, and Bion. However, the chapter also explores several new areas, including aspects of Fairbairn's contribution, the role of introjective identification in which I follow the recent work of Jill Savege Scharff (1992), and the seeming contradictions between Winnicott and Bion. These building blocks of object relations theory lead us to consider the clinical keystone of an object relations approach: the use of transference and counter-transference.

Transference and countertransference provide the vehicle for the object relations between therapist and patient, and between therapist and couple or family in the conjoint therapies. Individual and conjoint therapy both employ transference and countertransference, differing in this respect in consideration of which aspects of transference and countertransference are most in focus. We will return to our discussion of transference after examining some of the major tenets of object relations theory that put them in context.

FAIRBAIRN'S CONTRIBUTIONS TO AN OBJECT RELATIONS THEORY OF THE PERSONALITY

Fairbairn's revision of Freud's notion of individual development posits that what organizes the baby in the beginning is not the unfolding of a sequence of innate drives, but the baby's innate need for a relationship (Fairbairn 1952, 1954, 1963). The vicissitudes of the relationship to the mother (or other primary caretaker) in the beginning, and subsequently the relationships to the few primary members of the child's closest family, determine psychological development. Fairbairn thought that there was no death instinct causing aggression. He held instead that aggression arises in response to frustration of the need for attachment or affiliation. In homage to Freud's great contribution, Fairbairn retained the terms *libido* and *libidinal,* but where Freud used these to refer to the sexual instinct, Fairbairn used them to refer to the child's active search for attachment figures. In Fairbairn's view, the child progressively internalizes experience with the mother and family, modified by the developing child's limited capacity to understand.

Fairbairn wrote that the child begins life with "an original unsplit ego" in relationship to a "preambivalent object" (1952, pp. 134–135). Because the object is in some measure inevitably disappointing, the child defends against the pain by internalizing it. The child then treats this originally unsplit internal object by (1) splitting off from relatively rational and conscious experience those aspects of the object that are too painful to be tolerated; (2) repressing them precisely because they are intolerably painful; and (3) when the child thereby modifies experience of an original unsplit "preambivalent object," it thereby modifies its own unitary ego. The ego is split at the same time and by the same process that the unacceptable object is split into part objects. Fairbairn thought that the first action of introjection, and the subsequent splitting and repression of bad objects, were primarily defensive functions. The child also takes in aspects of good or acceptable experiences with the object and organizes mental structure around them. Fairbairn wrote that the child only internalized the good experiences with the object as a secondary action to compensate for the bad experiences already internalized. However, it seems to me that the fact that every child also internalizes good experience makes it likely that both good and bad experience are internalized from the beginning on an equal footing and that this basic process of mental structuring is part and parcel of a basic psychological sorting of experience with others (Scharff and Scharff 1987, Sutherland 1989). The difference between the handling of good and bad objects—"good" and "bad" meaning emotionally satisfying or not—is that relations with a "bad object" are relatively subject to repression or "defensive exclusion" (Bowlby 1980) because they are painful, whereas "good object" experience remains relatively available to consciousness to suffuse the ego with satisfaction and energy.

In Fairbairn's model, what is split off and repressed in each case is (1) *an image of the object* along with (2) *a part of the self in interaction with that object* (which Fairbairn called a part of the ego) and (3) *the affect that characterizes the painful interaction* (Sutherland 1963, 1989). This constellation can be termed *an internal object system*. There are three principal internal object systems identified by Fairbairn (1963) and shown diagrammatically in Figure 3-1:

1. **The central ego and its ideal object.** The central ego and its object constitute the relatively conscious and reasonable set of relationships that each of us has internalized. The ideal object represents the unre-

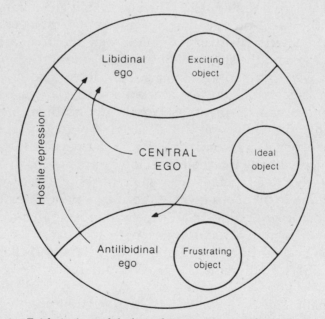

Figure 3-1. Fairbairn's model of psychic organization, by D. E. Scharff, from *The Sexual Relationship: An Object Relations View of Sex and the Family.* Reprinted courtesy of Routledge and Kegan Paul. The central ego in relation to the ideal object is in conscious interaction with the caretaker. The central ego represses the split-off libidinal and antilibidinal aspects of its experience along with corresponding parts of the ego that remain unconscious. The libidinal system is further repressed by the antilibidinal system.

pressed core of the originally unsplit preambivalent object, that part characterized by being neither excessively rejecting nor excessively exciting of need.

The other two systems are both "bad object" systems in that they are associated with painful affect:

2. **The libidinal ego and object.** The libidinal object is felt to be excessively exciting of need for a relationship. As Ogden (1983) has noted, it is felt to be "tantalizing." Part of the self (or ego) is attached to this object by an affect of painfully unsatisfied or unrequited desire.

3. **The antilibidinal ego and object.** This term, which seems difficult to many people, was introduced by Fairbairn for the sake of consistency. It refers to the aggressive side of relating (that is, the antiaffiliative part that tends toward separation) and to the kind of "bad" object that is felt to be rejecting, negligent, or persecuting. A part of the self, which Fairbairn originally called the *internal saboteur*, adheres to a relationship. The relationship is characterized by anger, frustration, and hate, but the internal saboteur is devoted to the relationship with the rejecting object nevertheless because parts of self can no more tolerate losing their part objects than a child with an angry mother can risk losing her.

These three types of structures described by Fairbairn are in themselves dynamic. That is to say, they are structures that internalize the ebb and flow of experience with relationships, not simply a freeze-frame view of objects. However, Fairbairn described an additional dynamic aspect. He noted that desire for the exciting object was so painful that the antilibidinal ego launched a further hostile attack on the libidinal ego and the exciting object, with the effect of repressing them further. This is indicated by the arrow in Figure 1 with the term "hostile repression" accompanying it. This formulation expresses the situation in which it is so painful to feel an unrequited longing for an unattainable object that a person finds it easier, less painful to be angry. Clinically, we find that anger felt toward an object is often a cover for yearning, that is, the anger has served to further repress the desire.

What is important about this formulation is that it elaborates on the fundamentally dynamic quality of internal object relations that comprise psychic structure. The antilibidinal system is in dynamic relationship to the libidinal system. But we can also continue on from Fairbairn's original observation to note a reverse configuration of dynamic relations between internal objects (Scharff and Scharff 1987). Clinically, we observe that some individuals—and some couples—maintain an excited or even manic mood that denies pain and anger, using an excessively desiring mode to cover feelings of persecution and rejection. Here the libidinal system attacks and represses the antilibidinal system. And the central ego or central self system relates to both sets of repressed objects continuously.

Internal object systems relate to each other in all directions at all times. What is important about these subsystems is precisely that they are in continual dynamic relation to each other, that they are all dynamic parts of a whole self. Many aspects of pathology occur when some aspects of the repressed self-and-object systems are excessively repressed, leaving the central self depleted, with an impoverished relationship to its ideal object. Other aspects of pathology can be formulated as representing the takeover of the central self system by one of the usually repressed systems, as in the case of a person whose relations are characterized by continual patterns of distance and rage with the apparent disappearance of rationality.

Kernberg (1975, 1976, 1980, 1984), Volkan (1976, 1987), and more recently Ogden (1986), Greenberg and Mitchell (1983), Slipp (1984), and Hamilton (1988) have led the way in popularizing Fairbairn's ideas in the United States and applying his ideas to the treatment of severe pathology, especially borderline states, and Socarides (1978) has applied Kernberg's work to homosexuality and the perversions.

Modifications of Fairbairn's Contribution

Some aspects of Fairbairn's formulation can be updated. The first of these involves his use of the term *ego* to denote an unclear mixture referring mostly to the self as a subjective organization containing the operating identity of a person, and partly to the executive ego mechanisms described by Freud (1923). Fairbairn later agreed with Guntrip that Fairbairn had been primarily referring to what would more accurately be called the *self* (Guntrip 1969, Sutherland 1989). Guntrip (1969) also elaborated problems of the self not explored by Fairbairn, and particularly the problems of what Guntrip called "the repressed libidinal ego" whose unrelenting search for an object is accompanied by the dread that none is to be found. In formulating the repressed libidinal ego, Guntrip extended Fairbairn's formulation in the direction later elaborated by Kohut (1977, 1984) who considered the area of the self seeking its own cohesion, integrity, security, and well-being through the use of an object. It is this aspect of the psychology of the self that has been more recently elaborated by the Self psychologists, by Tustin's (1986, 1990) work on the role of autistic objects in the formation of the sense of self, and Ogden's (1989) elaboration of Tustin's idea from which he suggests that there is a developmental position in the formation of the self. Ogden terms this *the autistic-contiguous position*. In the field of infant research, Stern (1985) has described the stages of growth of the self that develop during the infant's relationship with the mother.

Finally, Fairbairn's formulation of the ideal object, the object of the central self, is described in his clinical paper on hysteria (1954). He makes it sound as though the normal ideal object is synonymous with those he described for patients with hysterical organizations, shorn of its excitement and aggression, and rather deadened. I believe it would be more accurate to say that this kind of "ideal object" is pathologically constricted, the kind of object that an hysteric idealizes in a continuing effort to repress desire and aggression. The mature central object of a person with a mature central self would not be shorn of all exciting and aggressive qualities. Winnicott's (1960a) model of a "good-enough mother" offers a better approximation of the normal object of the central self. The "good-enough mother" is a mother (an external object) who can be less than perfect but who gets things just right some of the time and does so often enough that the child can transform experience with her—minor failings and all—into just what the child needs in an external object. Similarly, an internal ideal object modeled on a good-enough mother would be one that is *not excessively exciting or rejecting of need*, but that does have qualities of both—that is, it does have active appeal for ordinary needs of the central self, can be felt to be appropriately limit-setting on neediness with the central self, and can maintain an internal separateness from the central self.

In summary, the human personality consists of a system of internal objects and parts of the self that make up the organization of the individual's psyche and that have a dynamic relationship to each other. At a clinical level, we can say that relatively unmetabolized aspects of experience with the mother, father, and a few other central figures, and of the self in relationship to each of these, constitute the unconscious world. In consciousness, the central self manages relatively reasonable relationships in the day-to-day world. The degree to which central self-functioning is invaded by returning repressed aspects of relationships or is impoverished by overly stringent repression varies with the amount and type of splitting that the individual does. This is determined by the individual's experience during the entire period of development.

It bears repeating that an internal object does not represent a simple internalization of a concrete experience. Rather, it represents the imprint of experience as the individual understood it at the time. Thus a child whose actual mother (that is, its *external object*) is sympathetic to its needs but is temporarily too busy or too ill to attend to them is still partly taken in as an internal "bad mother," even if the child also consciously understands the reasons for her temporary rejection. Or a mother who incites a feeling of insatiable need by being overly teasing and arousing at a moment of play or who is overanxiously hovering is introjected as an exciting object. At other times the mother attends to her child in the way that is normally satisfying, but because of the child's upset, her comforting cannot be found useful at that moment. Thus every child, no matter how well parented, internalizes experiences of painfully exciting and rejecting objects.

By the time he completed his theoretical formulation, Fairbairn (1963) had built a model that extended beyond problems of pathology to formulate a general psychology. Although he had not elaborated the problems and structure of the self in great detail, his formulation has since been extended to clarify issues of self-development by Guntrip (1969), and more recently by Sutherland (1989). In my view, repressed object systems are not simply areas of pain and pathology, but are also, simultaneously, aspects or poles of normal functioning of the central self system. The central self must have excited or aroused longings for objects and must also have relationships with objects that value and put into action appropriate separateness and limit-setting. It is only the *excessively* exciting and aggressive relationships that are problematic. Figure 3-2 is a revised diagram of dynamic psychic structure that illustrates this model of psychic structure.

MELANIE KLEIN'S CONTRIBUTIONS

The Paranoid/Schizoid and Depressive Positions

Klein's work focused on the quality of relations between the developing child and its objects. Her writing is heavily weighted toward the effects of the child's inner experience on primary relationships and is relatively silent on the effects of external events on the growing child. One of her major

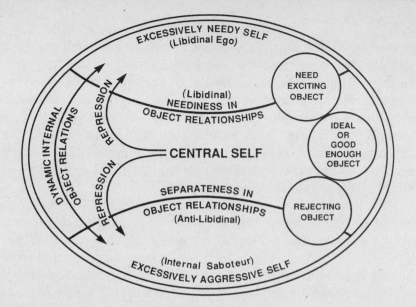

Figure 3–2. Revision of Object Relations Theory. Neediness and separateness are aspects of the Central Self. Exciting and Rejecting Objects partly communicate with the Ideal Object and are partly repressed. All aspects of self and object are in dynamic relation.

contributions was the notion of developmental positions. These are not stages in the sense in which Freud used the progression of psychosexual stages, but positions that are established early in life and are then organizations that persist throughout the rest of life.

The first of these, which begins at a few months, is the *paranoid/schizoid position* (Klein 1935, 1940) in which the infant is unable to comprehend a whole object possessing both good and bad qualities. Instead, the infant splits the object into good and bad part objects, often contained in fantasies of parts of the mother's or father's bodies, as the good or bad breast or penis. The infant then relates to these part objects through continued fantasies of splitting and projection, blaming, and fear of retaliation from the bad object, which has been located outside itself.

Later Klein noted that at about 8 months of age, the infant develops cognitively enough to become concerned for the mother as a whole object with both good and bad attributes. Klein (1935, 1940) called this new achievement *the depressive position*. It is characterized by concern for the object, the tolerance of ambivalence, the capacity to mourn losses, and the wish to make reparation to the object for harm done by the self. Klein also described the clinical situation of the "manic defense" against the depressive position, in which a person treats his or her objects with contempt and control rather than with concern and regard.

Throughout life, each of us struggles with the movement between these two positions, being drawn toward the paranoid/schizoid position in anger and blame, moving toward the depressive position with maturation or recovery. In 1987, Steiner examined aspects of pathology in movement between positions. Meltzer (1975) and Tustin (1986, 1990) have suggested that there is an earlier mode of relating to the objects that involves the formation of a self, which, as noted in Chapter 2, Ogden (1989) has called the *autistic-contiguous position*.

Projective and Introjective Identification

Klein (1946) coined the terms *projective identification* and *introjective identification* for large-scale unconscious communication of internal objects. (See Figure 3–3.)

Projective identification is a mode of relating that Klein thought occurred under the sway of the paranoid/schizoid position. Through projective identification, a person (the projector) puts an unwanted part of the self into the other, inducing behavior in the other that the projector unconsciously identifies with and attempts to control in lieu of handling conflicts inside him- or herself. As described succinctly by Segal (1973), *projective identification* "is the result of the projection of parts of the self into an object. It may result in the object being perceived as having acquired the characteristics of the projected part of the self but it can also result in the self becoming identified with the object of its projection" (p. 126).

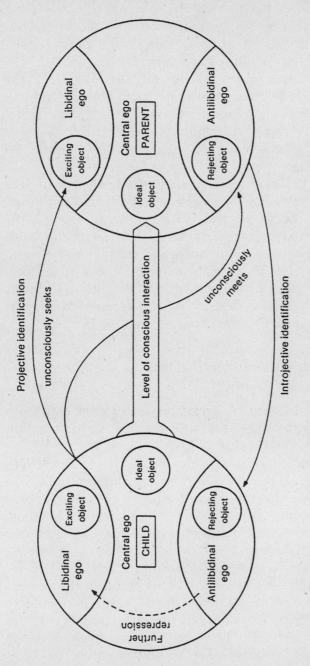

Figure 3–3. The action of projective and introjective identification. The mechanism here is the interaction of the child's projective and introjective identifications with the parent as the child meets frustration, unrequited yearning, or trauma. The diagram depicts the child longing to have his needs met and identifying with similar trends in the parent via projective identification. The child meeting with rejection identifies with the frustration of the parent's own antilibidinal system via introjective identification. In an internal reaction to the frustration, the libidinal system is further repressed by the renewed force of the child's antilibidinal system. Reprinted courtesy of Routledge and Kegan Paul.

There are many motives for projective identification: to get rid of a hated part of the self or to get it into a "better" object to control the source of danger. Projective identification is also a way of handling valued parts of the self that are felt to be in danger inside the self and to have a better chance of surviving if lodged in the other. As Ogden has put it (1986), what is projected in projective identification are parts of the self felt to be either endangering to the self (aspects of aggression) or parts felt to be endangered (victims of one's own aggression).

Introjective identification, the counterpart mechanism, occurs when a person takes in an aspect of another person as a way of adding to or controlling aspects of the person's own personality, and then identifies with these imported aspects and acts as if they were part of the self. As defined by Segal (1973), *introjective identification* "is the result when the object is introjected into the ego which then identifies with some or all of its characteristics" (p. 126). Thus an infant takes in the mother's function of handling its anxiety, a lover takes in characteristics of the loved person, and, as Freud (1917) described long ago, mourners take in their lost object that can displace their own egos.

Bion (1967) has described a continuum from normal to pathological projective identification. A normal infant projects its excessive anxieties into its mother to get help in tolerating them. She takes them in through introjective identification, tolerates them, and, through a process that Bion (1967) labeled her *reverie*, she transforms them into more manageable form. This allows the infant to reintroject them in this more tolerable form, so that the infant then identifies both with the detoxified aspect of itself it had originally projected, and also with the mother's ability to provide this transformation. This is the process of containment, in which the mother is the container and the anxieties of the infant are the contained. When the primitive anxieties are not contained, however, they may be fed back to the infant either in essentially unmodified forms, or even worse, magnified and sent back like hostile projectiles. This pathological process will be experienced by the infant with pain, the greatest pain being a kind of nameless dread in which the object becomes greatly persecuting and the infant faces a fragmentation of its fragile self.

Projective and introjective identification are the vehicles for unconscious communication in everyday life. Their excessive use is involved in pathology. Transference and countertransference are the names we use clinically to refer to the special form of unconscious communication in the therapeutic situation. Klein and her followers, using the notion of projective and introjective identification, were able to explore some of the reasons for and mechanisms of unconscious communication, leading to a view of the central role of unconscious communication from its earliest beginnings between mother and infant and to its continuing role throughout life in normality and pathology.

In the Kleinian view, the infant and mother use projective identification and introjective identification to communicate about inner states in a reciprocating cycle. As such, projective and introjective identification are the bases for empathy and are the vehicle through which the infant becomes psychologically organized. The infant puts into the mother, through observable means of communication, its anxieties and needs, impulse life, and growing understanding. She takes these in and forms what Bion (1967) called a *container* for the infant's anxieties. These anxieties and desires Bion calls *the contained*. The mother's function is to take in the infant's projective identifications, and in the process of introjectively identifying with the infant, to transform these anxieties to less toxic, more manageable form and then to put them back into the infant, now in the more matured form she can thereby "lend" to the infant. The infant then reintrojects these contained anxieties and is calmed, progressively organized, and led toward maturation. This process is like that described by Loewald (1960), who spoke of the mother as having the lead in a path toward maturation of her infant.

Projective and introjective identification are reciprocal processes, but in addition, they are simultaneous ones, occurring in a linked way (J. Scharff 1992). There cannot be a completed projective identification for one person without a corresponding introjective identification in the other.

In clinical settings, we often study the interactional paths through which these two processes combine. How do a couple find the fit in which, for instance, a wife puts her strength into the husband who puts his soft and vulnerable feelings into her? Bion's (1961) concept of *valency* is useful here. He described valency in referring to groups, where one person would tend to come to life to take leadership for certain unconscious impulse constellations, let us say, for using dependency to solve problems, while another person might have a penchant for leading the fight against the group leader. Bion did not describe the factors of personality that result in this capacity for spontaneous fit, but we can attempt to do so through the study of the process of introjection and projection (J. Scharff 1992).

Bollas (1987) has also recently added to our capacity to observe the process of introjection. His concept of *extractive introjection* describes the way one person takes away the feeling that originates with another, leaving the first person feeling bereft of a part of themselves. He gives the example of a child spilling milk whose parent responds with rage and blame. The child is left without an opportunity for appropriate sorrow over the error, and instead can only respond to the adult's affect. The adult has appropriated the original feeling from the child. Bollas does not present this clinical observation as the general mechanism of introjection, but his description moves us one step closer to observations of the general process of introjection (J. Scharff 1992). The study of couples and families has also contributed to the field of introjective identification, for there we begin to discern the way one person becomes what Lichtenstein (1961) called *the organ of expression* of another's personality, or in which a marital couple develop what Dicks (1967) called *a joint marital personality.* An extensive example of this is given in an assessment interview of a couple described in Chapter 4.

In this way we can begin to think of each person's internal

object relations constellation as operating as a scanning device that looks to the external relationships and searches for good fit with other people (Ogden 1986).

WINNICOTT'S MOTHER AND CHILD

Winnicott was a pediatrician and psychoanalyst whose studies of the maternal-infant relationship have contributed fundamentally to all ideas of reciprocity in growth-facilitating relationships including therapy. Winnicott (1971a) coined the term *psychosomatic partnership* to describe the quality of the mother-infant relationship in which there is an initial overlap of the physical relationship with the psychological relationship. It is through the physical holding and handling, and the almost physical qualities of gaze and sound that the mother communicates the essentials of the primary psychological partnership through which the baby is initially organized. Then, through the baby's contributions to the partnership, the mother becomes organized as a mother.

Projective and introjective identification operate in these first formative relationships, but Winnicott did not write in these terms. Rather, he described the infant's use of the mother (or other primary caregiver) in various ways, coining the terms *environment mother* and *object mother,* discussed in the previous chapter (Winnicott 1963b). These two aspects of relating, both present in every subsequent intimate relationship throughout life, form two aspects that we can describe separately. In her role as environment mother, the mother holds her arms around the infant and sets the conditions to facilitate the baby's being, relating, and growth. This "arms-around mother" sets the context of the baby's more specific activities and more focused relating.

Within the envelope provided by the arms-around mother, the baby is free to relate to her specifically as an object, to gaze into her eyes and "speak" with her in baby talk, to engage in eye-to-eye relating, which is also the beginning of the I-to-I relating, the relationship of an "I" and a "thou" of which the theologian Martin Buber (1978) wrote.

In the path toward the development of a self and an inner world of objects, *the infant finds its objects in the focused relationships of the I-to-I, but it does so with the emerging self that develops in the cradle of the arms-around relational context.*

There is a space between the mother and infant, described by Winnicott (1971a) as the *transitional space.* This is the external space between the mother and child where the child is allowed and encouraged to use things that are derived from the mother and that stand for her, but to use them freely for the child's own purposes, discovery, and manipulation, and to discover new things as though the child had invented them when they were actually placed there by the mother. This space has a characteristic mode of interaction: mother and child collaborate to make things the child's own. This space leads eventually to the zone that is the locus of creativity, the external space in which a child can "play" (Winnicott 1971b), and which is the counterpart of a mental space for playing with ideas and relationships in a creatively renewing way.

Figure 3-4 depicts the relationship of the transitional space and transitional relating to the holding and focused relationships of mother and infant.

WINNICOTT'S TRUE AND FALSE SELF

Winnicott (1960b) described two parts of self experience, that he called *true self* and *false self.* The true self was an experience of self which was an essential core of self. Under conditions that demanded compliance to the primary objects needs but that violated the needs of the true self, the child formed a false self that would look as though it represented the child's needs, but in depth represented compliance to the object over the needs of the true self. Winnicott is careful to observe that the

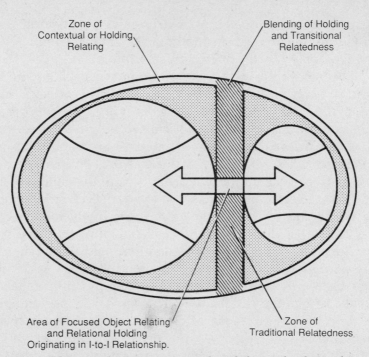

Figure 3-4. Diagram showing contextual and focused relationships. Focused (or Centered or I-to-I) relating occurs in and across the transitional space. The transitional space is in contact with both contextual relating and focused relating, and is also the zone which blends the two.

false self is not merely opportunistic or false in a moral sense, but that it also represents a caretaker self, mediating between inner needs and the demands of the outer world. In this sense, it safeguards the true self from extinction, doing the best it can to care for the self's inner well-being while maintaining the life-sustaining relationships.

What is important to see is that the notion of true and false self represents a universal part of the self (the true self) mostly loyal to one's own inner needs and expression, here divided from the aspect of self (the false self) that needs, in an equally universal way, to relate to primary objects. In health the struggle between these two aspects of self is creative and formative without feeling overly alien to the self's inner nature and potential. In ill-health, the division between being true to one's self and being true to the object may result in such strain that two selves alienated from each other can be observed clinically, resulting in the kind of personality that can be described as a *false-self personality* or an *as-if* character (Zetzel 1958).

RECONCILING WINNICOTT'S TRANSITIONAL PHENOMENA AND BION'S CONTAINER/CONTAINED

Bion's idea of the container/contained stands in an enigmatic relationship to Winnicott's idea of the transitional space and transitional phenomena. They seem similar, but they are not the same idea. Bion is dealing with an internal function of mental processing, with the way the mother handles the projection of part objects, projective identifications, and anxiety, and the way these are fed back to the child.

Winnicott is describing a feature of the external world, the observable exchanges and play activities between mother and baby, although clearly ones that embody internal components and implications. The child Winnicott is concerned with is using mental processes to construct something external, to modify it, to make something for him- or herself. The child Bion describes is focused on his or her internal world and trying to get it in control through unconscious communication with the mother. Bion takes for granted the external and transactional exchanges in writing his theory. Winnicott describes the transactions, feelings, and thoughts that accompany and flow from them, but he takes for granted and does not describe the inner process of personal transformation.

These two theoretical versions of the child are related, but just how is not clear from the two descriptions, focusing as they do on two different aspects of mental activity. If we begin with Bion's description of the container/contained, we see the mother "working" to take in the anxieties of the infant and modify them, returning them to the infant in a matured and detoxified form, which the infant can then reintroject. But the emphasis in Bion's description is on the psychic work inside the mother. There is a passivity inherent in Bion's infant whose anxieties are described by the term *the contained*, which seems to imply that the infant does not have to do anything to get the anxieties into its mother. Nor does Bion's discussion of the container/contained suggest that the infant has to work actively to get the anxieties back from the mother once she has processed them. At present, there is no term for that, just as, until recently, there has been little literature on the active work of introjection (J. Scharff 1992).

In contrast, Winnicott's description of transitional objects and transitional phenomena emphasizes the active work of the infant in the space between mother and infant, an activity that is missing in Bion's discussion. The working agency is the infant's self struggling to make something of the experience with the mother as an object. In so describing what is often an external activity, Winnicott implies the infant's introjection of the mother, but he does not tell us—at least not in the same description—what activities the mother herself is carrying out. The infant of Winnicott's concern is making something of the experience with the mother in order to create something external, and to introject a part of her, which is then under the infant's own control. In this process, a part of the mother, or more precisely of the interaction with her, is made the infant's own, and the capacity of the infant to do this means that the infant can "think" of its self as changed, too. So Winnicott describes an interactive process in which the mother sets the context for an exchange and holds the contextual space for the infant's play. Then in the transitional space—outside either mother or baby but inside their shared space—the infant carries out an activity through which the infant gets a part of the mother inside itself as an internal object. This suggests that the infant actively works in the transitional space to incorporate aspects of the mother, not as an unmodified transplant the infant passively receives, but as modified by the infant.

This is a description of introjective identification as an extremely active process, active in the way a cell actively transports substances from the blood into its interior, choosing some, eliminating others, and changing the structure of the substances as they are incorporated into the cell. So, in this description, Winnicott is dwelling and elaborating on the introjective half of the process, and while he is doing that, he ignores the part that Bion focused on—the activity of the mother as container. Mitchell (1988) has stated that Winnicott's focus tends to blame the mother for deficiencies left in the child's development, implying that the mother is at fault for these deficiencies. This criticism would hold if Winnicott did not also take up the position of the parent, as he does at other times in his writing (1965), where he points out, for instance, the need of the parents to survive the aggression of the child. Their so doing fundamentally promotes the very survival of the child. Neither Bion nor Winnicott discussed these two halves of a conjoined process at the same time, although we may infer that both understood other parts of the process than the ones upon which each focused.

THE THERAPEUTIC PROCESS

The description formed by putting together the contributions of both Bion and Winnicott also applies to the complexity of the therapeutic process. Therapy, like parenting, takes place in the context of the holding supplied by the therapist, although the patient must follow by providing a reciprocal holding. Within this jointly constructed envelope, patient and therapist together turn their focus to examine the internal world of the patient and the way that world affects the patient's relationships. This shared task is supported by the relationship between patient and therapist. In an intensive therapy or psychoanalysis, the shared relationship may become the main vehicle, but it will not—and need not—always be so. The relationship between therapist and patient is a cycle of projective and introjective identification. The patient projectively identifies with the therapist; the therapist introjects the patient's self and inner objects—and is influenced by the patient in depth—and then reprojects the therapist's own modification of this experience for the patient to reintroject. This process of projective and introjective identification is the vehicle of therapy. It is the in-depth process that supports the therapeutic process, and in many ways is the engine that drives it. In computer language, it is the processor that transforms understanding and meaning. It is this interaction of projective and introjective identification that forms the container for the contained.

The process of therapeutic containment begins long before a stage in which the therapist becomes the recipient of specific or focused part-object transferences from the patient, long before the patient comes to feel that the therapist is a new version of the old bad and repressed objects of his or her internal world. It happens from the beginning when the patient looks to the therapist, partly in fear and partly with optimism, for the help toward understanding and growth that parallels the expectations built into an infant toward its caregivers.

In order to examine the parallels between the object relations description of development and the therapeutic process, let us now turn to a discussion of the concepts of transference and countertransference.

TRANSFERENCE AND COUNTERTRANSFERENCE

Freud discovered transference through his work with Breuer on hysteria (Breuer and Freud 1895). In the original discussion, Freud (1895) viewed transference as a process in which the patient imposed past relationships onto the analyst. In this first view, transference was an obstacle to therapy. By 1905 he had decided that transference was the vehicle by which the patient taught the therapist about his or her past and that it was no longer simply to be understood as an obstacle (Freud 1905a). Patients repeated old patterns that embodied things they carried unconsciously but could not consciously remember (Freud 1912a,b, 1914, 1915). Transference had now become transformed into the path of psychoanalytic progress, the broad avenue to understanding the patient.

Countertransference has had a similar evolution. Freud's own discussions of countertransference are much less extensive than those on transference. From his first mention of countertransference in 1910, Freud locates it in the domain of the therapist's problematic inner life, in those unresolved areas of the therapist's own that call for more analysis, whether self-analysis or therapeutic analysis with another analyst (Freud 1912a, 1915, 1937). In contrast to his stated position, Freud's extensive case reports (1905a, 1909, 1918) indicate that he learned a great deal from his feeling states. In making sense of affective aspects of his experience with patients, he was able to understand them in ways that went beyond the confines of his narrow reported view of countertransference.

After Freud's death, the seminal work of Heimann (1950), followed by Money-Kyrle (1956), Tower (1956), Winnicott (1947), and Racker (1968) began to shape countertransference as far more valuable than when it was viewed only as a sign of the therapist's pathology. These writers described countertransference as the therapist's in-depth receptivity to the patient. They saw that the richness of unconscious resonance led the therapist to the most important ways of understanding the patient. Although the debate has continued about whether the word *countertransference* should be reserved solely for the pathological or destructively distorted elements of the therapist's response, or should be used as the broad umbrella term for the whole range of therapist affective response, the fields of psychoanalysis and psychoanalytic psychotherapy have moved on to make use of the broader point of view nevertheless.

Racker (1968) made an important contribution to our understanding of the identifications of the therapist, noting that a therapist might identify either with the patient's self or with the patient's object. In a "concordant identification," the therapist identified with the patient's self, feeling sympathy or anger, for instance, on the part of the patient when the patient claims to be mistreated. At other times, a therapist identifies with the object of a patient, what Racker called a "complementary identification." In this case, the therapist will identify with the object in relationship to the patient's self and the therapist might feel sorry for the objects of the patient's wrath or mistreatment.

In addition, during therapy a patient may behave in ways that are not solely generated by the patient's central self, or even by the repressed self-systems. At some times, patients identify with their own internal objects and treat the therapist as they feel treated by their internal objects. In this situation, the therapist may be projectively identified with the self of the patient while the patient has become identified with his or her own object. This occurred in the vignette of Mr. D. in Chapter 2, the patient who wished to fix me to a spot and pour contents into me as his mother had done to him. When he did this, I felt treated as he had been by her. In this complex concordant identification, I introjectively identified with an aspect of his self, while he became his persecuting internal maternal object. The free-floating nature of these identifications conveys the intimate relationship between self and object and the way both are fundamentally organizing aspects of the patient's self, both capable of generating activity (Ogden 1986).

In the last 30 years, the work of Searles (1965, 1979, 1986), Levenson (1983), Joseph (1989), Bion (1967, 1970), and others has added to clinical and theoretical writings on the therapist's in-depth responsiveness to the patient. Sandler (1976) and, more recently, Jacobs (1991) have, from the classical tradition, elaborated on its usefulness. The current thoughts of Searles (1986), McDougall (1985, 1989), Ogden (1989), Bollas (1989),

Segal (1991), Joseph (1989), Duncan (1981, 1989, 1990, 1991), Casement (1991), Williams (1981), and J. Scharff (1992), among others, have informed my own use of countertransference far more than can be acknowledged by references in this book. The modern expanded use of countertransference also overlaps with discussions by Self psychologists of the role of empathy and the exploration of intersubjectivity (Kohut 1984, Stolorow 1991, Stolorow et al. 1987).

   This movement in psychoanalytic theory and therapy finds a parallel in family therapy. Born originally out of and in reaction to psychoanalysis, family therapy came to dwell on the field of observable interaction between family members, downplaying and eventually disbelieving in the usefulness of transference. Nevertheless, in recent years, family therapy, like psychoanalysis, has focused on the use of the therapist's self — namely, the use of the responsiveness of the therapist in generating an understanding of the family and of its individual members (Aponte and VanDeusen 1981).

   Writing with Jill Scharff, I have been interested in exploring the use of transference and countertransference in couple and family therapy, in applying object relations theory to make more specific what happens inside the therapist, which enables this therapeutic use of self (J. Scharff 1989, 1992, Scharff and Scharff 1987, 1991). Our investigation required an elucidation of the similarities and differences between the use of transference and countertransference with the individual patient and the couple or family. What we learned in the course of this work also offered new perspectives on transference and countertransference in individual psychotherapy and psychoanalysis. That work is summarized in the next section.

A CURRENT VIEW OF TRANSFERENCE AND COUNTERTRANSFERENCE

The therapy situation is an intimate one of personal relatedness over time. The processes of projective and introjective identification provide the vehicles for the unconscious communication of transference and countertransference. In the beginning of any intimate relationship, the potential for its growth is borne in mind by both participants, rather like the way the mother keeps in mind the potential for growth of the infant. In a similar way, a patient and therapist begin with fantasies about the possibilities for growth of their relationship, and these have immediate transference and countertransference implications. For instance, from the beginning, the patient will have fantasies about people in therapistlike roles. These fantasies will embody the patient's hopes and fears and will be based on past experience with people in similar roles, including parents, teachers, and mentors. These transferences will be active from the beginning or even from before the first meeting, from the time the person begins to seek a therapist. When patient and therapist do meet, the patient will project aspects of these prior object relationships and the anxieties they contain into the therapist, who will have the job of taking them in, containing them, and putting them back into the patient in detoxified form. This is not merely a cognitive matter, not just a matter of the therapist's intellectually understanding the patient's worry, but of taking it in—of being open to the introjective process—of responding at both conscious and unconscious levels and helping the patient move to a gradually more trusting or open position.

CONTEXTUAL AND FOCUSED TRANSFERENCE

The hopes and fears for the therapist in this way form a transference, which I have called the *contextual transference* (Scharff and Scharff 1987), the transference to the therapist as a provider of arms-around holding, of a context for building "a continuity of being" (Winnicott 1960a, p. 54) and for growth. Patients come to therapy with positive expectations and hopes for the therapeutic relationship, and they come with fears about the consequences of the relationship and even dread at the possibility of failure for their wishes for acceptance and growth. This mixture of feelings and attitudes, this expression of patients' selves, constitutes the contextual transference and is present from the beginning of the therapy. If the contextual transference is positive, the therapist will experience the patient as trusting, open, collaborative, and perhaps grateful. In the countertransference to the contextual relationship, the therapist will feel benignly regarded, positively valued, or simply useful in the positive way that a loved mother feels securely valued most when taken for granted. The assumption of this willingness and intention to be helpful will lend something of a rosy glow to the relationship. If the contextual transference contains a predominance of negative elements—fear of persecution, scorn, or envy—the therapist will find the patient suspicious, untrusting, quick to criticize or express feelings of being criticized, or spoiling and rejecting of the therapist's efforts. In this negative contextual situation, the therapist's countertransference will consist of a sense of rejection and devaluation, frustration and disregard. In reaction, therapists may wish to be rid of the patients and may feel depressed, hopeless, or angry much of the time.

In the ordinary situation, the contextual transference is a mixture of positive and negative elements, although there will usually be a prevailing attitude with noticeable fluctuations. This aspect of transference is closely related to the concepts of the *working alliance* (Greenson 1967) and the *therapeutic alliance* (Zetzel 1958). These two concepts also describe the "glue" that makes therapy possible. Zetzel noted that the patient's capacity for an alliance was rooted in early experience, which she generally identified as preoedipal. By applying object relations theory, we can now be more specific. The capacity for an alliance and the infringements on this capacity, either at the beginning of a therapeutic relationship or later on, derive from the patient's early experience with the environmental mother—and with both environmental parents—and with the parents as containers. The contextual aspect of relating reflects prior experience of the environmental parents and is carried inside us as a component of internal object relations. Clinically, it is possible to observe and describe it separately from the relationship to our parents as discrete objects of our love, hate, fear, and desire.

That aspect of transference originally described by Freud (1912a, 1915) is more essentially what I have called the *focused transference* (Scharff and Scharff 1987). In this aspect of transference, the therapist is seen as a repressed bad object to be loved, feared, and regarded with frustration, wariness, contempt, or excitement. This is the part of the transference that has taken its inheritance from the infant's relationship to Winnicott's object mother (1963b).

The two aspects of transference can dissolve into each other. Indeed, the use of one may be substituted for the other. For instance, the hysterical patient who quickly assumes that the therapist is an erotic love object has substituted an excited focused transference of sexualized desire for an underlying contextual one that contains the fear that the therapist will not be able to contain his or her anxieties. Fearing that a positive maternal holding is not possible, the patient jumps to substitute a sexualized physical holding to cover his or her fears concerning what will be painfully and inevitably missing.

In psychotherapy we work mainly with contextual transference. It concerns the safety and reliability of the therapist as a person who will provide arms-around holding that respects the self of the patient and yet promotes maturation and a growth of understanding with minimal sense of threat. In my view, early interpretation of the transference, such as that advocated by Klein (1975a,b), Gill and Muslin (1976), and Kernberg (1975), should be about the contextual transference, that aspect of the relationship required to foster the therapy. Only when the relationship has grown and survived is the patient free to projectively identify intimate parts of his or her object world with the therapist, and then to recognize these relatively discrete aspects of self and internal object in the therapist. And it is only slowly that the therapist, who from the first allows him- or herself to take in aspects of the patient through introjective identification, can realize the shape of the patient's objects foreign to the therapist and that do him or her an internal injustice, in order to help the patient separate out these experiences.

This is the work of long-term, intensive psychotherapy and of psychoanalysis. Even while the hallmark of these depth approaches is work with the focused transference or transference neurosis, this only fully crystallizes after patient and therapist have established a long-standing relationship. When the focused transference and the countertransference that is its counterpart do come, they are delivered into the circle of the contextual relationship, the holding that has been mutually supported and nurtured by therapist and patient. The focused internal object transference is born into the waiting arms-around relationship and is then nurtured and supported by it. When this happens, a new kind of transference and counter-transference interplay is possible, but throughout this work, that is, for the duration of the therapy, attention will still fall periodically on the contextual transference, on its stability and viability.

THE RELATIONSHIP BETWEEN PATIENT AND THERAPIST

There is a further note about the reciprocity of the relationship between patient and therapist. We have been describing the situation from the patient's point of view, as though it were the patient who did all the projective identifying, the therapist who introjected first and only later reprojected, and that it was only then that the patient took something back in. Critics might charge that if this is a real relationship, the therapist must be projectively and introjectively active from the beginning, with his or her own unconscious agendas, perhaps in better matu-rational shape than the patient, but active nevertheless.

And the critics would be right! Racker (1968) labeled this situation the *therapist's transference* and described it as the expression of the therapist's immaturity and areas of difficulty. But I believe it is more than that. It is an inevitable component of the process, even in a well-analyzed therapist or analyst. We hope that the therapist is projecting a more mature image of him- or herself than is the patient, but—just as with an ordinary mother—it will not inevitably be so. Better to acknowledge that the therapist must projectively and introjectively identify with the patient simply because this is an inevitable component of all relationships! It should, as should the mother's activity, be the fainter theme and subject to modification by the therapist's previous growth, training, and experience. But it happens, nevertheless, and just as the mother must put her stamp on and into her child, who becomes the organ of expression of her identity (Lichtenstein 1961), so, in a successful treatment, the patient will be in part a reflection of the therapist's identity.

The view of the therapist's role that I am advocating here is controversial, relying as it also does on the therapist's inevitable introjection of aspects of the patient and the patient's inevitable introjective identification with the therapist (J. Scharff 1992). In my examination of the interplay of transference and countertransference throughout this book, I illustrate the ways in which this plays a fundamental role in the relationship between self and other in psychotherapy and psychoanalysis.

TRANSFERENCE AND COUNTERTRANSFERENCE IN CONJOINT THERAPY

Separating the two aspects of transference is also useful in differentiating the use of transference in individual therapy and family therapy (Scharff and Scharff 1987, 1991). Whereas the focused transference built of projective identifications of discrete parts of self and object is an appropriate level of consideration in individual therapy, in family therapy the therapist needs to organize the experience at the level of the family group. Since a family or couple has shared holding functions for and with each other, the therapist can best understand them by assuming that the aspect of transference that most needs to be understood stems from the difficulties the couple or family have in providing a context of holding for each other. This is expressed in the family's or couple's pooled contextual transference. Although each individual in the family contributes to this group transference, the therapist's countertransference represents a response to the family as a group struggling to provide holding to each other. If the therapist first attempts to understand his or her countertransference as relating to the group, it will subsequently be easier to understand individual contributions to the shared family transference.

The therapist's understanding in group therapy should also draw on the contextual transference. Each member of a therapy group has discrete projective identifications with the therapist, but each one also experiences them with other members of the group. The pooled group transference to the therapist represents the group members' shared doubts and fears about their capacity to provide holding to each other and to themselves as a group. Ezriel (1950, 1952) has described how the individual member's contributions to a group can be understood and interpreted in terms of an overall group transference. Attention to the therapist's countertransference as an indicator of the group's fears of deficits in its shared holding will lead the group therapist furthest in understanding the group's shared difficulties and the way their shared fears about environmental provision express and stem from their individual issues.

ADAM'S EVOLVING TREATMENT

Adam, an out-of-work engineer, was my first analytic patient. His opening dream about playing for the Los

Angeles Dodgers, described in Chapter 1, posed ambiguous questions about whether he was playing for me or against me, whether I was there to approve and coach him, or to try to get him out. Would he be able to hit my pitches, and would he drop the ball? He had sought therapy for his difficulty in getting himself to work after finishing graduate school and for his repeated pattern of depending on women for financial and emotional support.

In the transference during the first months of analysis, Adam regarded me as a benign parent, a combination of a mother with whom he could talk for hours, and a father to whom he could talk man-to-man. But the material about his own father was harsh. His father did things better than he did and was impatient with Adam, never explaining adequately, expecting too much. His father was a critical pitcher–coach who was Adam's ideal but who never offered enough support. Growing up, when he could not satisfy his father or feel satisfied by his father's support, Adam retreated to his mother, finding a sympathetic and supportive ear.

After several months, under the sway of consciously positive feeling for me, Adam reported another dream, the first in which I appeared.

I had a neat little dream. You are tinkering with a car with a teen-aged boy. It was my car, and I'm there trying to tell you where to look. The car has engines at both ends. I am telling you different places to look—maybe so you won't find anything?! Then I worry, "They're experts and won't they find anything?" The other person helping turns out to be me, too, only younger. You're the chief of the operation.

Adam liked the dream. He was struck by the partnership between me and the boy in a mechanical project. Adam said, "I think I was hoping to mislead you, but I also hoped you wouldn't be fooled, that you and I could find out what was wrong with my car together."

"The dream sounds like parts of the relationship you had with your father. Did you work on cars together?" I asked.

"No," he answered, "but I got him to advise me on buying a used car, which turned out to be a lemon. The dream also reminds me of the summers I worked in an automobile plant to pay for college. Dad wasn't very sympathetic to the danger I felt I was in. One time I did get slightly hurt and he didn't seem to care."

"Feeling your father gave bad advice and was unsympathetic adds something to the dream," I said. "In the dream you and I have a partnership about fixing this car, but you are also trying to throw me off the track. Then you're worried I'll be fooled by you, so the car won't get fixed. Part of you is with me, and part of you is against me in the job."

"I think that's the way I felt about my father," he said. "I wanted him to be with me, but lots of times I felt he was against me."

"And would you try to mislead him?" I asked.

"When I felt mad at him, I'd go to my mother, who was sympathetic," he said. "I'd say things to her I wouldn't tell him. So in that way I did."

"What about the car having engines at both ends?" I asked.

"It could go forward or back. Or if both engines worked, it would just rev up its motors and stand still at full speed. It's a funny image, like a 'Push-me-pull-you,' the animal in the Doctor Doolittle books Dad read me as a child. You couldn't tell if it was coming or going. It had heads at both ends."

"You haven't made up your mind whether to go forward in analysis," I said. "You're not sure if I'm a sympathetic coach or a cruel father. And you just may want to go in the other direction if things get rough, or just rev up your motors so you can stay where you are at full speed while I'm a frustrated Dr. Doolittle. But you also hope you can't fool me, so that I can help you."

Adam hoped he could depend on me despite his fearful withholding—a fear for himself that drew on the image of the rejecting object father. But he had another image of his father as a clever mechanic or coach, clever enough not to be fooled by his ploys. And he saw his hopes for his own growth as dependent on that father. At the same time, the image for a supportive object was based on his mother, the mother to whom he retreated when buffeted by the threatening father. This image of the environmental or contextual support was also made up of the parts of his father he felt did support his efforts, but he tended to split the images vigorously so that his mother was assigned the role of support and his father that of assault.

So far, the contextual transference was benign: I was the combined supportive and helpful aspects of father and mother. In fact, I felt suspiciously well treated. I was untainted by the anger that was directed at the focus on the critical and criticized bad father whom Adam accused of failing to support him. I was still the idealized aspect of father, but the envy that lurked in the shadows of the idealization was covered by and split off into the attacks on the rejecting object father. I had an eerie feeling of being protected from elements that could form a transferential attack, one now outlined by the dream.

Despite the ambivalence depicted by the dream, it mostly gave a sign of a positive contextual transference, for it demonstrated that Adam had enough trust to deliver his dilemma into the arms of our relationship. Through it and later in association to it, he revealed to both of us aspects of his internal object relations that had influenced his relationships with men who might be available to help him, and of his retreat to women, as he had retreated to his mother and his wife for support and protection from the threatening world of men.

I was aware of another current that was ripening, of a pull toward me in a sexual vein, of two heads linked together as in the analytic situation, two engines in a single machine, two men working together. Partly it was this homosexual element that made him—and me—uncomfortable. I still did not highlight this element, especially the hidden sexual tie I now began to feel lay underneath the ambivalence about the working alliance. Much later, this element came to the fore, as he longed for me. It was expressed in a fantasy in the second year of the analysis about putting something through a mail slot in my office door, which we agreed was a "male slot" for a sexualized union, and in the image of biting my genitals in reaction to the pull toward me.

But in these early days of the analysis, Adam was first concerned with the adequacy of the arms-around relationship to provide for our work. He wondered if I would be the easily misled mechanic or the one he could not fool. Would I support him against his competitors and enemies as his mother did? We can hear his concern for his developing self and its fate in these questions, both as he was growing up and now as he hoped to set things right for himself with me. Here the old transferences about his parents' adequacy were relived, brought to us by the emergence of his internal object relations into the context of the therapy.

But already, at the beginning, we can see the pull of the longing for father, a sexualized pull that also frightened Adam. The father who was the object of Adam's desire and the aspect of Adam who longed for him enviously when he felt unsupported and denied is lurking in the wings, threatening to attack the holding of the therapeutic relationship. Much later, we would discover that this aspect of an oedipal father was built on early rejections Adam felt from his mother when three siblings were born in rapid order, and that, in an internal dynamic way, pinning the blame on father was an unconscious attempt to spare mother from his rage and retaliation so that she could be available to shore him up (see Chapter 6).

What about my countertransference in this early stage? I have said that I already felt uncomfortably spared. I was the benign supportive father he longed for, whereas his reports of a rejecting father were full of resentment. I sat a bit nervously in my chair, waiting for the resentment to come home to roost. In time, of course, it did, but not until we had built an alliance through work on the contextual transference and countertransference. There I was able to work with my uneasiness, which led us to his, to the fear he could unseat or mislead me, and we were slowly able to catch him at games of deception—mainly to his relief.

But there were other aspects of my countertransference that remained less comfortable for me. The threat of the homosexual pull. My hopes for his help in our two-headed task. And mostly, my own doubts. Adam knew of my training status. He had been referred for a low fee analysis that he knew I offered because I was in training. His doubts about my skill in fixing the car and in understanding his attempts to throw me off the track echoed my own. Of course, I had my supervisor who was supportive and clever. She worked with my self-doubts, helped me to sharpen my skills. But neither of us quite understood the way Adam's doubts and dreams expressed my own, were in their own way the product of my own. His dream of the two-headed engine also could have been mine, could have expressed my own yearnings for a supportive father or parent. The partner I had was Adam. How could I know if he would support my efforts at learning car repair? Was he with me or against me? Were we on the same team or were we opponents? And how would I look to my supervisor?

The dream issues could be understood as his introjection of my issues, of my transference to him, and at the same time, his own issues gave him a valency to take mine in. He worried if I would support his efforts and needs, just as I worried if he would support mine. He experienced these as problems for the growth and repair of his self, whereas I might have told myself that my own worries were about a merely professional task outside my central self. But my concerns were at the center of my growth as an analyst. In this way, the issues were central to both of us. In the resonance between them lay the greatest intensity of our relationship, the greatest potential for mutual understanding and growth, the greatest potential for my becoming the analyst I wanted to be by helping him.

My situation with Adam was like a mother's with her baby. To become a mother, a mother needs her baby's help, as I needed Adam's to become an analyst. The fate for each of us was held in our shared interaction and work. We were each becoming the other on whom our selves depended. The vehicle for our mutual evolution was the shared projective and introjective identifications that formed the transference and countertransference interplay of our work. They are the vehicle for in-depth communication in therapy and analysis, the foundation of an understanding of the relationship between self and object.

These forces do not only operate in individual therapy. The next chapter illustrates their similar operation in a couple, and the way the understanding of projective and introjective identification leads therapists toward an understanding of a couple.

PART TWO

Therapy of the Self in Relation to Objects

4

Using Transference and Countertransference to Understand Projective and Introjective Identification in a Couple

It is through the use of the therapist's own experience that patients' self and object experiences can best be understood. A vivid example is offered by a couple I saw with Dr. Jill Savege Scharff for a videotaped assessment. Replay and review of the tape have allowed us to study the processes of projective and introjective identification and of countertransference with a fullness not ordinarily available.

Michelle and Lenny were in their late twenties or

early thirties. She was blond, chubby, dressed in a flamboy-
antly colored blouse of bright turquoise with red, yellow, and
orange flowers; he was thin and bald, wearing a muted
turquoise shirt with thin stripes of red, yellow, and orange.

Despite their dramatically obvious physical differences, I had the
experience of seeing them as variations on a theme, almost as fraternal
twins.

As soon as the interview began, the impression that there
was a visual paradox extended to their relationship. They had
been referred by a colleague, a Mrs. Taylor, who was Lenny's
therapist and who had also occasionally seen them as a couple.

Lenny explained what brought them to therapy.

"We first went for therapy because of Michelle's question:
'Why can't I dump this guy?' She figured she could get the
answer in one session. That was a year ago."

Michelle crossed her legs. Kicking her right foot furiously,
she said, "I tried to get Mrs. Taylor to tell you to dump me, but
it didn't work. Basically I'm interested in ending the relationship, and he's interested in getting married. So we should do
something about that." She turned to me and said impishly,
"Do you have a cure? Maybe you can prescribe a pill?"

Dr. Jill Scharff asked, "Would you take a pill to get married
or to break up?"

Michelle answered, "To break up! I don't want to marry
him. Even though he did buy me a lovely engagement ring. I
wish I had it to show you. It would make a great visual for a
tape." She held up her hand as if showing off the ring.

I asked, "What happened to it?"

Michelle said, "I had to try it on, but I decided not to
accept it. That was about six months ago."

"Yeah," said Lenny. "In December."

Michelle continued. "We decided to break up on New
Year's. Basically I don't want to marry him, for reasons I'm sure
an hour isn't enough to get into. My problem is this: I'm here
because I can't seem to dump the guy, but I don't want to
marry him. So you could say, 'Michelle, get on with your life!'
But there's a lot of good in him, so I can't dump him either.

And he's in exactly the opposite spot. So we really need a cure."

Jill said, "I notice you get a lot of pleasure from taunting each other."

"We have an ongoing act," Michelle agreed. "You could probably book us into a few theater houses."

Lenny nodded. "We have it down pat." They laughed.

Jill continued, "Do you find your friends enjoy that or is it mainly for each other's benefit?"

Michelle answered, "For each other. Our friends don't enjoy it."

Lenny added, "She doesn't do it that much in front of her friends. They think she's cruel."

Michelle was a bit more thoughtful, saying, "I admit I am being mean to him, although there's affection in it, too. He does bring it out in me."

THE INITIAL COUNTERTRANSFERENCE

I found this couple extremely amusing in a way that was exceedingly uncomfortable, reminiscent of Jackie Gleason's "Honeymooners." They shared an extremely aggressive sense of humor, full of confusing contradictions, so that right at the beginning of the hour I found myself feeling that they were a good match, yet I was jolted by the sadistic humor. It was disquieting right away.

Jill continued the line of questioning. "How does he bring the cruelty out in you?"

Michelle said, "It's a mutual thing. We're diametrically extremely different people. That's why this relationship is doomed for failure. But it's been almost four years because, although I've dated other guys a bit, he's the one that stuck around."

Jill said, "You can't dump him, but you can't kill him off either."

Lenny confirmed her way of putting it. "You can't live with him and you can't shoot him, as they say."

Michelle said, "He just seems to be so resilient. He just pops back. And I hate that. My problem is that I hate people who like me. And, of course, he doesn't only like me, he loves me a lot. Which I can't stand! So basically, I mean this is one for the books!"

Jill said, "You make it sound funny, like a cartoon. But basically, you feel you're a person who really is. . . ." She hesitated before finishing. "You feel you're horrible, don't you?"

I was hit with the directness of my wife's language, but once she said it, I recognized it had to be said. I, too, felt a need to cut through the confusion and tantalizing quality of the comedy routine.

Michelle was not flustered. She said, "I'm only horrible to him."

Lenny said, "She says I'm the only person she's like this towards."

Michelle nodded. "He is! I'm not really horrible, but I'm not the greatest altruist in the world either. I'm ambitious, assertive, and I have no patience for people who aren't. And he's not. He's a wonderful human being. I've never quite had a boyfriend this good. He's a born husband, but it's never been enough. I want someone on my level intellectually, with the values my upbringing gave me. We have opposite kinds of upbringings, so that's not likely."

I was now struck by the pervasive paradox of opposite–likeness. The metaphor of the shirts had been organizing my thinking about their variations on a theme. So Michelle's introduction of the ideal of opposites appealed to me. But I felt intuitively that these were cartoon opposites—opposing yet dovetailing projective identifications in a raw caricature of intimacy.

I asked, "How were your upbringings opposite?"

Lenny answered, speaking more than he had so far. "Michelle was a middle-class child. She considers my background upper class. I lived a sheltered life. Michelle was thrust out into the world, yet she still had the protection of her family. There were stronger family relationships in her family than in mine. We're very different people, too. I'm laid back, where she's type A, quick to get going, can't sit still. She says I don't meet her three criteria for a man: fun, funny, and intelligent."

Michelle agreed. "You're not fun; you're not funny. And you're definitely not intelligent. I mean," she said, turning to Jill, "this is 3½ years and we can talk to each other fairly brutally and honestly."

Lenny said, "You might say she's been brutally honest."

I asked, "How do you feel when you're bantering like this?"

"It passes the time," said Michelle.

Lenny said, "It depends on my mood. If she gets me in a bad mood, she can make it worse. Most of the time, I ignore it and don't take it personally. She has difficulty expressing affectionate emotions, so she uses opposites. Rather than give me a kiss, she'll give me a punch."

Jill asked, "So that's how you know she loves you?"

Lenny nodded. "That's how I look at it. Those are her words of affection."

Michelle gave an expression of equivocation with her hand. "Well, sometimes."

Lenny continued, "But of course sometimes she does mean the abuse."

Michelle said, "That's right. I'm not exactly forthcoming. But then again, I'm not in love. And that bothers me. I mean I'm fond of Len, affectionate, all that stuff. At times I love him. But I'm definitely not *in love* with him. Mrs. Taylor said, 'That's fine.' But it really bothers me because I think you have to be in love to have a good relationship. I know that lots of times, opposites attract. Well, we're opposites, but. . . ."

My hopes were raised by her hint of insight. I asked, "How are you opposites?"

Michelle loved the questions and our interest in them. "In every way. Like Lenny said, his family is upper class. He's the youngest boy of four children. His mother is a Jewish mother and he's her golden child. She did everything for him, so he never learned to do things for himself. He grew up sheltered, so he didn't want to socialize. He didn't assert himself. I was the opposite. Our family isn't intimate, but it was intense."

Lenny's role was to punctuate her narratives. "Extremely intense!" he said.

Michelle went on. "My family dealt from crisis to crisis. They're a kind of depleted middle class. My parents were idealists who married young. We were a young family, but a family of thinkers. Very different from Lenny's family. That would be fine in a normal relationship. But I resent him because I have to do all the work. Lenny depends on me for everything. He needs a mother, not a wife. So that would stand in the way of getting married. If I marry Lenny, I'm going to spend the rest of my life lighting a fire under his . . . under his tush. It sounds funny, but it's true."

Jill asked, "Do you see it that way, Lenny?"

Lenny said, "I'll admit that I lack motivation. The only time I'll push myself is when someone else relies on me. Otherwise, I don't just for myself. I'm lazy. Michelle says I should meet other women to see what I'm missing. I never wanted to. I'm happy with Michelle."

Jill continued to probe. "Does Michelle rely on you for anything?"

Lenny sighed. "I give her security. I tell her I'm the rock in the river. And I won't move. I'll always be there for her. If she ever needs me while she's running through the river—both up and down stream. I give her the security she needs."

Michelle laughed. "He's a great date! The hell with security! He takes me out nice. He treats me like a queen. He's wonderful! Always the best. He was raised first class, and he's the classiest man I've ever met." She raised her hands in a gesture that seemed to discount what Lenny had said about offering security. "Fascinating so far, huh? You're both riveted!" she said sarcastically.

I was now finding this couple fascinating! An oddly jarring combination of theatrical amusement and insight. Lenny's formulation of the rock in the river caught my attention. They were articulate and insightful, and yet Michelle was always destroying the meaning and attacking Lenny. Her nastiness was getting to me, upsetting me as I identified with his steadfastness and with his fascination for her theatricality. I felt this tied to the theme of the shirts, which had been on my mind from the beginning of the interview.

I said, "I'm interested in the question of whether you're really opposites. I've been looking at your shirts."

Lenny laughed. "She bought this for me."

Michelle said, "That's not his personality. It's mine."

I said, "Well, maybe." Michelle laughed again.

Lenny said, "But I like her taste. When she buys me things, there's hardly ever a time I don't like them."

I said, "What I noticed was that the shirts are the same colors. Yours, Michelle, is bold and right out there. And Lenny's is a quiet statement of the same colors."

Michelle was still laughing. "It was a *total* coincidence. Total!"

I quipped, "I'll believe you. Thousands wouldn't."

ENACTING CO-THERAPY COUNTERTRANSFERENCE

My quip is an expression of Jill's, which I co-opted here. In retrospect, I realize that in using it I had introjectively identified with Michelle's sarcastic jokiness. Using this phrase was an act of "stealing" from my wife, which echoed the way this couple took things in from each other. In retrospect, I could see that I used the remark in an introjective identification with the bantering of the couple. I had taken in their way of relating and, in an elaboration in my own coupleship, had also magnified an introjective identification with Jill.

Michelle took my joke in stride. "It is a total coincidence. But if you send Lenny to the store, he would never in a million years bring that shirt home. I bought it for him. It's not his taste at all."

Lenny agreed. "I'd bring home the solids, probably, and blues."

I wanted to give a trial interpretation to see how well they could work with it. I said, "Let me tell you my thought about the shirts. I had the idea you might share a lot, but in ways that reflect the opposite poles of things. You, Lenny, might be the quiet, deeper statement of some of the same characteristics and emotions that Michelle has. Something about you, Lenny, helps hold the two of you together. This has been going on a long time."

Lenny nodded and Michelle sat listening. I continued.

"So all these statements about how impossible the relationship is, that it's ready to break up—even if they're true, there's still something important about why each of you is so strongly attracted to the other."

Lenny said, "Probably if she knew the reason why we were so attracted, she'd find a way to get rid of that reason." Turning to her, he continued, "You keep wondering why you can't break up. So If you could find out. . . ." He smiled at her.

Michelle shook her head. "It's just a matter of time. This is so cruel. My own reasons for *not* breaking up are purely selfish. They have nothing to do with him. It's because he's a great boyfriend, great to have around."

Lenny grinned. "Why get rid of a good thing?"

Michelle said, "Exactly! How much does it interfere with me to have him around? Well, it interferes with meeting other guys. But even when I meet them, they're not that great. And I don't view myself as such a hot proposition that I could just go out and meet the man of my dreams or someone I'd be truly attracted to. But it also drives me nuts. I can only tolerate him for two or three days at a time, and then I go berserk."

Jill asked, "Am I right, Lenny, that Michelle *is* the woman of your dreams?"

Lenny answered, "Yeah! She is, although she would argue with that. . . ."

Michelle, again laughing with sarcasm, interjected, "Because you probably don't have any dreams. Look, you say opposites attract. But not if they resent each other. He doesn't resent me. But I feel like he's a vacuum cleaner, you know. I'm going to be empty because he's removing everything I have because he's hollow himself. And that's not right. What I have is golden. It's like buried treasure because of the way I was brought up. I'm proud of it. There's a lot of substance there. I'm independent, emotional, and I'm looking for someone that can communicate back to me, on my level. I'm from a family of discussers. Lenny's from a family that didn't talk. . . . It's fine to blame your parents for your upbringing, but when you get older and discover how empty or lacking your life is, you do something about it. And that I would respect. But he doesn't. And so I don't respect him."

Michelle was going on in this vein. We were about twenty minutes into the interview. Our attempts to make sense of their sadomasochistic pattern were being rebuffed. In fact, Michelle upped the ante, and here was charging full force at Lenny's lack of good qualities. Our naming of his steadfastness and our pursuit of her use of him through projective identification led to an intensification of her attack. Feeling helpless and deadened, but without realizing it, I got sleepy and had to fight off fatigue for the next fifteen minutes or so. The agony of the struggle between sleep and wakefulness dulled the pain of experiencing the contradictory seductive and murderous attachment to this man with whom I rapidly developed an identification around his valuing of reliability and caretaking.

The interview moved onto other topics: Michelle's idealization of her father and family; her parents' divorce five years ago; the way Lenny's sister is a soulmate to Michelle, so understanding of her impatience with Lenny. Jill led the interview, and it now turned out that Lenny was a successful architect with a dozen employees, earning much more income than Michelle. Yet Michelle, who worked in a social agency, was scornful of him here, too, for "being uninterested in the world" and in social causes. I listened to her, feeling that she was inflating the worth of her own social interests.

Still fighting my sleepiness, I grew annoyed that each of Michelle's characterizations was more extreme. She was the brightness, the verve, the value. He was the stalwart, the blah, the dullness. I was glad my wife was there to carry the work while I, not quite

grasping it, felt disabled by the murderousness the couple tolerated in
the heart of their relationship. I had taken in the deadliness. My
capacity to work was, for the moment, killed off.

They were now discussing Michelle's previous relationship to a man she said she had loved. Jill asked, "Lenny, what
do you understand about that last relationship of Michelle's?"

Lenny said, "The only thing I understand is she was in
love with him. She saw fireworks and felt true love. She said
she was close to marrying him when she saw that it wouldn't
work and got out."

Michelle said, "It was the same thing, only worse. The guy
was passive! Actually, I read a book, *Smart Women, Foolish*
Choices. He's on page 57. I sent a Xerox to all my girlfriends.
Passive dependent! He couldn't even signal a waiter. The first
thing I liked about Lenny was that he had no problem signaling
a waiter. Why do guys that need self-confidence get attracted to
me? I obviously have a need to feel needed. So I tend to settle
for less when I go out with guys because I don't think highly of
myself."

WORKING THROUGH COUNTERTRANSFERENCE

Jill said, "I certainly have heard in what you've said, Michelle,
that you don't like yourself. You can't bear to be loved. You
expect people to find the way you treat Lenny horrible. Before
we began the interview, you said that you were afraid if people
saw you act like this, they'd say 'What a bitch!' At the same
time, the two of you cooperate to push Michelle forward,
hoping to be really fascinating. For instance, you said, 'Are we
riveted?' "

Lenny and Michelle looked at each other and laughed. Jill
continued, and what she said finally woke me out of my
stupor.

"At the same time, David, I looked over and saw you
looking rather sleepy. I wondered if you were experiencing

another side to it while I was listening attentively? Perhaps something that would help us understand their polarity?"

I was shaken awake instantly by my wife's turning attention on me. She kept talking long enough for me to gather my wits, and in the process, I suddenly realized what had been possessing me.

Michelle discounted Jill's question. "Maybe he's tired," she said.

Jill continued, "When I saw you, David, sitting there in an uncharacteristic way, it led me to wonder if you were experiencing a feeling that Michelle carries inside, closer to a passive feeling, or an image of being a rock herself with the water running over her."

My wife was being quite specific in asking what projective identification I had taken in that could help us understand the couple's experience. She and I share the view that fatigue in a session almost always represents a countertransference feeling, which, if understood, helps us recover sufficiently to demonstrate the underlying anxiety that produces the defense. I was grateful by now for her intervention. I felt rescued from the rocks.

Michelle quipped, "How about boredom?"

Finally I was able to speak. "I think not boredom," I said. "I don't think it's a boring problem. It's sad." Michelle laughed, and Lenny joined her.

Jill nodded. "I agree."

"I love this!" said Michelle.

I said, "Well, I felt a couple of things. Earlier when we began to talk, I felt I was supposed to persuade you, Michelle, to stay with Lenny. That's not my job, but . . ."

"No," said Michelle. "You were supposed to persuade *him* to dump *me*."

"That's what you say," I continued, "and the louder you said it, the more I thought that so many of the things you said about him were kind. He has so many virtues, and you describe yourself as ungrateful and difficult but stuck on him. It did sound like a plea to persuade you to stay with him, which isn't my job."

I was perseverating on how getting them to stay together was not my job. I felt guilty for having a wish to keep them together, as though that would be for my needs. I could not yet recognize that they had put that wish into me while Michelle continued to speak consciously for ending the relationship.

Michelle shot back, "No!"

I continued, "I don't think you're literally saying that, but I do hear that underneath. When I had to fight my temptation to try to persuade you, feeling irreconcilable contradictions, I drew back and got sleepy. Because it's hard to know what to do. You present such a good case for leaving, so why are you here?"

Michelle said, "Because I'm stupid."

I was suddenly struck with Lenny's broad grin as she made this self-effacing joke. I felt I had caught him colluding and could almost feel myself springing a trap.

I said, "Well, no. But Lenny, you're smiling. You seem to be enjoying Michelle's jokes."

Lenny said, "I love listening to her."

I said, "Even though it's about how she's going to leave you?"

Lenny nodded. "I know." They were both smiling broadly.

I said, "The more you say you love listening to her and find she's the woman of your dreams, the more I feel that what fits is sadness."

Michelle nodded. "Contradiction is one of the things I'm working on in therapy."

"Let's work on it here," I insisted.

Michelle turned up one side of her mouth quizically. "That's a big one! I'm a walking contradiction."

She was a slippery one! She was trying to scoot out of talking with us in this session by referring it elsewhere, to her individual therapy. I could feel how hard it was to confront her despite her show of insight. I could feel a pull to confront her more openly, more sadistically. I had to check that pull, to keep it confined to limit-setting in the interview.

I said, "What I'm saying, Michelle, is that I find you contradictory, right now."

Michelle said, "I know."

I said, "In the same way that there's the theme of the 'same-but-different' in the colors of your shirts, there's this theme of the wrong colors being used to say things, of bright dancing colors being used to express . . . almost a dirge."

Michelle laughed with disbelief. "A dirge!?"

I said, "Yes, about your relationship."

It was Lenny who confirmed my interpretation. "It's like in New Orleans where they have the jazz bands playing at a funeral!"

I felt a sudden relief, a gratitude at Lenny's association to the New Orleans jazz bands. His association, which was humorous without being a joke, let her relax and speak in a more straightforward way.

Michelle said, "I'm so sad, frustrated. Sometimes I look over at him and I think, 'Why do I have to leave him. It would be perfect. He would be a good husband, and we would be such a good team.' "

I said, "Really? That's a strong statement."

Michelle said, "I know it is. And I've known it for so long. This relationship started out on a horrible note. I was dating several men. One of them was the man I was in love with. And Lenny wouldn't leave me alone. I liked that about him. The fact that he stayed consistent for three and one half years drives me nuts. It makes it harder to leave him. Because I don't like myself as much as he likes me. So I lost respect. Here I am telling him he doesn't have a snowball's chance in hell, and I told him that from the start."

Even in this more serious tone, the sentences in which she confessed attachment and gratitude to him came right next to the ones blaming him for exactly the same behavior—his steadfastness—which she immediately claimed she hated. This impossible contradiction seemed to be the knot that must be understood.

I said, "The main strike against Lenny is that he's stayed."

Michelle nodded. "That he loves me. That's pretty bad, too."

I said, "Anybody who would want to be involved with you . . ."

Michelle finished my sentence, ". . . has gotta be a loser! Yeah. I'm working on that, too. Because intellectually I've known it's not so, but emotionally obviously it is. . . ."

Jill said, "I think the question is if you felt better about yourself, and if you were then able to accept his love for you, would that change him?"

Michelle said, "No, it wouldn't change anything, but it would certainly help my development as a human being."

I asked, "Is he unchangeable?"

Michelle, full of certitude, said, "I believe the guy's unchangeable."

Lenny said, "I change. Just too slowly for her."

I said, "You're like the rock in the river."

Lenny agreed. "Yeah. I change, but very slowly."

I said, "You could be worn down, but it would take a few millennia!"

Lenny nodded in agreement.

Jill asked, "But I still think that's a question, too. If you knew Michelle accepted your love, would you still love her? I think that must be what's worrying. . . ."

Michelle said, "That's a really *good* question."

Lenny said, "Do you mean if things changed and all of a sudden she started loving me? I don't know why I would change."

Jill asked, "Could you accept that?"

Michelle said, "Yeah. How would you deal with that? If I was nice to you all the time and I never called you names?"

Jill shook her head. "Oh, no! I don't think that's what love is."

Michelle laughed. "It is in our case."

"Do you mean it would be the opposite of what happens now?" I asked.

Michelle said, "Right. I wouldn't call him names and ignore him half the time, and treat him somewhat like. . . ."

"You'd probably keep the names," said Lenny in a self-deprecating joke. To Jill he asked, "You mean if the challenge wasn't there anymore? That wouldn't change my feelings toward her."

Jill said, "I hadn't thought of it as a challenge. But I'm interested in your using that word."

Lenny said, "I look at it as a challenge. She keeps saying. . . ."

Jill said, "It sounds like this is your way, Lenny, of taking on the world. It's all right there in Michelle."

Lenny nodded. "She's more than the world to me!"

Jill said, "I got that feeling."

Michelle asked, "Would you conquer me?"

Lenny said, "I never conquer. I always say, 'You don't have to win as long as you come in as a tie.' I'm happy enough to just tie. I don't have to win."

I said, " 'Tie' is an interesting word. You don't have to win if you get tied together. You're just hanging on for the long haul."

Lenny shook his head. "No. I'm not hanging on for the long haul. I love her. I like being with her."

Michelle said, "Because I entertain you twenty-four hours a day."

Lenny said, "No, you don't." Then he smiled, back in the old joking mode. "Twenty-three, maybe!" He turned to me, pleading. "She's different, very different. I don't mind her being in the forefront. I guess it's good protection. But I'm also there *I feel* as a support for her. Maybe she doesn't feel that."

Jill said, "That's clear: she's very different. She's entertaining and she certainly fills the time. She fills any void you may feel in terms of not being interested in what's out there. You don't have to look out there when you've got it all right here! But there must be a worry about what is there if there's no entertainment. And it relates to what David was saying about the sadness, and to what Michelle said earlier about an emptiness in Lenny. There's a great worry about a bleakness you would discover if you stopped this bantering."

I said, "The way you said, Lenny, 'I'm also there *I feel* as a support for her,' made me think that what you were saying was that you only feel, only come alive, when you're functioning as a support for Michelle. That's what makes you feel most alive."

I found that Lenny's language had clarified for me the way in which his relationship to her gave him a sense of purpose. From his point of view, she did him an enormous favor in allowing him to be a support to her, and the greater the odds against him, the greater the victory, the more alive the triumph. She was split into two objects for him: the one who fought him and over whom he could triumph, and the one he loved and who was grateful. She was the rejecting and the exciting object, and his victory unified his inner world in a perverse version of repair that gave his self life.

At the time I was able to say this, I was feeling considerably centered myself by Jill's highlighting of Michelle as "all the world" to Lenny. Her formulation catalyzed my own work, and thus our work together on the way in which he was dedicated to finding his internal world in Michelle—that is, dedicated to projecting his own lost inner worlds into her and then refinding them, hoping to introjectively identify with the life he found in her. It was the reason he put up with the bruising while finding himself in her unknown world. This recognition came as Jill and I were pulling together to make sense of our experience. Putting the couple's perversely split relationship into perspective constituted our own reparative work.

CLARIFYING THE COUPLE'S ENVY AND SEXUAL RELATIONSHIP

We now tried to pull together a picture of the pattern that the couple enacted together, one made up of their efforts to shore up Michelle's self-esteem and conviction that she was unlovable, and Lenny's need to introject a sense of being alive.

I said, "We'd like to see if you can hear what we think without having to banter it away. This pattern is something the two of you maintain together. When Michelle gets frightened, Lenny acts like more of a rock because he's given you, Michelle, all the flow. He stands firmer, digs in as the rock that makes the ripple possible, and you, Michelle, ripple faster. Then you get bored—which is a terribly deadly feeling."

Michelle said, "Yes. I think that's right."

Jill continued, "The two of you form this pattern together. It's as though the two of you are one personality. He stands firmer, more solidly so the rapids don't wash everything away. You, Michelle, would feel the terror if you weren't bored. But the terror you have covered with your boredom returns when you then begin to fear you'll end up your life in a relationship with a rock."

I felt relieved that we had been able to pull together an image of the two of them that described their mutual contribution to their dilemma. I felt I could now see it instead of being caught in the whirlpools around the rapids their pattern formed.

Michelle threw off our formulation with a quip. "So how do we improve on that? Any medication?"

My satisfied feeling was thrown by her defensive banter.

I said, "That joke expresses your sense of hopelessness."

Michelle said, "Yes. It does."

I said, "You're hopeless about being able to do it any other way. Then you turn and blame him for being boring."

Michelle said, "There's one point I want to bring up about the boring that ties to my upbringing. Being boring is being average. I've always considered Lenny average. I was brought up thinking I was special. My whole family was special. I believe I'm special and destined for . . . I don't know what. But how can a person who's so special hate herself as much as I do? Somehow because I was the older child, I got it from my mother. My brother, who is two years younger, has that specialness and all the confidence to go with it—a complete winner! And I really envy him because of it. Because I'm missing that little part! There's a part of me that constantly finds holes in herself."

This language, about envying 'that little part' of her brother's and 'finding holes' in herself, is the kind of language that makes analysts sit up and listen, and we did. One needs the experience with analysis (such as the portions given elsewhere in this book) to grow the conviction that a woman like this has tried to solve her own feeling of emptiness by the early and persisting fantasy that if she only had a penis, she could be whole. Once one has that conviction, the language leads us to this constellation. Here, near the end of the interview, at the point of loss of us, Michelle volunteered material with deep unconscious resonance, and in the interview, we were pulled to stay with her and with them for a while longer.

I asked, "What little part of your brother?"

Michelle said, "Whatever it is that he has—the confidence that makes him a complete mensch—I'm missing."

The language was focusing on his genitals as making up for everything. In the countertransference, I experienced it as arousing of interest; that is, it had the standing of being an exciting object and an interpersonal seduction.

I asked, "Do you envy his being a boy?"

Michelle said, "I used to, as a child. I used to see the world as a man's world. And I used to be an extreme tomboy. I dreaded becoming feminine. Now I wouldn't trade it for the world, but I used to see things as a man's world. Maybe I do envy his being a man, but I also envy his confidence. I just don't have it."

Jill said, "This envy you feel for your brother, we can see you feel it for Lenny, too, who is also his mother's great little kid, right?"

As always, the envy was not just for the man's penis. It was for the things that boys and men seem to have. In the hour, it was a sign of the couple's forthcomingness that they could bring the envy so clearly to the surface after they lived out Michelle's envious attacks on Lenny, which he tolerated for still unknown reasons.

Michelle laughed.

Lenny said, "I was brought up by women, my mother, my sisters, and my grandmother. My father didn't bring masculinity into the family the way Michelle's father did. In my family, I'm the more confident male."

Jill said, "So it's a kind of phallic quality Michelle's brother has?"

I experienced Jill's use of the word "phallic" as jarring, as too technical and too far from the couple's experience. I feared it would increase their defensiveness. But Lenny proceeded to translate it into their own language, and they moved right on.

Michelle said, "I don't know about that, but. . . ."

Lenny cut in. "Cocky! Self-confident! Her brother knows he's good."

Michelle said, "Yeah. He's self-confident and cocky. But he also has an incredibly sensitive side. It's not just me that's jealous of him. Lenny is, too."

Lenny agreed. "Yeah, I'm jealous of him, too. I'd love to be like her brother."

Here were more clues as to what Lenny saw in her. At the same time he was continuing to fill in for the missing masculinity of his father as in his family growing up, he was identified with Michelle's internal object of a man, tied to her brother. He was trying to get that into himself through sticking with her.

Michelle continued, "I'd love to marry someone like my brother. He's the epitome. He's not completely perfect, but he's that kind of guy. He has that chemistry I'd be looking for in a man. It's not the kind of men I've gone out with. It's the men I'm chicken to go out with. It's the men I never let be attracted to me—by gaining a lot of weight or whatever. So this settles it. Lenny doesn't have that confidence. When he's called on to be a mensch, he's not. Well, he is in certain cases, but not where it counts to me."

Jill asked, "What about where it counts in bed?"

Michelle was visibly hit by her comment. "Excuse me? In *where?*"

Jill repeated, "In bed?"

Michelle said, "Ahh. Umm. . . . You talk about that, dear."

Lenny shook his head. "Why should I talk about that?"

Michelle said, "Because I don't want to."

I said, "See if you can, at least in general terms. It may be embarrassing, but it's important."

Michelle vigorously agreed. "It's as embarrassing as hell!"

Lenny was able to begin. "I think I'm her release in bed. I free her of tensions."

Lenny's beginning also released her to talk in the session. Michelle said, "That is something that's grown in our relationship, because at first I couldn't stand him."

Lenny looked at the floor. "At first you couldn't stand it."

Michelle said, "I hated it. It was awful."

I asked, "And was that different than with other men?"

Michelle said, gathering steam, "Completely different! There hadn't been that many." She looked down at the floor, too. "The guy I was in love with couldn't function at all in bed, but it didn't seem to matter to me at the time. I was new to the whole experience. I loved him, so it didn't matter. But when I went with Lenny, I realized how lacking that guy was. So I learned a lot. It wasn't easy. The transfer from the man I loved to the man I definitely couldn't stand."

I asked, "In bed especially?"

I was confused again here, by now a familiar feeling with them. She seemed to be saying that Lenny had taught her some pleasure in sex she had not known before, but while saying that, she maintained her disparagement of him as though he were contemptible for doing so.

Michelle said, "Oh, it was awful. It took a couple of years before I realized 'This isn't so bad.' So obviously there wasn't a lot of sexual activity. Sex isn't one of my favorite things because I'm one of those self-conscious people that hates her body. So who's going to love me and my body? We don't have to get into the details. You can assume the rest. But Lenny has taken the time to find out what feels good, so I gotta give him a little credit. Although it's still not number one on my list, there has never been anyone quite like him. So I can't complain about that. Because sex is really more a pain than anything else to me."

I asked, "Literally painful?"

"Yeah," said Michelle. "Physical pain. Real pain. It's not highest on my list of things to do. But with Lenny, I have learned to enjoy it more, though we're still not real active."

Jill said, "But that's not because the passivity lies with him in this instance?"

Michelle said, "Oh, no! He's certainly not passive there."

Lenny said, "I'm probably too aggressive. She says I'm always horny."

Michelle said, "Well, you are."

Lenny said, "She generalizes and says, 'All men are.' "

Michelle said, "There's one thing I love. He's attracted to me no matter how fat I am. How many men would be like that? They always want skinny people, and I've never been skinny. I take everything out on my weight, and this man is still wildly attracted to me. When I look horrible, he thinks I'm beautiful, even if it's a lie at that moment."

Lenny said, "It's not a lie."

"And that makes me feel like a million dollars."

I asked, "How do you feel about her body and her looks?"

Michelle laughed. "Don't be specific, please."

Lenny said, with a new confidence, "I think she's beautiful. There's nothing about her that makes me cringe or anything. Everything about her I love." With humor, he added, "It probably makes her sick to hear it, but I enjoy being with her, touching her, feeling her."

I asked, "How do you feel about her sexual reluctance?"

Lenny said, "I understand part of it. The pain is a big thing."

Jill asked, "What do you understand the pain is due to?"

Lenny said, "I don't know. It's physical. No! It's in her mind, which is always running and not always on the topic at hand. At a certain point during sex, her mind wanders. . . ."

Michelle said, "We just lose it."

"Lose the arousal?" I asked.

Michelle said, "He doesn't lose it."

"That's right," said Lenny. "But I'm always sensitive to any pain she may be in."

I asked, "Michelle, is the pain you have only on penetration or with continued intercourse?"

Michelle answered, "Intercourse isn't high on my list."

I said, "Because it's painful?"

"It's painful and a pain in the neck. It's a nuisance to me. I like to get it over so we can do other things."

"Like holding and cuddling?" I asked.

Lenny said, "We love to cuddle and snuggle."

"Only nonsexually?" I asked.

"Sexually, too," Michelle volunteered. "Lenny has never been with any other woman, so I don't know how he learned. But he can make it a release for me. It used to be a stressor, but now it's a release."

"In intercourse, or in other ways?" I asked.

Michelle said, "It almost never happens in intercourse. But otherwise I'm completely comfortable with him. Well, sort of. I'm never completely comfortable."

I said, "You're not comfortable with yourself, so there's no way."

Michelle agreed. "Right, exactly! I'm as comfortable as I can be. You know for a girl who had penis envy as a child, I hate them now. So there's something obviously wrong with me."

"One thing about Lenny you appreciate is that he doesn't force himself on you in this way," Jill said.

Michelle said, "Right. He's very good to me."

Jill said, "But as a child, you saw the penis as a source of power."

Michelle said, "I don't remember anything about the penis itself."

Jill said, "I mean the boy's world, the things boys had that you didn't. What I'm saying is that now that you've taken possession of your adult femininity and enjoy a woman's world, it's sad for you that you can't take pleasure from the penis. You see it as a source of envied and threatening power."

Michelle said, "I see it as an intrusion! I hate it. I've come a little distance, but I used to see it as a man sticking it to a woman."

I said, "Now you don't *see* it that way, but you still *feel* it like that."

Michelle said, "Not as much as I did. I used to see it as another way of a man's control, which I hate. But it's never, ever been like that with Lenny."

This discussion of the current status of Michelle's attitude toward sex and the penis revealed more than we could have expected to learn in a single interview. She had converted her envy of men generally because as a child she thought they did not feel the empty longing she did because they had the things she was missing, including a body part, the penis, whereas her vagina seemed to capture the hole, the emptiness she felt in her inner longing. In her adulthood, the penis continued to be threatening because it could enter that painful hole, and because her envy of it meant she was in danger of feeling the hatred she felt toward it and toward the man who had it. In this way, the better Lenny did with her sexually, the more she had to attack enviously. But being able to see this in the first hour was a good prognostic sign. It led me to feel she might well be able to work on this in therapy.

I said, "The two of you share this idea, too, that men can be harmful, their aggression and their penises can be harmful — that unless you're careful, sex will mean sticking it to a woman."

Lenny said, "That's true. I don't like the way men treat women. I was brought up with women and was taught how to treat them. I take the man's world on my shoulders, the way men act. I don't like their games. I never did and never will."

I said, "But the cost to you of bending over backwards to make sure you are never aggressive is that you can't do things. And then Michelle says you're just passive. Although she requires that bending over backwards of you in bed, for instance."

Michelle said, "That's not passiveness."

I said, "But he's so caretaking, it's hard to separate out the passivity."

Michelle said, "The passivity I would see if he wants to make love and I don't. He doesn't give me one minute of pain in the neck about it. What we're hearing about right now is part of him I just adore!"

Jill said, "There had to be some parts of him."

Michelle countered once again with a joke. "There's a lot. He's sensitive. He's got credit cards."

I said, "He's got a lot of credit, period."

Michelle now agreed. "He's true to his word. He wouldn't do anything to hurt me. And he does handle it as a man of the world, whom I do usually see as sticking it to people. I'm just scared of men in general. Not real men, but the ones I have intimate relationships with, even nonsexual relationships, I'm scared of them."

Jill, signalling that the session had to close, said, "The point is that there's a lot of work needing to be done here, both in individual therapy for each of you, and in couple therapy if you care to work on it together."

Summing up, I added, "In these last few minutes we've been hearing about the loving and caring that have been encapsulated in the sex. It was as though the caring part of your relationship had to be saved for the end, where it could not be fully considered but also would not be fully exposed. Until then it was as though your relationship was made up of envy, anger, the feeling that men will damage women—all to be countered by Lenny's holding firm like the rock in the river. These aspects seem to call out for understanding."

Michelle said, "It certainly does! So what should we do?"

Jill answered, "There's a lot of positive feeling covered up by a lot of fear in your relationship. If you dared to hope you could have a better relationship, therapy together would be worth it. In any case, individual therapy is also a good idea for each of you, too. Thank you both for coming in to talk with us.

We'll talk with Mrs. Taylor, as we agreed, about our thoughts. Good luck!"

Lenny shook our hands. "Thank you."

Michelle could not part without a joke about whether they had been interesting enough to us. "Nice meeting you both. I hope you got something for a book out of this. No real names, please!"

CO-THERAPY AND COUNTERTRANSFERENCE

During this interview, the flamboyance of the couple's dress and behavior, their use of mutually deprecating humor, and the caricatured quality of their projective and introjective identifications became quickly apparent. The couple and their way of relating got inside us, as it does in every hour with a therapist or with co-therapists, where it influenced our attempts to understand the couple, to join with their request to be understood and with their defenses against that request.

During the interview I was taken over by a fatigue that represented an introjective identification with them, which disabled me in a way that ultimately gave me an experience inside myself similar to their disability. In working my way out of this momentary disability, I was able to obtain insight into the strength and experience of the couple's relationship system, and especially to understand the crippling emotions that characterized it. In this process, work with my co-therapist added enormously to my capacity to understand the couple. Without her, I would have had to absorb the total experience and work my way out of it alone.

However, I usually work alone and have to struggle with similar countertransference situations by myself. Usually the internal struggle eventually results in the same end point, yielding—often with a similar relief—a sense of understanding a patient or couple from inside of my own experience. This

often goes on silently and preconsciously—outside of awareness—when I work alone. The co-therapy relationship requires
an open, more verbalized demonstration of the issues to be
absorbed, metabolized, and given back to the couple. For this
reason co-therapy is particularly useful in demonstrating the
work of countertransference and in training therapists to use
countertransference.

5

Changing Internal Object Relations in the Psychotherapy of an Adolescent

In this chapter, I outline the way in which alterations in the self are marked by and dependent on changes in the internal object during an adolescent therapy limited to once-weekly sessions during the course of one school year. During this relatively brief psychotherapy, the teenage girl, Tammy, found a new set of identifications, images of herself and, at the same time realized differences in her internal objects. Her parents, who had provided the experiences that became the makings of these objects, did not themselves change in any substantial way during this year, although both mother and father had made therapeutic gains of their own through therapy and analysis during her pre-teen years. It was the changes in her self that enabled Tammy to see her objects differently, but things did not stop there. Once she saw her objects in these new ways, she in turn saw her self differently again. Self and object continued to alter in a mutually reinforcing cycle. We could then see how views of her objects had impinged on developments of her self throughout her previous development.

Incidentally, changes in Tammy paralleled changes in my own growth as a therapist, providing another level of interest for me in the growth of my own self and my therapeutic objects. I had treated her when she was younger and had received sporadic reports about her from her mother over the ensuing ten years before I saw her again in therapy.

TAMMY'S TREATMENT AS A YOUNG CHILD

I first met Tammy when she was 6 years old. Her mother, Miriam, brought Tammy in, saying, "We just can't get along. It's a terrible loss. We battle about everything. Tammy thinks I don't do anything right."

I saw Tammy in psychotherapy for two-and-a-half years. In the beginning, she was so anxious that she couldn't come into my office without one of her parents. Her parents had been divorced two years earlier when she was 4 and her brother, Russell, was 1½. It had been an angry divorce. Miriam said that John, the father, had been like a child, unable to think of her needs or the children's needs. Now Tammy, Russell, and Miriam were living without him in a small apartment. Miriam fought with John over his inconsistent visitation and his sloppy care of the children. In many early sessions, Miriam had to come into the room with Tammy in order to get her to see me. When John brought her, he also had to come into the room with her. Although he was concerned about Tammy and Russell, John preferred to relinquish responsibility in many small ways. For instance, although he did pay a portion of the therapy bill, he left it to Miriam to deal with the insurance company, even though he held the policy.

Tammy never liked coming to see me, but with her parents there she would play nevertheless. I sat on one side of a table while she played with her father or mother. After a while, Miriam could sit in a chair across the room and Tammy would play with me. It was often difficult to discern from her play what the issues were. After a few months of therapy aimed at simply managing her insecurity and developing an alliance, Tammy made a collage of a picture with a heart with a hat sitting on its head and with smiles all around it. (Figure 5–1.) This particular picture was especially interesting because she did it in a session with her father present, while she smiled coyly at him. Tammy then demonstrated to her father and me that the hat could be lifted away, showing us that the hat made a phallic insertion into the V of the heart. (See Figure 5–2.) Although I did not say so to them, I felt that this picture could be interpreted as representing Tammy's unconscious age-appropriate wish for intercourse with her father.

Tammy's collage suggested that her oedipal longing for the father that her mother had let go was at the base of Tammy's battling with her mother. Miriam told the story of John's neglect during their marriage. She thought he took Miriam for granted, erupting angrily at her whenever she did not carry out his wishes or meet his needs. Engrossed in other aspects of his life, he had no sense, she felt, of the needs of his wife and children. He had the same lack of thought when it came to taking care of the children. After the divorce, he showed up late for his visits and kept an old, hard-to-clean house that was so dusty and full of dog hair that Tammy, who

Figure 5–1. Tammy's "Heart with a Hat," age 6

had allergies and asthma, was constantly at risk for bronchial attacks while visiting her father.

After the session in which her oedipal longing was revealed, Tammy could tolerate seeing me alone without her parents. Now her underlying insecurity became the focus of our work. As she worked on separating from her mother, she learned that she had unconsciously blamed her mother for her anxious attachment. Now Tammy felt closer to her mother—and went sour on her father. During the therapy she struggled with her reluctance about going to his house. Miriam reported that John didn't seem to take Tammy's interests to heart. He refused to remove the physical irritants that Tammy was phobic about. So her mother, who was upset about his failure to comply with medical instructions, found it hard to send Tammy to see him. Tammy also found it more and more difficult to go there.

Figure 5-2. Tammy's picture with hat removed

In a session toward the end of therapy, Tammy built a village compound out of blocks. It held many members of a family who got along well together. Tammy told me that none of them was ever allowed to leave. The underlying issues about separation bound her closely to her mother, although she was able to do well in school and now had friends whom she could also visit. On most fronts, she seemed to be doing well. In retrospect, the anxieties in her attachment were handled by a split: good mother and bad father. I was unaware of the way Tammy unconsciously constructed this split because I believed Miriam's account that John was extremely difficult, and I agreed with Tammy's reservations about her father. Their accounts of him echoed my own experiences with him of his inaccessibility and unreliability.

In any event, there wasn't much I could do about this split. Now that she had after-school activities, homework, and friends to visit, therapy was even less appealing. As she approached her ninth birthday, Tammy grew hardened against it. Her feelings about her father had the transferential effect that she was more reluctant to see me. She seemed to be doing too well generally for me to insist on continuing therapy. By the time we terminated when Tammy was 9, her presenting symptom was resolved. She was getting along well with her mother and had no difficulty with school or friends, but she was still kicking up a fuss about going to her father's house, partly for good reason and partly out of reaction to her repressed longing.

I did not see Tammy again for many years. I did see her brother Russell a year after Tammy stopped therapy. Miriam brought him because he was isolated and friendless, doing poorly in school. He was 6½. He didn't get along very well with his father either, and he was unenthusiastic but not phobic about visiting him. But he got along well with Miriam. I concluded that Russell had a childhood obsessional neurosis, and I referred him for analysis. He had an interesting and largely successful analysis, but that is not part of this story. Now, as the parent worker for my colleague who was Russell's analyst, I resumed working with Miriam. The child analyst periodically saw the father, John, and his second wife.

In my work with Miriam, I was able to deal with her continuing difficulties in forming intimate relationships. I urged her to think about more intensive treatment. Reluctant at first, she finally decided that she was stuck, unable to form a permanent, satisfying relationship. She asked for referral for analysis herself. With analysis, she was able to move relatively quickly into a steady, caring relationship with a man whom the children also liked. They married soon after Russell finished analysis. Tammy was still doing well in school and in friend-ships and Miriam reported that the children related to their natural father about as well as could be expected, given his arbitrary and difficult personality.

Incidentally, during the period of Russell's analysis, his father and his new wife asked Russell's analyst for a referral for their marriage. They began marital therapy with another colleague, who later told me that there had been considerable improvement in their marriage and maturation for both of them individually.

After Miriam's marriage, she and her new husband, along with Tammy and Russell, moved away from Washington, a business move that they had anticipated. But a year after that, I got a phone call from Tammy's father, John, asking that Russell's analyst and I evaluate the two children for school placement. Tammy and Russell were now living in an isolated, rural area with Miriam. The school year had been difficult for them. They wanted to move back with John and go to their old school. Miriam was in agreement with their wishes because she agreed that the school where she lived was inadequate and she felt that John had matured and was now living in a suitable new house without any animals. She told me that she did not want the happiness of her life to interfere with the children's education. However, because John's new house was not in the children's old school district, they would require a special exception to return to their old school. John and Miriam both hoped that a psychiatric report might help with that request.

So I saw Tammy, who had been so wary of seeing me in the many years since treatment as a child. She was now almost 16. She looked like a little girl with braces and a broad but shy smile. She told me that she was getting along beautifully with her mother and stepfather, as was Russell. But the small town they lived in was isolated. There were few resources. There were no kids she or Russell felt comfortable with, and both found the school situation painful. Although she would miss her mother a great deal, she felt it made sense for her to spend the last two years of high school living with her father and returning to the school she missed.

I asked Tammy if she thought this move would also give her a chance to know her father better. She said that would be worth doing, although she was nervous about it. Russell's analyst and I agreed to recommend that the children be permitted to return to their old school. The request was granted, and they moved in with their father.

THE COURSE OF ADOLESCENT TREATMENT

It was in the summer of the following year that Tammy called me. There were some things she would like to think about. Her father and mother had agreed that she could have some psychotherapy. Would I be willing to see her? We agreed over the phone to meet as soon as school resumed in the fall.

On the 4th of September, Tammy was in my waiting room. Although she was 17, she still looked like an immature 14-year-old. It wasn't just her prominent braces and her little-girl curly hair, or her shy tentative smile. She was small and dressed in young clothes. Her grin seemed characteristic of the happy 9-year-old I had known when she had not been annoyed at me for making her come to therapy eight years before. This and her frilly short dress reminded me that her mother usually looked like a little girl too.

Tammy said she was glad to be here now, but when she was 6, she had thought I was the enemy. She hadn't wanted to see me then at all, but her mother had said, "You're going! That's all." She remembered telling her mother then that she was afraid that I would do something to her that would make her a different person so she wouldn't be herself when she grew up. It had helped in the interval to see that her mother had gone to analysis and found it so helpful. She could see how much her mother had grown and changed. So coming to see me now ought to be a good thing.

The impetus this time was that Tammy's boyfriend was going to a counselor and had said to her that she ought to go to therapy, too. She thought he was right, but she still wasn't sure why she was here. She felt that she really didn't have a good enough reason. That made her feel badly, because she didn't want to waste my time.

Quickly, this confusion became the theme of our first interview. Tammy said she never knew what she wanted because she wasn't sure who she was or what she should want for herself. She said that when she had a decision to make, she called her mother who gave good advice. Sometimes, Tammy said, she objected to what her mother said, but her mother always turned out to be right. She would say to her mother, "Is that what I should do? Is that the right thing?" And her mom would say, "If it's the right thing for you." Then Tammy would feel that she must do what her mother said because her mother was always right. But she would be left with the feeling that she wasn't quite sure herself.

Tammy said she was glad that she had come to live with her father. She liked his brand-new home. She didn't get sick around him. She didn't fight with him. It was going well. On the other hand, she hadn't really been able to talk to him. However, on a recent trip to see his family in New England, she was upset about something and her dad was able to talk it through with her. This confirmed something she remembered I had said to her when I had met with her a year earlier—that if she lived with her father, she might get to know him better.

Tammy went on to tell me about the boyfriend, Ed, who had recommended therapy for her. I was interested to note how she would treat her boyfriends as an externalization of her internal object status. In this report, I want to demonstrate how her way of dealing with her self and the objects who were her peers also changed over the course of the treatment. Although I was predisposed to like Ed on the basis of his support of psychotherapy, Tammy was wary of him. Ed was the first boy that she had dated in a long time. He came from a disturbed background. He was an orphan and had been on drugs. But most alarmingly, he neglected and verbally abused Tammy. As she got to know Ed, she found that she didn't like him. When

Tammy went on the recent trip with her father, Ed got furious. That ended her interest in him. When she finally broke up with him, Ed begged to get back together.

Tammy seemed confused. She looked immature, yet in some ways she was curiously mature. She had seen by herself that Ed was abusive and had been able to break up with him rather promptly. Yet, she did not know who she was or what she wanted. I found myself remembering her play from eight years before when she had built a whole family being reined into a compound that nobody could leave. Having left her mother, Tammy was being confronted with not knowing who she herself was. I said that these questions—not knowing what she wanted or who she was—were important reasons for therapy.

The theme of this first interview was how much Tammy did not know who she was or what was right for her. Questions about her self would be the main concern of therapy. Her uncertainty about her identity showed up in the need to have her mother make major decisions for her and in her turning to her mother and then to Ed to define her self. It showed up in her transference to me as a person who might dismiss her needs or else tell her what to do instead of discussing her doubt as to whether she deserved therapy or was wasting my time when she did not know why she wanted to see me. Although she knew she wanted to see me without knowing why, she felt sheepish baring her confusion to me. Her identity diffusion and her consequent overreliance on her external objects were continuations of herself as a young child who literally could not let her parents leave the therapy office, and later who symbolically placed her family in a compound that no one could leave. Now in adolescence she was struggling with the same issues in her internal world, with resulting depression and confusion that left her feeling badly in my presence and in the presence of her wish to know her own mind and direction.

Over the early weeks of the therapy, Tammy worked in the way that adolescents do, mostly through talking about her own issues as they are displaced onto others. Having broken up with Ed, she distanced herself from him further by examining the way that Ed had passed on the abuse to her that he had learned in his own orphaned upbringing. Ed lived in a home for parentless children. A foster parent was demanding of him. On one occasion when Tammy and Ed had scheduled a date, the foster parent grounded Ed, who did not call Tammy. Ed had not bothered to consider the consequences to Tammy of his failure to let her know he could not meet her. She realized that she didn't want to be treated like that. Although she didn't think well of herself, she didn't want to feel *that* badly.

She now moved on to a new boyfriend, Pete, who was in the process of going off to college. She was infatuated with the idea of an older, college-bound boyfriend. I noticed that Pete also provided her with a safer distance in the wake of her feeling abused by Ed, but I did not say so to Tammy.

Tammy also examined herself through contrast to a girl-friend, Mary Lou. This relationship provided a second area of interest in external object relations over the course of Tammy's therapy. Mary Lou was an overweight girl who accompanied Tammy to her second appointment with me. Over the next weeks, Mary Lou became an object of Tammy's study. Tammy felt loyal to Mary Lou but came to see her as a foil for herself. Mary Lou clung to Tammy, expected Tammy to accompany her wherever and whenever Mary Lou was anxious, and expected to be included in every aspect of Tammy's life, just as the young Tammy had used Miriam. Mary Lou's father was a teacher at their high school, and Tammy felt that he often appeared to be a "jerk" in class. This word was particularly interesting because it is also the word she had begun to use to describe her father's behavior when he was self-centered or not particularly attuned to Tammy. But Mary Lou's father seemed to care about Mary Lou, even though he did jerky things.

Finally, Tammy began to consider her life with her father and stepmother. In a session after two months of therapy, she told me about her step-mother, Faye. Faye was somebody who wasn't used to children, having none of her own, and Faye felt displaced now with the two new adolescents in the house. On one occasion, Tammy asked Faye if she could have several friends sleep over. Faye had been distressed, saying, "Well, okay, if they don't use the telephone, because I need it. If I don't have to clean up, it's all right. But on the other hand, they might eat a whole box of cereal and drink a whole gallon of milk." Tammy had said angrily, "So I'll buy the cereal and the milk!" Faye lost her cool. Her father had taken Tammy aside and told her not to argue with Faye because, he said, "You and I and Russell are on a team, and she feels on the outside." Tammy said that Russell intentionally provoked Faye, but that she, Tammy, tried—and usually succeeded—to consider Faye's point of view. "It must be hard for her," she conceded.

Tammy now turned to a conversation she had had with her mother about Pete, the new college boyfriend. Her mother had said to her, "You understand that he won't really write you back when you write him. He'll find people in college he's interested in." Tammy had said, "Mom, don't tell me that. I know that it's true, but I don't really want you to tell me that."

I said to Tammy that she wanted her fantasy left intact for a while to enjoy, and she agreed.

A month later, Tammy was talking about another new boy that she wanted to date, one who was closer to home. She compared him to Ed, the orphan whose rudeness and self-centeredness she now said reminded her of her father. In the middle of this discussion, I asked her about sexual issues. She grew silent and embarrassed. Finally, she spoke about something else. A teacher in school had said to her, "You know, you look terribly sad." She related her sadness to being away from her mother. When she went to this school in ninth grade, her mother had been around. She had a wonderful year. This year was so much harder without her mother.

Thoughts of loneliness and sadness had been triggered by

my question about sexuality. Perhaps she wanted me to know that she wished to have her mother with her during the threatening transition to adult female sexuality. She acknowledged that she talked about sex with girlfriends, but she remained too uncomfortable to talk about it with me. I got the impression that she wasn't sexually active beyond mild physical interaction with the boys. It was never possible to discuss this directly.

Tammy treasured the psychotherapy. She came on time reliably despite the long commute to my office, and she was a steady, enthusiastic participant. I found myself looking forward to the hours with her, feeling the work to be collaborative and valued. The contrast to the feel of the sessions when she was little was an unceasing source of amazement. Her experience of me as an external object was now totally different, colored by shifts in her internal object representation of the rejecting object linked mainly to her father.

Increasingly, Tammy talked of needing to separate from her friend Mary Lou in order to branch out to more adventurous and varied friends, yet she felt a loyalty conflict because Mary Lou needed her. Boys came on the scene and then disappeared, but without urgency. Steadily, the peers seemed to be more mature and more capable of mutual regard for individual needs. Yet Tammy did not, as do many teenagers who change in therapy, easily and heartlessly discard her old friends. Whereas Mary Lou or an old boyfriend still had a place in her life, they were no longer the external objects against whom she defined her emerging self. They were old and valued relationships, worthy of regard, but no longer in the center of the object relations action.

Tammy now began to talk a good deal about her father and the arbitrary things he did. When she asked permission to go out for an evening, her father assessed it in terms of whether or not Russell had to be taken care of, since her father was intent on going to a concert. As she presented it, the decision seemed to ride on her father's convenience. He made quirky demands on her, Russell, and Faye. He would insist, for instance, that the entire family clean up after dinner, but he would take a quick swipe at the table with a sponge and then sit and read the newspaper while Faye and the children cleaned up. It didn't even matter if they had homework.

Tammy found herself a college counselor to work with about her choice of college. She did all the work herself, getting the information and doing the applications without prompting. Her father was uninvolved. He was vague about whether he would underwrite the effort to visit colleges. In the end he did so willingly, and they had a close and pleasant trip together.

Through the years I had shared the view that John was irresponsible. Tammy's description of him as a "jerk" might not have been far from my more technical description of him. For instance, in the past he had almost always been late paying my bill, and during this year he continued to leave it to me to collect her share from his ex-wife—not an arrangement I liked or would usually accept. So I had considerable sympathy with Tammy's description of him.

In retrospect, I am somewhat chagrined to think of how much I accepted Tammy's description of her father as fact instead of seeing it as a projective identification born of her internal object relations. Partly, I suffered from the same situation growing children do who treat their parents as though they were still the same as they were in the children's earlier internalized memories. I remembered John from my contacts with him, which came soon after his divorce and before his therapeutic growth. It was only in the last few months of Tammy's therapy, scheduled to continue until shortly before she would go off to college, that this became clear in the therapy. Only then did I become convinced that the view I had all these years was structured from Tammy's internal object of a rejecting and persecuting father—grafted to be sure on a valency John had to fit with this description. In turn, we could see that Tammy's view of her father as so negligent and rejecting had its origin in her mother's view of John, which was modeled in turn on her mother's relationship to her own rejecting and arbitrary father.

TAMMY REFINDS HER FATHER

In early March, we had a landmark session. Tammy began with a question. Had she been unfairly taking her mother's side against her father? She had been thinking about it clearly since the previous session when I had raised the question of her anger at him. I had done that more out of a sense of duty to be fair, or guilt over my own unbalanced picture, than out of any conviction myself that John was other than Tammy painted him.

But Tammy had been working on things. She said she could see the idea that she might have taken her mother's side out of a sense of loyalty after the divorce. That would make sense to her. She didn't feel it, but it made sense to her that she might have sided with her mother because she was living with her during her growing up years. Mother would say from time to time, "You really ought to get along with your father. He loves you too." It made sense to Tammy that she did not feel it, because he overlooked her needs. His old house was dirty and it triggered her asthma, and he seemed to be more centered on his own needs than hers. She also felt that he took Russell's side; he seemed to care about him more.

But, said Tammy, she could see that Mary Lou loved her father, even though he did jerky things. She noticed that she got quite exercised about Mary Lou's father, more than Mary Lou did herself. Tammy talked about feeling that she did not love her father as much as she did her mother. I said I had wondered if, strangely enough, she couldn't admit hating her father as much as she could her mother either. She said there were two kinds of hate. There was the kind when you wanted to get rid of somebody. There was another kind that just sort of erupted and then was gone. I said that the second kind happened when you were free to hate someone because you really loved them, so being angry had no major implications. For instance, I had the impression that Tammy could be angry with her mother—hate her—and not expect anything awful would happen between them.

Tammy jumped on this idea enthusiastically. "That's true. If I'm mad at Mom, I can tell her to drop dead without thinking it means anything. But with Dad, I do mean it, so it really bothers me."

Tammy now moved rapidly. Perhaps she had never given her father a chance. She recalled that when she was small and said to her mother, "I don't want to go with my father this weekend, I don't want to be with him," her mother would say, "He loves you and you love him. I can see the gleam in your eye when he gets ready to pick you up." Tammy said that she couldn't remember feeling that way.

I now reminded Tammy of the session when she was 6. I told her that when she came in with her father, she had drawn a heart with a smile on it and the little hat on top of it. I told her that I remembered her warmth and her coyness. I did not speak to her about her sexual longing for her father in that phase of oedipal development, sensing that would have been provocative.

Tammy was struck by what I told her. She remembered the heart, which had come from a school project she had been doing. She paused and said, "It must have been hard for Dad. I can see he tried to do things for me. He wants me to love him. I don't think Russell and I give him a chance. It must have been terribly hard for him to know that I hated him! How could anybody not know that? He tries so hard to have us love him."

Now she began to cry. She didn't want to cry. But with some urging she talked about how she hated him all those years and never gave him a chance. And he had tried so hard to be close. How painful that must be for him.

I said she had reasons.

She said, "I needed to be on Mom's side. It was so hard for

her to be alone during the divorce. I remember they would have these fights. Dad wouldn't want me to be there during the fight. I can see his point about that. But my mother didn't say that I should go away, so then I would feel that it was him not wanting me. He was rejecting me and maybe I loved my mother too much."

I asked if perhaps she thought she needed to be a parent to her mother, to take care of her.

She said, "Yes, oh, sure! I had to take care of her. There wasn't anybody else to take care of her. Then I would feel it was her and me against Dad, and why didn't he take care of her?"

Tammy promptly went on to consider the relationship with her mother. The way her mother had clung to her was like the way Mary Lou clung to Tammy.

I said that this maternal clinging was the aspect of the relationship Tammy was trying to fend off at age 6, when her mother first came, saying that the problem was the mutual hostility between Mother and Tammy. Tammy had seemed so oppositional, really pushing against her mother's attempt to rely on her after feeling so rejected and hurt. Tammy must have felt impinged on by her mother's neediness.

The session now ended. Tammy wiped away her tears. She said it was good to talk about this. I said that her hatred for her father had not fundamentally come from a wish to hurt him. We agreed there was more to investigate about why she had been in this position.

Over the next weeks, Tammy experienced a revelation in the way she saw her father, although he was behaving much the same. It now seemed clear that, although he had his limitations, they weren't particularly severe. He had had her interests in mind all along. During the next two months, she consolidated this new image of her father as somebody who cared about her and did his best to express that care. Furthermore, she now saw that he had done so despite the considerable opposition that she had mounted for years.

A major piece of work had been done. Tammy's realignment of her view of her father constituted a revision of her internal object relations. Her image of the rejecting father had softened, bringing a significant advance in the sturdiness of her self image. It was now my turn to wonder why she was still coming.

Here is an example of the projection of part of the patient's self into the therapist while the patient now becomes identified with her object and heals her self. I was now identified with an aspect of her mother in which I began to wonder if I were clinging to Tammy for my own pleasure. But Tammy still had something to learn, and in turn to teach me. She did it by combining her memories of me as an internal object with her current view of me as an object that provided therapeutic holding, to examine the way her overreliance on her mother had prevented her from metabolizing that aspect of her mother she had unconsciously experienced as rejecting.

A NEW SELF AND A NEW RELATIONSHIP TO HER MOTHER

In a session in May, Tammy told me that she had enjoyed her senior prom with another boy, one with whom she only wanted to be friends. Going to the prom had been a big night for her. She had managed it in a balanced way that I admired. After some time in the hour, she began to tell me that she used to have a memory of the coffee pot in my office when she was little. She remembered that she used to take a whole lot of sugar in her coffee. When her mother said she shouldn't do that any longer, she didn't like the coffee. Then she began to remember her mother being very critical and demeaning. When she had drawn pictures in therapy and showed them to her, her mother would criticize them or laugh. On one occasion, Tammy had copied a picture that another girl had drawn and showed both pictures to her mother. Her mother had said that she thought the other girl's was prettier. Tammy was devastated.

This was the first time that Tammy had ever been critical about her mother. She went on to say that somehow her mother hadn't understood. She remembered throwing herself on the floor and having a temper tantrum because of her mother's not understanding.

This screen memory of the kind I had thought about (Chapter 6) was of additional interest because I had known my patient at the time of the formation of the memory. I said, "This is not about something as small or inconsequential as a cup of coffee. That memory about the coffee pot might stand for a whole set of feelings that you found painful."

Immediately, Tammy said, "Yes. It must have been about the divorce. I must not have wanted to go to my father's when she was critical of me."

I said, "This seems to be the first crack in the picture of your mother as perfect. You know how you've been able to see your father as more complete and complicated. Maybe you could look at your mother that way, too."

She said, "Yes. I can see that with Mom. Maybe I had better talk about her some more."

I said, "Do you know that your mom brought you in when you were 6 because you and she weren't getting along very well?"

Tammy said, "I don't remember that. All I remember was feeling misunderstood and criticized by Mom. But I don't remember that I acted badly." She grinned and shook her head with humor at her presumptiveness. "Maybe I acted badly after I felt so upset and disappointed, and I must have blamed Mom."

Tammy's ease in talking about this and the comfort with which she admitted that she might have had a hand in the difficulty with her mother because she felt so misunderstood made me realize how far she had come in the therapy. It was one of those times I felt grateful to her for benefiting from my efforts.

We agreed that it might be of interest for Tammy to bring her mother in when Miriam was visiting Tammy for graduation. Tammy called her mother to invite her to join in a session. She was surprised when Miriam was hesitant. She would come if Tammy wanted her to, but she clearly had misgivings.

Without knowing why Miriam had these misgivings, Tammy began to talk about her difficulties being angry or disagreeing with her mother. She was afraid if she said something to her mother, especially if she said it in front of me, her mother would take it badly. It would do something destructive to their relationship. She remembered that previously she would think, "Oh, my mother must be right," whenever Miriam would have said something Tammy didn't agree with. Then Tammy would wait for her mother's opinion to be validated.

I was still struck with the difference between this idealizing attitude about her mother and the initial presentation some eleven years before when Tammy was pushing her mother away. Tammy had used idealization of her mother to cover over all those struggles, to repress them further in order to avoid the pain of facing this angry maternal internal object. Now, in the wake of the work Tammy had done to rehabilitate the image of her father, this defensive mutually idealizing and dependent relationship was yielding, with reluctance on both sides. It did not unravel their central relationship, which was basically good—a relationship between central selves and good-enough objects. It was touching to see the loss both Tammy and her mother had to take in giving up their defensive idealizations, and it was gratifying to see the integration each of them was now capable of.

Tammy and I were now able to talk about how giving up her stereotyped denigration of her father led her to realize that idealizing her mother could not last either. She said that in the day-to-day relationship with him, she could see that he did care and that he had her best interests in mind a lot of the time, even if at other times he could be foolish. This also led her to feel closer to her stepmother. She was enjoying Faye more. Faye had given her a present of a little china box with hearts and flowers on it, and Tammy said to Faye that she was glad they were getting along better now that she felt closer to her father.

Then Tammy returned to her feeling that any anger, displeasure, or disbelief would threaten her relationship with her mother—not that they wouldn't love each other, but that something precious would be damaged. For instance, Tammy said to her mother that she was going to keep coming to therapy through the summer, but that she didn't have a lot of problems. She wasn't sure what she was working on. Her mother had said, "Well, I hope you do keep coming. You have problems. You don't handle stress very well."

In the session with me, Tammy erupted at this statement by her mother. She said that her mother would call Tammy when it was earlier on the West Coast, where her mother lived, and therefore it was late at night here in the East. Tammy would be tired, and if she had had a rough day, the call would be at the end of everything. So she would tell her mother things that were bothering her. On the occasion that her mother said she didn't handle stress, Tammy had actually been behaving very pleasantly, as she did in her demeanor toward her mother generally. Tammy thought that after a rather difficult day, she had been handling stress extremely well. So she didn't agree with her mother at all. She just thought that at times her mother didn't want to hear that she was doing well when she acknowledged and dealt with rough times.

With this minor outburst at mother came a stronger adolescent theme of differentiation than I had heard until now. Tammy was becoming a clearer person and was doing so without any fundamental erosion of her love for her mother. In fact, her love emerged more clearly and more durably the more she could differentiate. I talked with her about the process of becoming her own person, carving out her own positions from those of her mother. I pointed out the difference between her previous way of handling things, of always saying, "Mom must be right," and the new way of thinking that sometimes her mother was right and sometimes she wasn't. Tammy then linked this to the way that Mary Lou, in her clinging, had insisted that everything Tammy said was right. That wasn't right either, and it hadn't even been especially reassuring. Tammy had known that she wasn't always right, so it would have been better if Mary Lou had disagreed with her some of the time.

Tammy also now talked about despairing of ever finding a boyfriend who wasn't "messed up," since she found that all her friends inevitably turned out to be messed up and confused, like Mary Lou and all the previous boyfriends, once she got to know them.

I said it might have to do with her previous fear that men were all made in the image of the way she had seen her father. They wouldn't care about her and they would have many problems of their own. We discussed the way that her friends reflected her own inner state.

She said, "I guess people always have problems. But maybe that's different from being messed up like Ed." She connected this to another statement her mother had made some time ago, that she might find different friends if she were in a different place herself. She resented that statement when her mother had made it originally. Now she began to understand.

Tammy ended this session saying that she hated the idea of leaving therapy without all of this completely finished. But she was committed to going to college in September with her peers. She wanted to go away knowing who she was and what was happening, with everything worked out.

I said that there would be time later to work out things if we couldn't get to them over the summer.

TERMINATION

The work through July and August went on in this vein. Tammy worked at a concession stand and was praised as a reliable worker. At work, in conditions of modest adversity, she had the capacity of remaining cheerful. Now well into idealizing Tammy myself, I found the assessments of people she worked with, peers and supervisors, to be charming and insightful. I was defending against loss with a defensive idealization of her. I was introjectively identified with her characteristic defense. Once I recognized this countertransference, I was able to help her from inside my own experience of sharing the loss of therapy. We discussed how termination now carried the echo of earlier losses.

A couple of weeks before we finished, Tammy said, "I just don't know what life would have been like if I hadn't had the chance to come here. I'm so pleased that I had the chance to learn about my relationship with my father. It is different with him now. I'm glad that I understand more about my mother and me, too. I feel I could smile so wide that my face might break." In my mind's eye, I suddenly saw the smiling heart again (Figure 5–1) and realized that Tammy would leave with an idealizing defense partly intact as a way of dealing with loss.

In the final session, she said, "I thought I was ready to finish therapy, but now I don't know if I am quite. I think I need another month. But then again, I *am* ready. It's just going off to school is coming on me, and I'm worried about what I don't know." She reviewed our work, from her initial confusion in naming her problem, to defining it, then working on it, and getting over it. She had found out what she had come for: the work on Ed and Mary Lou, the rearranging of her relationship with her father and stepmother, and finally the chance to develop a sense of a realistic but good relationship with her mother. She hoped her brother wouldn't weaken and go back to live with her mother, who still lived in the isolated area that wouldn't be good for him academically or socially. Russell was still kind of difficult, as any 15-year-old would be, and he had become something of a loner. But she was still fond of him and hoped that he would come with her father and Faye to visit her at college in the fall. She was glad she had come for therapy. It had changed her impression of me from the age of 9 when she didn't like me. She thought that if she had a problem now, she could easily come back to me, or to therapy with someone else. On the other hand, she also felt she could solve things herself. She was ready to face what was coming, and she seemed eager.

We talked about the sense of loss and the worry about the unknown, feelings anybody would have. I said, for the first time, that her not liking me was the split-off part of her father that she could not face at age 9. How nice for me it was that she had been able to come back and do that piece of work and so get to know me as a friendlier person. She smiled in agreement. We both acknowledged the pleasure it had been to meet again with this chance to finish our work. She left cheerfully.

At Christmas, five months after termination, Tammy sent me a card. It showed two very cozy critters with long ears and fur, one hugging the other with a smile a mile wide. The inside said, "Squeezin's Greetin's." She wrote, "Dear Dr. Scharff, I just finished my first semester of college and I wanted you to know how happy I am there. It's a great place and I have made a lot of special friends. The main reason I wanted to write you was to say thank you for the self-confidence you gave me and the closer relationship you made possible between me and my father. You have been an important and special part of my life. Thanks. Love, Tammy."

The evolution of this treatment illustrates the reciprocal changes in a girl's self, in her identity formation, and her view of her objects. At certain points, shifts occurred directly in the transference, which, unlike the transference she had ten years earlier, was a warmly positive one not so invaded by the split-off rejecting images from both her mother and father.

This therapy went especially well because Tammy was ready for change and because her external objects—her parents—had had therapy and were now capable of different ways of relating than formerly. Previous role relationships had been kept because of their familiarity and because Tammy was not ready to change her internal objects. This therapy came at a time of adolescent developmental fluidity and readiness for change. It built upon her previous therapy with me—work that she carried in her own psyche. And it also built on her parents' growth in therapy and analysis—changes in her external objects who could now support her change in ways they previously could not. As a result of these internal and external factors, Tammy could allow her internal object relations to be modified by current experience with external objects and by her own maturing perceptual abilities. In this way, she established a new intrapsychic constellation from which she also defined a matured self.

Another kind of exchange between self and object accompanied this therapy. Tammy was the kind of patient who is a gratifying object for her therapist. As such, she healed the doubting parts of my therapist-self, at least momentarily. By her unconscious effect of improving me, she healed herself of uncertainty and became sure of herself as the kind of person who knows what she wants and can make others feel that they have it to offer. The repair offered to the therapist's ever-present doubts about his therapeutic effectiveness, about his power to promote healing, is like the relief experienced by parents whose children do well enough. Such children confirm the parents' selves against the continuing erosion of self doubt. Tammy became this kind of child and, in doing so, she was that kind of patient.

6

The Therapeutic Transformation of Screen Memories

Early memories, both painful and pleasant, tend to represent condensations of important early situations, relationships, and feelings that have been frozen in time. These memories, which are often introduced early in therapy and psychoanalysis, are condensations that convey the surface of internal object relations just as dreams and fantasies do. As such, they can provide important clues to events and relationships that subtly but surely continue to have a significant effect on a patient's life through their internalization as psychic structure.

The condensations that have made up these memories have particular meanings related to internal organization. They are carried forward as substantial components that have the vividness and feel of reality to the person who remembers them, but the reality they express is most often a psychic reality. From the beginning, psychic reality has built in exactly the kinds of distortions that the child's limited capacity for understanding and painful life circumstances require him or her to build into internal object structures. (We will explore these built-in distortions further in Chapter 11.)

Patients who explore even the most pleasant early memories in the course of psychotherapy and analysis discover that these memories are usually compensations for painful situations of rejection, frustration, family strife, or neglect. The memory is formed as a consequence of resolving an unpleasant circumstance, but the healing may have occurred in fantasy. For example, in therapy the remembrance of a fond embrace by a parent enlarges suddenly to include the parent's painful absence that preceded the fondly remembered reunion. Making such a therapeutic connection enables the patient to see how the pleasant memory, although expressing the treasured relationship to a parent, has also had a defensive role in supporting the repression of a painful event. Many patients' earliest memories have such dual functions. Pleasant, vivid early memories are not necessarily simple recollections of happy times. Often they serve to cover unhappiness too painful to be borne or remembered. They disguise the hopes for surcease of longing or feelings of exclusion from parental care. The memory becomes part of the lid on the repression of the painful aspects of the relationship. The progress of therapy can in part be marked by the progressive transformation of these memories as the patient comes slowly to understand more of the external reality at the time of the remembered events and more of the internal psychological reality concerning how the original situations contributed to the way he or she structured the memories.

EARLIEST MEMORIES

During therapy, recall of memories from earliest childhood usually involves events that occurred at age 3 or 4. Some patients claim recall for earlier events, but these memories have often been externally reconstructed or reinforced by family discussion or photographs. Some events, however, are undoubtedly recalled by certain people from the age of 2, such as the famous dream of his parents' intercourse recalled by Freud's "Wolfman" from his second year (Freud 1918). Memories for these early childhood events are almost always modified in meaning during growth and maturation.

The analytic term *screen memory* evocatively refers to the same kind of phenomenon as that of a dream screen, a surface on which internal events are projected with errors in scale. Experiences are projected and combined to form an image that has coherence and surface meaning and yet also contains the mystery of its latent meaning. The resulting early memory may be of an actual event, a fairy story, a movie, or even a childhood fantasy. Such memories are of particular interest because their existence underscores the fact that the person has forgotten the vast bulk of his or her experience occurring before and at the time of the early memory, including usually the context for these early life events. The forgetting involves not only passive erosion of memory, but active splitting off from conscious memory and repression, a process of exclusion that was Freud's (1895) earliest rationale for using dynamic psychotherapy and psychoanalysis.

Not all early memories are explicitly sexual, but sexual memories are most often subject to intense repression. For instance, patients who have witnessed parental intercourse during early childhood may be unable to remember the event. Instead, they remember another traumatic incident with all the emotion that would probably have accompanied the memory of intruding on the parents or of having slept regularly in their room. Recent work on childhood sexual abuse indicates that if sexual or other abusive treatment is sufficiently traumatic, repression will be strengthened so far that mental structure is changed into a dissociative form in the pathological exaggeration of the normal process of maintaining the capacity to split and repress painful experience (Terr 1991). For these patients and for those subjected to less extreme difficulty, examination of early memories in the course of psychotherapy will facilitate the emergence of the original meanings.

Adam, the 28-year-old man described in Chapter 1, began psychoanalysis to deal with his inability to work as an engineer after finishing graduate school. His unemployment meant that he was dependent on his fiancée Sheila for financial support, as he had been on his first wife during college and graduate school. It was not long before he told me of his consuming jealousy over Sheila. In his vivid jealous fantasies, Adam imagined Sheila in bed with each of her previous boyfriends. He frequently badgered her with questions about her earlier sexual experiences. He worried that she would not tolerate his insistent behavior and would leave him.

At the beginning of analysis, Adam easily recalled two early events from the age of 3. In the first, he was shut out of the house by his mother. The front door slammed in his face. Lonely and hungry, he wandered to a neighbor's house and was given some food, but he felt guilty for taking it because his mother would not have approved.

In the second memory, Adam's parents had taken him and his younger sister to see a new house they were building. Adam and his sister had been playing in the yard when he fell and cut his knee. He ran bleeding to his parents in the house. His father, seeing him enter the doorway, shouted heartlessly for Adam to stop. Even more cruelly, he kept Adam's mother from going to give comfort.

These two memories came up repeatedly in analysis because they were the earliest instances in which Adam could recall feelings similar to those that brought him to treatment. Slowly he shifted from a tenacious sense of outrage at his father to a dawning recognition that the remembered exclusion, hurt, and guilt were not justified by the events. It was only after two years in analysis that he suddenly linked this memory with what he had always known about his sense of childhood exclusion. His mother had had three children at yearly intervals beginning when he was 13 months old.

A memory now emerged in which his father barred him from a room in which his mother was nursing his baby brother. Adam was now able to make sense of the screen memory of being shut out, lonely, and hungry. He connected this to something he had been told but that had never struck him emotionally. He had apparently slept in his parents' room during his first year, until the birth of the next sibling, the sister who accompanied him in his second memory of the new house. That memory, too, now took on new meaning as he understood the sense of exclusion and anger he must have experienced when she was born. He had wanted not only to have more time with his mother, as in the memory of hungry wandering, but to actively challenge both this infant sister and his father for a place with his mother.

Expanding on the second memory, he now recalled the real story of the cut knee. He must have felt more and more excluded over those early years and must have felt particularly excluded when his parents entered the new house together, leaving him with his sister outside. He had begun to compensate for his loneliness and rejection by showing off to his little sister, trying to impress her in a "manly" way by jumping off a wheelbarrow. It was in attempting this narcissistic daredevil act with his sister as a compensatory object that he fell and cut his knee on construction equipment. Feeling hurt and belittled, Adam had rushed to his mother for solace. When his father shouted to keep the boy away lest the blood stain a new, as yet unsealed wood floor, Adam reexperienced the rejection of being kept from mother by father. In sum, he experienced a rejection by mother grafted onto an oedipal defeat. Thus this traumatic memory dating back to the age of 3 was a condensation whose simplicity belied the complex structure of painful object relations already built out of experiences with his family up to that point. The memory then structured and conveyed the internal object constellation, which expressed itself through repeated similarly painful longings and rejections that continued to dominate his adolescent and adult relationships. The reworking of these memories was both a vehicle and a benchmark in the transformation of his internal object relations.

At times the falsification of early memory that occurs when it is stripped of a context that would make it understandable is revealed by external life events. These moments offer opportunities for therapeutic growth, nevertheless.

A 36-year-old man, Eric, was certain about the facts of a particular childhood event. As an adult, he had often laughed at himself for the feelings that this event generated in him. The event was as follows. He remembered his enthusiasm over his brother's birth when he was 3½ years old. But when his parents brought the baby home from the hospital, they refused to let Eric hold the infant. He thought his parents had used reasonable caution in refusing to let him hold the newborn. In his own therapy, he had understood that his childhood outrage reflected the jealousy and displacement he had felt over many childhood years toward his parents concerning his brother.

Eric was surprised to discover, in a forgotten cache of family home movies, the film of his newborn brother's homecoming some 33 years earlier. In the crowning scene, his parents smilingly put the baby in his lap and doted on Eric, the proud and pampered older brother. It was only then that Eric could appreciate the extent to which his hurt during the intervening years had altered his memory to justify his jealousy toward the brother whom he also loved.

MEMORIES OF LATER CHILDHOOD

Childhood memories from the latency period are usually associated with better recall of the context of painful episodes. But splitting of the experience still occurs. People may isolate their memories from the full impact of a family context or may overload one episode with painful affect in order to make the surrounding period appear more benign. The most painful recollections usually represent condensations of circumstances and relationships. Latency-age memories may appear to make more sense due to the enhanced ability for rational thought and recall of the latency child. Memories of shame, humiliation, or inadequacy are particularly painful in later childhood. Since the older child has a greater capacity for remembering, these memories cannot be repressed as easily as similar earlier experiences.

> During the course of psychotherapy, Alan, age 30, recalled a shameful memory of fecal retention and soiling while attending summer camp for 2 months at the young age of 8. He recalled his fear of being ridiculed by the other campers while using the public toilets and his dread of a bully who slept next to him in his cabin. The thought of camp remained painful to him, fusing his sense of bodily shame with a pervasive personal feeling of inadequacy.
> In psychotherapy, Alan connected his fecal retention and sense of inadequacy during this first long summer away from home with a more general anxiety and realized that his parents must have been at war with each other during that period. Although they did not separate until a year later, he understood in retrospect that his father was

having affairs, his mother was lonely and angry, and that his father's harshness and rejection before Alan left for camp were a reflection of the father's difficulty in accepting his wife's preference for closeness with her son and guilt about the imminent break-up of the family.

Alan had developed the retention of stool because he felt humiliated by the public nature of the bathroom without walls between toilets, exposing him to the scrutiny of older boys and men. He had projected his father's anger and disapproval onto them with, of course, no awareness of doing so. When, in the therapy, Alan became able to understand his retention and the fecal leakage that eventually followed as expressing this situation, he could empathize with his childhood loneliness, the longing for his loving mother, and the fearful longing for his angry and anxious father. He could also grasp that his love for his mother had in some way come between his parents and so provoked attacks by his father at home and by the cruel father substitutes he projected into peers and counselors at camp. This realization, coming to him as an adult, considerably relieved his residual feelings of shame and inadequacy.

Following this work on understanding his projection of a parental transference into counselors, Alan was able to see his therapist as someone whose commitment he could trust. Alan decided to intensify his treatment, and began psychoanalysis a month later. When the camp memory came up for reworking a year later, Alan recognized that he had split his image of his father into the bad one he feared would haunt him in the form of contemptuous counselors and older boys, and the good one he tried to keep inside and hold onto in the form of a fecal object. His anal dilemma, which contained the attempt to hold onto an object no matter how threatening, diverted him from facing what would analytically be called castration anxiety, the fear about competing with the older boys at camp and ultimately about fantasies of challenging and ousting his father.

ADOLESCENT MEMORIES

In adolescence, unconscious falsification of memories still occurs. Severe falsifications are seen in adolescents who have disturbances that are already well developed. The following case presents the memories of a borderline girl in whom there was already a history of traumatic loss, illustrating the way in which sexual issues often intertwine traumatically with aggressive fantasies.

Judy Green, a 14-year-old girl whose family is described in Chapter 8, was admitted to the hospital following the ingestion of 100 aspirin tablets. She said that a month before the hospitalization she had witnessed a car backing over an infant who was killed instantly. She insisted that she could have saved the infant but had wished the baby dead and therefore had failed to shout. Judy seemed to believe this story, claiming it was the cause of her guilt and suicidal depression. Witnesses, however, clearly established that she had not been present at this tragic episode. She had falsified a memory to fit an otherwise nameless guilt.

In psychotherapy, we eventually came to see that this invented memory of near murderous intent was linked to many aspects of her inner turmoil. It gave form to her inner fantasies of destructiveness. She had had unprotected intercourse with a series of boys, flaunting her promiscuity and unconsciously begging her parents to stop her. She eventually acknowledged her disappointment that her mother unconsciously supported this desperate sexual acting out. The murderous intent of which

Judy's "memory" accused *her* in a distortion of her own
sense of reality was the taking on of blame that she really
felt toward her mother for letting her destroy herself. The
falsified memory embodied Judy's unconscious accusation
of her mother. We found further sources for this blame in
Judy's early sexualized attachment to her father, who,
though not abusive, was apparently seductive with Judy
when he felt rejected by Judy's mother. He had died when
Judy was 6. Later, beginning at the age of 10, Judy had a
year-long incestuous relationship with her brother, who
was then 13. The distorted memory of the baby's death
incorporated the feeling of these cumulative periods of
neglect, loss, and unfulfilled longing to be babied herself,
and the murderous yet longing feelings toward a fantasied
baby born of fantasized oedipal union with her dead
father and the fantasy's enactment with her brother.

The distortions of memory by Judy, which resemble
normal distortions of events by young children, are signs
of severe pathology in adolescence. Judy's dissociative
and borderline organizations are common in adolescents
who have had severe traumatic loss in earlier years, so
that the process of formation and storage of memories, the
severe splitting of self and object become prominent. In
the course of therapy, the mending of the memories is a
sign and path to the mending and integration of their
selves and their object relations.

DISTORTION OF ADULT MEMORIES

It is not only memories of childhood and adolescence
that are distorted in painful circumstances. Adult memories are subject to similar influences. Therapy with Judy's
family two years later revealed distortion of painful memories by the adults, in this case her mother and stepfather.
In the absence of borderline conditions or psychosis, the

distortions usually represent failures to establish connections between events, rather than overt falsifications.

Judy could by now test reality normally. The family was hard at work trying to understand its earlier history. In a family session, Judy's mother, Mrs. Green, recalled that several years earlier, her 2-year-old son Bob had wandered out of the house and onto a median divide of a highway. To her, this showed how uncontrollable Bob had been. But something clicked for Judy, who was now well schooled in making therapeutic connections. She remembered that this event occurred not long after the period of her incestuous relationship with her older brother. With this contribution to the family picture, they were able together to draw back the curtain on a larger memory of a time of shared loneliness and fear. Mr. and Mrs. Green now recalled their unhappiness during the early days of their marriage when Mrs. Green was unable to take care of her five children and languished in bed while Mr. Green, an older man who had been a bachelor until age 40, felt overwhelmed with his sudden new responsibilities. Following these revelations, the family achieved an enlarged capacity to digest the past, which had continued to haunt them because up to this time they had unconsciously agreed to suppress it lest the events overwhelm them again. In this session they admitted to themselves that the baby's unsupervised wandering happened in the context of parental neglect, which was the consequence of the desperation each of them had felt through those years, feeling neglected and overwhelmed themselves. Once Judy's adolescent symptomatology was no longer split off from the context of family memory, the Greens and Judy herself could understand it as an expression of the shared despair of the family as a group and could move to offer each other a strengthened holding built now on mutual understanding. The family's enhanced individual capacity to rework old memories, which is demonstrated in Chapter 8, contributed directly and substantially to the family's enhanced holding capacity.

Just as adolescents find memories of inadequacy or shame before peers painful, so adults, exposing childish vulnerabilities during therapy, find the process threatening. Incidents of feeling weak or unloved may also be the subject of painful recollections and retrospective falsification, as in Judy's family. Some of these may be memories associated with post-traumatic stress disorder, traumatic episodes of war, or episodes in which the person was helpless to prevent a mugging or rape. Recurrent nightmares, flashbacks, or ruminations offer an incremental reliving of the event in attempts at psychological mastery.

In the case of familywide distortion of experience, family members can work therapeutically toward sharing memories of a painful period or circumstances. In their previous need to minimize the pain felt by each individual member through a combination of defensive processes and patterns of interaction, they have constructed altered psychological realities that explain the events in superficially less painful ways (Reiss 1981). The Green family-wide distortion had been perpetuated by a series of interactions among various members and with the wider world. The trauma was then lived out in Judy's sexual behavior and in other family symptomatology, for instance, in the poor school performance of a younger brother. Action and interaction had thus become a substitute for remembrance, both collectively and individually (Freud 1914). The incestuous episodes between Judy and her brother and her later adolescent turmoil and suicide attempt all served to keep alive the family's "memory" of unhappy relationships and events, but also to keep it buried from view by the family. Individual and family therapy enabled each member, and the family as a whole, to review and revive their memories and to locate their meanings in the family's history. Once this was done, family members were empowered to remember and digest instead of continuing to act out the forgotten events.

Painful memories are handled differently by the growing child, the adolescent, and the adult. As we have seen, these memories most often represent condensed images of a time of distress and conflict. They may occur at any age and involve the pain of feeling weak, unloved, or humiliated. A young child can more readily repress the context of the memories or the memories themselves because repression and forgetting are appropriate to this stage of development and the contemporaneous kind of psychological organization. Repression is less feasible for adolescents or adults, who instead employ subtle or overt forms of retrospective falsification unless they already suffer from ego-splitting, dissociation, or borderline personality organization.

Families often unconsciously agree as a group to try to "forget" or falsify certain events. But when this occurs, we often see the memory preserved silently by a series of repetitive interpersonal interactions. Therapeutic investigation of the retrospective falsifications and corresponding interactions among family members leads to an examination of the experience of self and object in the intrapsychic dimension of each family member and in the pooled unconscious organization of the family group. This work is illustrated further by the Green family in Chapter 8.

7

The Birth of the Self in Therapy

Internal objects are born into the relationship with the analyst. The analyst is experienced as the background facilitator, the parent of opportunity and of space for growth. The patient also experiences the analyst as the object of desire and hate, the object mother and father. In the confusion and synergy of these two lies the patient's struggle. In exploring the relationship between them, the patient may find his or her self.

The process of therapy or analysis delivers the

internal object as a focus of study and revision. Thus within the safety of therapy or analysis, we hope to provide a haven and creative work space for the recovery and revision of the repressed, hidden, and often lost internal world of the patient.

We have already noted that it is within the arms-around holding of the mother that the infant is free to find itself, to become and then to have a trial of *going-on-being* as Winnicott (1971a) has put it. Just as the mother provides the arms-around holding to the child, so the therapist provides the therapeutic space within which the patient can explore and develop.

The process of therapy, from an object relations point of view, occurs by an examination of the patient's objects and object relations. Initially, the analyst or psychotherapist provides the context in which this revelation and examination of the objects occurs. Together, therapist and patient look at the objects the patient has delivered into the arms of the transference where they can turn them over and around and begin the process of looking also at the patient's relationship to them. In this derivative form, the therapist begins to find out about the part of the patient's self that is revealed by implication through the verbal description of the object. The therapist's preliminary comments about aspects of the self that are indirectly revealed often need to be couched with tact, especially if the patient is narcissistically vulnerable and easily wounded.

The experience of transference and countertransference that accrues as the work proceeds is the other source of information about the patient's self. At first, the therapist is generally treated as a parental holding object, one that is expected to facilitate the process and to be sympathetic to the patient. As noted in Chapter 3, when the patient makes the therapist the early focus of projections of discrete internal objects, that is, the target of a focused transference, the most important information he or she provides for the therapist concerns the patient's fear of the deficits in the therapist as a provider of holding.

Only later, in the security of a stable and proven container for the therapy, should the process naturally lead to the projection onto and into the analyst of the discrete internal objects that are in intimate relationship with parts of the patient's self. This heralds the middle phase of a long-term intensive psychotherapy or a psychoanalysis, which is supported by the tempered but flexible steel of the holding object, the therapist who has the confidence of the patient won slowly in their arduous and time-tested working relationship.

DELIVERING THE SELF: THE CASE OF FERNANDO GONZALES

The patient does not so much deliver the object into the nest, as deliver his or her self into a nest by finally trusting the therapist enough to put the object into the therapist. The patient asks the therapist to provide the holding, and later to house the patient's internal object, allowing for the emergence from camouflage of the self that had been in hiding behind the previous description of internal objects. This reversal marks a qualitative difference between early exploratory psychotherapy that deals with problems of the self indirectly through discussion of the object, and later, more intensive work that focuses more directly on the self as it emerges. The therapist is actually experiencing the life of the internal object because it has been thrust into him or her through projective identification, and the therapist has introjectively identified with it.

From the standpoint of the patient, both internal object and this part of the self have equal standing as parts of the self or ego. Intrapsychic organization recognizes some of these parts as parts of the self, and others as internal objects that carry a legacy of the external objects (Fairbairn 1952, Ogden 1986).

The patient I describe here was unusual in a respect that became a dominant theme of his long analysis: he had no particular feeling about or for me. He mentioned this not long after beginning the analysis, when I first wanted to say something about the transference. At the time, I wondered if perhaps I had prematurely pressed his lack of feeling, as though it were my issue, my wish that he care for me. But it gradually became clearer that his absence of positive feeling for me was an extension of his incapacity to feel positively for anyone in an intimate, long-term relationship. This patient exhibits the way that fundamental early difficulties in a maternal-child relationship can later form the nuclei of a perverse and homosexual organization (McDougall 1985, 1986). In the description of this man, and especially of the session we will examine in detail, I want to illustrate his use of the therapist to define his forming self.

Fernando Gonzales

"Do you think I'm homosexual?" Fernando asked, almost out of the blue during the evaluation.

"I don't know what you are. You don't seem to have conviction about whether your sexual partners should be men or women," I answered.

Fernando found my statement curiously encouraging. He latched onto it. "I've never given up hope for a wife and family, even though I've always found men more exciting than women."

Fernando Gonzales was a 39-year-old economist, the son of South American parents; his father was a diplomat who had married the beautiful daughter of a wealthy Latin family. He came to me because he could not maintain erections in homosexual relationships. He had been exclusively engaged in homosexual sex for the past seven years, but previously had emotional and sexual relations with both men and women, having been engaged as a young man before breaking it off because he could not face the marriage. Nevertheless, he had continued sexual relationships with women as well as men through the next several years, and then after the failure of a previous psychotherapy, had slowly slid, as he experienced it, into homosexuality.

Fernando's social relationships had remained long lasting with both men and women. His many close friendships lasted over many years, but he could not link personal intimacy with sexual intimacy. His sexual relationships with men were fleeting and unsatisfying. The men he wished would show an interest in him did not, and those he pursued were compromised objects. He was driven toward men for sex in anonymous, furtive encounters that he found degrading.

Gradually, we came to understand that Fernando's lack of feeling for me was more than coincidental. It echoed the affective withdrawal from his mother whom he resented and accused. He held her responsible for the impositions and constraints of a lifetime, the discouragement of his masculinity, the interruptions in his attempts to develop other significant relationships — and most especially for getting in the way between Fernando and his father. Fernando described his worldly father as meek and passive at home, belittled by his wife's pettiness and controls, reaching out weakly and infrequently to his son. Fernando's longing for his father had been submerged by the resentment and fury at his mother, and could scarcely be found. In the transference, it was embodied in the lack of positive feeling for me. He had no difficulty being angry at me over my fee, cancellation policy, my belongings, and lifestyle. He had no trouble voicing his respect for me, his desire that I would be able to help him fashion fundamental changes for which he had not dared to hope prior to analysis, and his gratitude that I was willing to confront him man-to-man over many issues. But he emphasized repetitively that he did not feel any warmth for me. Slowly, we began to understand that the absence of feeling for me was linked to his inability to feel erotically for anyone in an intimate relationship.

Eventually we understood that it was not actually the same as the fear of intimacy with women, but that it constituted the object relationship of feeling he had no father with whom to identify, no father to guide and back him. I had been the missing father. Warm feelings for me were impossible because he despaired of a father who could receive and reciprocate them. This was the basis for his desperately urgent homosexual search, but the objects he sought were younger men to whom he was a father, or else men turned into disembodied penises—blow jobs in the woods or at a sex bookstore, pickups with no future. He longed to get a penis from a man, to get a penis that would magically make his own penis erect, because he despaired of getting a fatherly object who could live inside him. Without this, he despaired of being a man who could love a woman and whom a woman could love in return without dominating and extinguishing him.

A dream heralded the transition between despair and collaboration. He dreamt that he was sodomizing a man who was having intercourse with a woman at the same time. The dream, he felt, was bizarre and exciting, frightening and revealing. He could get an erection from the experience with another man and could then reach out through the man into the woman. In this way, the other man did the sexual relating for him while Fernando was not in danger of being engulfed by the woman. I felt the dream also held the hope that the man would put his penis into Fernando so that Fernando could take the other man's power, but it was this longing that Fernando was blocking. He could let neither man nor woman inside himself—that is, he could not experience the desire for male or female objects—lest they take him over.

This was the transference. Although I sat behind him in the literal arrangement of the analytic consulting room, emotionally Fernando stayed behind me, hoping to steal my erection from behind or to enter intimate relationships without letting me enter him. By entering me without letting me enter him, he could take from me what he needed to become potent himself, or at least he could get to the woman vicariously through me. The longing for a relationship with a woman was still filtered through me, still distanced by his use of me. I had become the self he longed to be.

Fernando still could not have reliable erections, even in masturbation. In the initial evaluation before beginning analysis, tests had indicated that his erectile difficulty was primarily psychological. I doubted this. His capacity for intimate relationships was initially so limited that we agreed to hold off any physical medical intervention until such time as he could sustain an emotionally intimate relationship. In the first months after he moved away from men, he was so frightened of the women with whom he began relationships that he lost his erections. Although analysis lessened his fear, the erectile difficulty persisted. Fernando attributed this to embarrassment about the unreliability of his erections. I still wondered about an organic component and said that I thought it was time for a second urologic consultation for the organic aspect of his erectile failure. This time, two consultants agreed about the organic origin of the erectile difficulty. One recommended pelvic vascular surgery; the second suggested instead that Fernando try papaverine injections into the body of the penis, an approach that had been standardized over the previous few years (Virag et al. 1984). Fernando chose papavarine injection therapy and regained his capacity for reliable erections, with some improvement in his capacity to maintain erections even when not using the papaverine.

Fernando was soon able to try a sexual relationship with a woman who had been hovering in his life for many years. He felt his potency confirmed with her, but she was not the woman he would have chosen. Grateful to her for the first sustained sexual relationship in twenty years, he broke off with her nevertheless to see if he could manage relationships that he found more satisfying beyond the sex. In this time of stretching his boundaries, he felt a tentative and frightened hopefulness.

The hour that is the focus of this chapter occurred in this time of hopeful but uncertain transition. It began with a dream that gave a picture of Fernando's experience of the therapeutic holding relationship as a matured place for work and growth and of what I had come to mean for him. A new woman had appeared on the horizon, but when this hour occurred, it was still unclear whether they would be able to consummate an intimate relationship. That new relationship did ultimately mature. It ripened into the first relationship of his life which was both sexually and emotionally satisfying. But at the time of this hour, he could not be sure it would proceed. He was doing his best to hope in a time of uncertainty.

In the following session, Fernando frequently used the word "you" to mean *himself.* Since grammatically *I* would have been the "you" in the room, I believe this use of "you" was in the service of using me as an object through which he was building a self. Embedded in the grammatical ambiguity was a penetrating confusion between himself and me that characterized his search for a self. I have italicized those parts of the hour that illustrate this process.

Fernando began the hour with a dream: "I dreamt of a building, as I so often have. There was renovation going on, and there was a man there who was part of the scene, a secure part. It wasn't sexual. He was helpful, in the background. I don't really remember the dream well.

"I have two thoughts about the dream. I wonder if perhaps I don't remember the dream so well because there is something homosexual in it, and I suppressed that. But it could be that it's a fine dream—that the man in the dream is you. I have a secure relationship with you and it makes me happy. The renovation is my search for a home, my psychological renovations. But I don't know if it's true. This is what I've dug up. It may not be, but it is what has come to mind."

I said, "You're worried. You hope the dream is a sign of the positive, of the hard-won good feeling for me and for yourself, but there is also the lurking bad feeling, your suspicion of a homosexual element, which carries the conflict you're still in."

He was silent for a few minutes. "I took your comment as though I had no reaction, no feeling. That's the 'no feeling' I had about you for so long. I think I don't want to hear that I'm still in conflict. I want out of this!

"My friend Ted lost his job a few weeks ago. He's deeply depressed, and then yesterday his wife said she might ask for a divorce. He said he's so deeply unhappy about the way his life is going that he can't even have much of a reaction about the latest downturn. It's a feeling I'm familiar with. *You're so tired of being the way you are, so burdened by it.* I read that Freud said that sometimes symptoms just die of exhaustion, wear themselves out. I feel like that myself sometimes."

When he first used "you" to mean himself or someone in his position, I felt jolted, as though he had reached right into me to get a self. As he continued over the next few minutes I felt I almost *became* him.

"I do want to jettison my burdens. But that's not the right image. It's like . . . *You have a space inside. It's filled with effort, filled with things that have cost you something. The effort was a drain. Or that space can be filled with things that give you energy, a source that fills you, gives you strength instead of making you weak. So it's not just getting rid of a burden, but it has to be replaced with something that gives you something positive.*"

Then at times he let me go, speaking *to* me of the ambiguity about his self, almost as if allowing me my own skin again.

"I see that as being the relationship with you. I continue to insist that I don't have that point of reference inside my own personality that gives me dignity. I don't have a model or standard. So what I have is a mish-mash of things. Some things I believe in, some I don't. Some are things that reveal themselves just by repetition.

"I allowed to Mary Ann the other night that I'm a diamond in the rough. I didn't have a theology, a code, a right-or-wrong. No, I *do* have a right-wrong code, but I don't know why. All the evidence, all the resources are there, but I don't feel it. I don't know my own weight and form, my substance. And I miss that. I envy people who just seem to have it. I never had it as a child and I don't as an adult. That's what I want from or through you—an adult point of reference, something that will let me know how to function in the world.

Now he began using "you" for himself again, dizzyingly alternating "you" and "I."

"It seems to me it comes down to a search. My lack of self-confidence, poor self-image, it all revolves around an empty point. *Where does your personality start? The strength emanate from? Your conviction? Your self-confidence? When you get down to that point for me, it's empty!* So parts of my personality are like hungry dogs circling around an empty food bowl—hungry and lost. It's supposed to be there, but there's nothing there to eat. I have all these ideas and parts of my self, but nothing holds them together. Nothing gives me that consistent conviction I can refer to when I am shaken. I'm offered choices and I don't know what to do. I look for it in church, but I haven't found it there either.

"I'm fortunate to be here, in analysis, searching for something to fill it. I'm not a scientist, but I have this image of loose atomic particles zigzagging in a defined space without coordination or coherence. *Then you do something to that space, zap it, give it order. Then they establish an order.* I feel like I'm an atom and I've been smashed. All these particles whirling around, not knowing what to do."

I felt drained, used to "zap" him with a self, as though he had committed a sexual act of extracting his self from me.

I said, "I don't think you heard yourself using the word 'you' to mean yourself instead of referring to me. Do you feel you need me inside to form yourself? Am I the father whose zap you want?"

He paused. "I have a fundamental desire for a center, a home, a father—'a master's voice,' an image I can feel I am coming from! That is to say, a father. And I can't do that. That's where the conflict comes from. I'm fighting as hard as I can with and for a father. There was so little in my father I want to be like. But in many ways I am like him and I don't like it: his timidity, his passivity. I scream against it! I don't want to be that way.

"If you're screaming and fighting with all your might against something that is supposed to be your source, what do you do? How do you stop the fighting and acquire the source you want? All my life you try to build without him, which you can't do! You have to accept him for what he is. You don't have to be like him. I don't have to be like him! But what do I put in his place other than the person who was naturally supposed to be there?"

I said, "The struggle isn't over. If I'd be your father and your source, you're afraid I'd take you over, use you for my own purposes."

"That conflict is still there, and it's key because *I will not be like him!* And I'm committed to that, but then I don't know what else to do. How do I keep him out and still keep someone or something that a father is supposed to be? Perhaps I lay too much on my father. I try to describe what I want. It may not come from him. I guess you'd argue it can't. But I don't have to accept that I can never have self-confidence. I'm here because I believe that I don't have to be like him. I can be competent and productive. Yet, I can't resolve the two. I can't get rid of the fear of being like him. And I can't give up on the wish for a father, for a God. That's why I go to church. It's another part of my search for something I haven't found yet."

We were near the end of the session. I said, "It's still a mystery to you how you can find a satisfying self-image. You still feel you have to find out what and who you need to make up for the feeling you didn't have, the father you missed for so long. Without him, you can't find yourself, that zap that will bring you together around a point. You want it from me but it terrifies you."

"Yes!" he said. "Practically speaking, I think sex could help, like with Mary Ann, a woman who cares about me and who I can stay with to care for her. Over time it would help establish my self-image. There were times I began to feel it with Helen last year before I felt I had to break up with her. Before then, we'd have sex for a few days and I'd begin to feel a source of power. I don't have a source of power. I broke up with Helen because I began to feel I no longer needed to be captive of the weaknesses in both our personalities. But the source of the strength was sex with her. I don't regret breaking up with her. It was healthy, but it's left me in limbo, and I haven't replaced the source of strength I had in the sexual part of the relationship with her."

Both of us experienced this session as an hour of confirmation. In this hour, Fernando summed up the leading edge of the transference, the relationship with his father, which was its major precursor. And he clarified the analytic situation for me in words that were beyond my own, yet that fit with my experience of our work.

The hour began with his dream of a building in renovation, with a man identified with me who was a helpful part of the background. Fernando often dreamt of buildings, an image he viewed as his personality, his search for himself. There was some lack of clarity in the dream, but, as he told it, he was clearly saying that I was the helpful man. He had a secure relationship with me, and he felt a dramatic shift from the years of having no positive feelings for his father or for me.

This is the description of his finding me as the contextual parent, embodied in the father who could hold the situation and provide Fernando space in which to live. The discovery made him happy.

Yet there is a partly repressed conflict. He is worried that it is a homosexual relationship. During the hour, I thought of the years in which he sought a father and an identity through a search for homosexual relationships. He was embarrassed and threatened by those longings now, but they are still a feature of his feeling for me as the provider of holding. He is still haunted by his unsatisfactory defense of sexualizing the relationship with the contextual parent as his way of dealing with the kind of despair he described early in the hour in terms of his friend Ted—no job, no one there for him.

Fernando's despair developed originally in the relationship with his mother by whom he felt dominated from the beginning. He felt that it was her intrusiveness that deprived him of his self, that she had scooped out the core of his self and had at the same time denied him access to others who might have provided him with the space in which to find a self. In this situation, he unconsciously developed the strategy of turning to men, not only for arms-around holding, which he desperately wanted, but for the insemination that he had come to feel was required for the birth of a compensatory, new self. I believe that he was actually identified with his mother, who must at bottom have also felt that she needed insemination from a man to form a self. Frustrated with her passive husband, and probably with her father before him, she seems to have attempted to get a self from Fernando by taking his masculinity and personality from him, introjectively extracting it from him (Bollas 1987). What Fernando experienced as her control, I believe, was her attempt to get his liveliness into herself. Nevertheless, Fernando experienced being controlled. He felt that his mother tried to mold him in a rigid die and then stole his self from him.

In the hour, Fernando then discussed the internal corollary of the external holding space I provided for him. It is the space inside which he described as "filled with effort, with things which have cost you something . . . or that space can be filled with things which give you energy, a source that fills you, gives you strength instead of making you weak." This is the creative reservoir, the place inside the self that corresponds to the external transitional space that is Winnicott's "locus of creativity" (1971b). It is here that Fernando describes a positive self that derives from the external holding. He can identify what is growing in his self, but it is not yet secure. Once it is more securely installed, he will not look for ways to describe it. Analysands are most eloquent during their search for self.

Fernando then discussed the use of the analyst in building a secure self. "I see that as being the relationship with you . . . I don't have that point of reference in my personality that gives me dignity . . . a model or standard."

It still comes by outside reference, but increasingly, the outside is being installed at the core, partly by the analyst's role of being in the steady background and partly by being available as an object for identification who can be used through introjective identification. But in another way, it is not only through taking in the analyst. Fernando wants to find his self, not the analyst's self. That was the trouble with his mother and father. He felt he kept having his mother's self and her preformed image of who he should be foist on and into him, so that she could extract it from him for herself. Meanwhile his father, a man of the world who was a shy violet in the family, offered too little to identify with.

Fernando wants to find his self, the things that "reveal themselves just by repetition." But to do so, he has to be helped to hold steady to find them. In this part of the search, I am the platform on which he stands to see the self displayed, which he hopes to assemble. He sees himself, now, in a new way, in a way he had hardly dared to hope for, as a "diamond in the rough," an unshaped gem that might have structure and integrity if it can only be found. "All the evidence, the resources are there, but I don't feel it. I don't know my own weight and form, my substance."

What had brought Fernando to treatment was his desperate need to depend on others, on external objects, for a view of himself. Unconsciously, he fantasied that the longed-for erection would be the defining embodiment of a self. Now he no longer converts an image of a self into another man's erect penis, but he still feels he needs another man to help him see who he is. We all need our external objects to help us see and be ourselves throughout life. We realize that when Fernando says it, but he means it too literally. He has not yet internalized the sustaining function of the object, so he feels he must have a constant external supply of internal objects to confirm his sense of self. "That's what I want from or through you—an adult point of reference, something that will let me know how to function in the world." For many years, the disembodied penis had been the "adult point of reference" he imagined would be the answer to his search, enter his center, and infuse him with what he needed to organize around it.

So he tells us: "My search . . . revolves around an empty point. The place my personality should start is empty." And he then describes his ravenous search for the seed crystal of personality, which he, as so many others, envision as food: "So parts of my personality are like hungry dogs circling around an empty food bowl—hungry and lost. It's supposed to be there, but there's nothing to eat. I have all these ideas and parts of my self, but nothing holds them together. Nothing gives me that consistent conviction I can refer to when I am shaken."

BUILDING A RESILIENT SELF

Again, Fernando draws a picture of what would be necessary to form a self. He would have to introject something like food to form the glue to his splintered, disorganized, lost self. And being left hungry for a lifetime, because he cannot feed himself and cannot maintain a relationship with those who could help him achieve cohesion, he remains not only hungry, but filled with a pack of voracious dogs who would destroy any food that came their way.

Fernando is still lacking in his capacity to derive benefit from feeding his others, helping others to establish their selves in a reciprocal way. His friends felt that Fernando actually did nourish them and that he did it better than most people—but he was unable to derive a reflected self-cohesion from these relationships because he felt giving to others emptied him. It emptied his self because he felt it was demanded by the internal needs of a controlling mother.

In the next moments of the session, Fernando gave another graphic fantasy of what I would have to supply to give him coherence: "I have this image of loose atomic particles zigzagging in a defined space without coordination or coherence. Then *you* do something to that space, zap it, give it order. Then they establish an order. I feel like I'm an atom, and I've been smashed. All these particles whirling around, not knowing what to do."

Here is another image that gives a clue to the sexualized longing for a penis, the moment of creation of a self that is an atomic "big bang." He needs me to give him this bang, to "zap" his disorganized fragments. This is the form of his dream for the father who is "a center, a home, a father—'a master's voice,' an image I can feel I am coming from!" But this desire also leads to his dread that he is issuing an invitation for this object to exploit his craving to enter him and take him over at the core. It is here that his fight is against his father, to be *not like* him in refusing to be taken over by his mother as he feels his father was. He tries to be like the father he longed for, not like the one he felt he had, through being in a relationship with someone while not taken over. He told me how much he wanted me to be firm so that he would not take me in deceptively, and yet that he did not want to have to be like me:

"I'm fighting as hard as I can with and for a father . . . If you're screaming and fighting with all your might against something that is supposed to be your source, what do you do? How do you stop the fighting and acquire the source you want? All my life you try to build without him, which you can't do! You have to accept him for what he is. You don't have to be like him. *I* don't have to *be* like him! But what do I put in his place other than the person who was naturally supposed to be there?"

The inextricable puzzle of how to identify with others without having to be them in their fallibility tied Fernando in a Gordian knot. He tried to solve this conundrum by the quick and anonymous homosexual episodes that denied the individuality of the men through whom he nevertheless desperately hoped to get the "zap" he needed for formation of his self. With failure came desperation and futility.

But he found what he needs to begin the process of building a resilient self: "I can't resolve the two. I can't get rid of the fear of being like him. And I can't give up on the wish for a father, for a God. That's why I go to church. It's another part of my search for something I haven't found yet."

In the last minutes of the session, Fernando mentions two areas of continuing search. The first occurs in church. It was true, I thought, that his life-long search for God carried the same elements: a greater being who could contain and oversee his search for himself, who would love him without intrusion, and who would support his search for meaning and a relentless devotion to higher values and service to others, so characteristic of Fernando.

The second occurs in sexual expression. Like John Donne, whose religious and sexual longings were so intertwined that his sacred and profane poetry drew equally from sexual and religious sources, Fernando looked for a higher self in the gutter to which he was brought by the baseness of his longing. But in the renewal of a search for a woman who could offer what he wanted from his father, he fantasied the coming together of his longing to be a man who could penetrate, who could be the "zapper" organizing the other, like the father he longed for, with the external object who could reflect back to him the images of a fragmented self and integrate them in her holding gaze. Both religion and intimate sexual relating are like intensive therapy in offering opportunities for the coming together of self with its objects in moments of conjoined intensity, which at the same time support the separate individuality of both. In this way, they speak to Fernando's search for objects that will help him become whole beyond the confines of his treatment.

It was an enormous relief to Fernando, and to me, that in the ensuing months he found a considerable degree of this in his developing relationship with Mary Ann.

REFINDING THE THERAPIST'S SELF

It is in the nature of our work that when it goes well, patients give us what we need for reassurance and confirmation. In this session, Fernando gave me the confirmation that something had been happening during the years of our work that had enabled him to change fundamentally. He was not made in my image—something I came to realize that both he and I feared was the only way out. He had found himself in the struggle with and against me. In doing so, he helped me to find *my* self—the self who did not have to impose an identity on an emerging other, yet who could hope for a better way of life for him. A self who had not been a fool, as I had often felt I had been, for instance, when I said to him in our first meeting, "I'm not sure what you are."

And he gave me as beautiful a description of the ideas I had been struggling with as I could ever hope for. He described for me his need for a holding arms-around parent to provide the context for his growth, the contextual parent toward whom he had felt so cold and guarded through the first years of our work, but toward whom he could now feel warmly grateful. This was the parent by whom he wanted to be fed, to be held from the inside, and to be "zapped" by in an organizing, integrating infusion of love for his emerging self.

But this self was also confused with the object parent by whom he wanted to be loved and whom he wanted to love and nourish in return. He wanted to be validated without feeling controlled.

Ultimately, the focused, loving, object-relating parent who holds and suffuses with love and meaning from the center turns into the contextual, holding parent. The quandary in which Fernando began is solved by learning that in surrendering to being defined by those we love, we find the context in which to find our self-definition. They must give our selves to us and we must give their selves back to them.

PART THREE

THE OBJECT RELATIONS
OF DREAMS

8

The Dream as

Communication between

Self and Others

Dreams told in the interpersonal setting reveal a new aspect of the unconscious: family members know things unknown to the dreamer. Using this perspective, we can apply the use of dreams to the communication between self and object in family and marital therapy.

Use of the dream as communication in the interpersonal field was first brought home to me in a session with the family of the first psychiatric patient assigned to me as a resident. Judy Green was 14 upon admission, an acting-out girl with the diagnosis of borderline personality. As a fledgling psychiatrist, I found her immensely appealing. I treated her individually for almost two years when difficulty that her younger brother, Bob, was having brought the whole family to therapy with me. At the time of the session reported here, I had been seeing the family for almost a year. Their treatment was about to terminate because I was moving from Boston to Washington, DC.

The family included Judy's mother and stepfather; Judy, who was now 17; her 12-year-old sister, Deb; Bob, age 11; and Sam, age 6, the only child of Mr. and Mrs. Green's marriage. An older brother was away at college and did not attend. The family as a whole had been intensely dedicated to the therapy. As the session began, Mrs. Green said she had had a dream that followed her guilt that the family had picked on 11-year-old Bob in the car on the way home after the previous week's session.

Mrs. Green dreamt that there was a friendly purple lion near her son Bob. In the dream, she was unsure if the lion was a threat. She wondered if she should protect Bob, who was a baby in the dream, or even if she needed to evaluate the situation. She was so unsure. Was the lion really friendly?

Mrs. Green related the dream to her neglect of Bob when he was little. She remembered a time when he was 2 years old. He had been unsupervised and had wandered into the middle of a main road in his diapers.

Mr. Green thought the dream had to do with his wife's lack of trust in men, including himself. Then Mr. Green, whom the children often teased for his bad jokes, quipped that perhaps "lion" meant "lyin' " and he cited the pun in support of the idea that he, who was often not believed, was the menacing lion.

Mrs. Green replied that she felt that in the dream Bob was saved, although perhaps she would not be. Perhaps it was she who was threatened.

Bob, who had sat quietly so far, now countered his mother's earlier focus on him as the endangered one in the family by saying that perhaps the lion was really his little brother, 6-year-old Sam, who was, after all, the baby of the family. This was a particularly interesting idea, because it ran against the reality of Sam's charmed life in the family. It was rare for anyone—except Bob—to direct aggression at him.

Meanwhile, Sam was having a ball. As soon as his mother had reported the dream, he had gone to work drawing a picture of it (Figure 8–1). He asked if anyone had noticed that his father's tie was purple. We could all now see that Mr. Green indeed had a purple tie. Sam drew a picture, which he called "Andy, the purple lion." As with many youngest children in family therapy, Sam had an ability to speak the truth without remorse and

Figure 8–1. Sam's "Andy the Purple Lion"

without anyone minding. It must be her husband who was Mrs. Green's original "purple lion" and her dream revealed her sense of him as a threat to her and her children. She had held this view for many years, both when Bob was small and now too, when Sam was the current baby.

Meanwhile, my own association was to the words "David in the Lions' Den" with the complete conviction at that moment that "David"—not Daniel—was the name of the Biblical hero so endangered in the lions' den. In another moment I realized *I* felt in the lions' den, that the Greens had become threatening to me.

While I was countertransferentially taken over by the sense of danger and confusion in the family, Judy, who had lately often taken the role of resident therapist, spoke up. She thought that the dream represented the way the family blamed Dad when things got tough. Now, in the therapy, it was not so clear that Dad really was the bad guy. She thought that just as Mom was confused in the dream, so were they all in the session, but it was better that they were thus confused. They used to blame each other with conviction, she said, but now they weren't so sure there was really a raging lion to pin everything on. Grinning at her stepfather as she copied his way with words, she quipped that maybe the lion was "lyin' in waitin' " inside each of them. With Judy's interpretation, I also felt relieved.

During the rest of the session, the projections of aggression onto Bob and Mr. Green, were considered, with the result that the family felt less like a "lions' den"— less that way to me and less so to them. At the end of the session, the family agreed that "Andy, the purple lion" had indeed become considerably friendlier.

I knew at the time that this dream was an interpersonal communication. It provided material that led to insight into the family as a group.

With the passage of time and further experience, I now

realize that the dream spoke to the family's transference to me. They knew, because I was moving away, that I could not provide an adequate holding environment for much longer. This already presaged their fears, which soon surfaced in the termination phase. And in this session, they were trying to deal with shared anger at me for leaving, which then threatened them all.

This dream was more than a report of an intrapsychic experience. It was more than the intricate combination of day residue with internal fantasy or the fulfillment of an infantile wish as Freud originally described in *The Interpretation of Dreams* (1900). It did not merely represent the comparison of old and new affective experience during the matching process fundamental to the storing of new information in the memory tree (Palombo 1978). Beyond these individual functions, it also expressed something for the family group, especially in relation to the therapist.

FAIRBAIRN'S DISCOVERY THAT DREAMS DEPICT THE STRUCTURE OF SELF AND OBJECT

For me to make a case in object relations theory for that dream I heard more than 20 years ago and described in the previous section, I present here an overview of the status of the dream in, and its extension into, object relations theory.

At the end of his project of building an object relations theory of the personality, Fairbairn (1954) emerged with a six-part model of psychic structure: a central ego and its ideal object, characterized by reasonable internal harmony; the rejecting object and the internal saboteur (which he later called the antilibidinal ego), characterized by anger, the anxiety of persecution, and frustration; and the exciting object and the libidinal ego, characterized by longing and the anxiety of excessively aroused neediness. (This theory is pictured in Chapter 3, Figure 3–1.)

These internal structures were built around the images of the parents or other primary objects and later modified by new experience with primary objects such as spouses or children. But what is crucial to this view of psychic functioning is that the internal structures of the ego are capable of generating meaning and action and that they are in constant dynamic relationship with each other (Fairbairn 1952, Ogden 1986).

The development relevant to consideration of dreams is the step taken in Fairbairn's 1944 paper, "Endopsychic Structure Considered in Terms of Object Relationships." Through analysis of the dreams of his analysands, he demonstrated the action of the six internal psychic structures and drew his conclusion that dreams were to be understood not as wishes, but as *statements of internal psychic structure.* He was then able to demonstrate the nature of the relationship between the elements of the psyche as illustrated in the dreams. For instance, in the dream of a woman (1944, pp. 94–101) he located her central or observing self; an ideal object in one rather reasonable version of her experience with her husband; an exciting object as another image of her husband; and an image of the persecuting object in the form of her mother attacking her.

In a later paper (1954), a patient, "Jack," now understood to be Fairbairn's analysand Harry Guntrip (Hughes 1989), dreamt of being tempted with enticing but poisonous milk, being caught between the exciting object and the persecuting one.

In none of these cases did Fairbairn say that these dreams, or the internal objects they depicted, gave form to the actual mother or husband. They were painful internal versions of these figures, constructions of the dreamer, which represented internal objects, not the actual living people.

Fairbairn reasoned that for dreams to express either wishes or conflicts, they necessarily must express aspects of the structure that derive from those wishes and conflicts. This led Fairbairn to the idea that the dreams could, themselves, be seen as statements of the underlying psychic structure. Since he defined these structures as made up of self and object in relationship, the dreams described the nature of internal object relationships, which, in themselves, made up psychic structure.

THE DREAM AS INTERPERSONAL COMMUNICATION

If we accept this view of the dream as a statement of the internal object relations of an individual, then when a dream is reported in the hearing of others, it will convey the dreamer's internal object relations. When Mrs. Green reported her dream in the family situation described in the opening section of this chapter, her husband and children understood intuitively that it gave expression to the way images of them lived inside her. In describing her internal psychic situation, she was describing her internal family and her internal family was made up of primary objects based on her images of the people in the room with her, namely, her husband and children, who had inherited their role relationships in her intrapsychic realm from her original primary objects based on experience with her own parents. So this dream, reported in the therapy setting, formed a communication from Mrs. Green's internal object relations to her external objects.

In the first instance, the dream is a statement of Mrs. Green's internal object relations to herself. She began by considering her relationship to her son Bob, who probably stood also for her own needy self. She projected her own "lion bits" onto her husband, the painful part of herself that was a rejecting, angry, or negligent mother. We also heard about her in the dream as an observer, wanting the best for her child, Bob, who is her ideal object. But in the dream Bob also represents herself both as needy and as exciting of a longing for need and protection. She is unsure if she can function parentally under the threat of the lion—the persecuting object—but she is also unsure of the nature of the threat: the lion is friendly looking and should perhaps be trusted.

This confusion between threat and trust of parental figures was a feature in this family throughout generations. Here represented in a dream is the telltale combination of a parental figure who is seductive and threatening at the same time, and a negligent parent who looks the other way. Her dream revealed Mrs. Green's internal constellation, but it was her children who had acted out the unsolved conflict between dynamic structures: Judy and her older brother had had intercourse several times a few years earlier during the height of family distress.

THE FAMILY'S OBJECT RELATIONS

When Mrs. Green reported her dream, it became a communication between family members. It informed them about her individual conflict at that moment, and in the ensuing discussion, it facilitated expression of the way internal relationships between self and objects influenced the family group.

When the family heard the report of Mrs. Green's dream, they heard it through the ears, as it were, of their own internal objects. Children in a family therapy setting are in the room with the very people who are the stuff of which their own internal objects have been fashioned. These internal objects act as a kind of scanning device (Ogden 1986) or lens through which events are perceived. So Mr. Green heard the dream in terms of what it said about him. He understood that he was cast as the ambiguously threatening object. That made Mrs. Green his accuser, as she had often been. Their previous therapeutic work had let him develop an observing part of his central ego so that he had enough distance to see the situation and deal with it, which he did by employing the helpful defense of humor.

Bob understood that he was being placed in a threatened position. In a way he was being offered to the lion by his mother, who was, in the dream, failing to protect him.

And Sam understood a great deal about the situation: that the proposed lion was none other than his father, whom he was determined to rehabilitate by coloring him a friendly and perhaps royal purple.

The index patient, Judy, saw the dream as a picture of the family's projective identificatory system in which her mother was putting parts of her own internal quandary into other members of the family, who for reasons of their own psychic economy introjectively identified with these.

And finally, although I did not see it then, the family as a group were letting me know of their alignment in regard to me and my leaving them.

PROJECTIVE IDENTIFICATION AND UNCONSCIOUS COMMUNICATION

For the individual, projective identification is the mental process in which hated or threatened parts of the self are put into the other person as a defense against one's own aggression or as a way of controlling oneself and therefore the other person unconsciously (Klein 1946, Segal 1973). Here we can look at the process as applied to the family. In Chapter 3, we reviewed the way projective identification, along with its counterpart, introjective identification, is the mechanism of fundamental unconscious communication, the vehicle through which each person makes unconscious identifications with others. In the couple or family, the group divides up personal qualities and lodges some more or less in one person, others in another (Dicks 1967, Zinner and Shapiro 1972).

In this dream, and especially through Judy's interpretation of it, we can see the way that the telling of the dream demonstrates projective and introjective identification in action. All of the family members in the room had a response to the dream in terms of their understanding of Mrs. Green's quandary. But most important, each of them interpreted the dream in terms of the meaning for his or her own relationship to her. Since she was a primary object for each family member, each association from a family member has to be understood in that light of their implications for that person's internal object relations and psychic situation.

THE TRANSFERENCE MEANING OF THE DREAM

Finally, there is the matter of the transference implications of
the dream. From an intrapsychic perspective on the dream, we
might speculate that Mrs. Green felt threatened in the therapy
and that I was being experienced as a lion.

The family's combined transference was first spoken for
by Mrs. Green as an ambiguously combined hope and fear. But
the family members, who understood this, worked to modify
her opening statement and developed a mature view of hope in
the presence of uncertainty about the object. The dream was
reorganized as belonging to them all. The whole group, including the therapist, worked on the dream through the
sharing of associations to uncover the unconscious themes,
much as a dream might be dealt with by a single dreamer in an
analytic session. The result was a gain in understanding about
the nature of relationships inside the family, and, by implication, about the family's relationship to the therapist as well.

THE DREAM AS INTERPERSONAL
COMMUNICATION IN INDIVIDUAL THERAPY

Dreams convey interpersonal meaning even within the intrapsychic focus of individual therapy or psychoanalysis. Three
examples underscore the point that the telling of a dream in
psychoanalysis or individual therapy is an interpersonal communication. Dreams join in the conversation of the therapy and
express the issues between therapist and patient, now expressing the resistance of the dreamer, now the shift in psychic
structure. And on occasions, therapists have dreams about
their patients that indicate they have joined in the process, as
in the following example.

A male supervisee reported that his patient had the
following dream:

A guy at work had control over me. He was involved in sexual abuse along with a woman who was there at his apartment. He took me there. He had captured my girlfriend and forced me to have sex with her against my will. They took her pants off, and I was excited at the prospect of finally making love to her, especially since it wasn't my responsibility. I moved my mouth toward her genitals, but then I rebelled against the man so that at least she would know it was done with a struggle.

In the rest of the dream, the patient overcame the man and took him to the police station. In the process, a boy assisting the man was killed.

The patient associated the abusing man with the therapist, who he remembered had recently said that the patient regarded the therapist as a "cockteaser." Patient and therapist were able to connect the patient's ambivalence about genital sexuality with his ambivalent attitude toward therapy and to his fearful, yet aroused feeling about his therapist.

A few days later, the patient extended the theme when he had fantasies during his therapeutic hour of a car crash while he was driving his girlfriend, and of performing fellatio on a childhood boyfriend who, in the fantasy, did not respond. He linked these fantasies to feelings about the therapist.

That night, the therapist had a dream, which he reported to me in supervision with an embarrassed forthrightness. He said the following:

I was with a baby. I moved down to kiss or suck its small, retracted, and gentle penis. Surprisingly, I felt no revulsion, and I had a sense on waking of empathy for the patient you and I discuss, and for a homosexual patient I see as well. I thought of "mouth-to-mouth resuscitation" and of trying to bring my patient to life through this act, which I would in fact find personally repulsive.

The patient's dreams and fantasies had gotten underneath the skin of the therapist. In a way, this dream was a communication from the therapist to himself, a countertransference

dream of the kind reported by Searles (1959). But the therapist's dream had expressed itself *in the language of the patient*,
indicating an introjective identification, which had reached a
depth of resonance that touched the therapist deeply and that
touched me in the supervisory hour. The therapist's dream
demonstrated that the patient's dreams and fantasies had gone
further than merely reporting on his inner condition. They had
penetrated the therapist to convey a message that altered the
therapeutic relationship itself. The dream's representation of
the patient's object relations had also been a communication
to the therapist about the relationship of the patient's self to
the therapist as an object. And in making this communication,
the patient had modified his own object relationship with the
therapist. The therapist felt that his understanding of the
patient was changed—as must happen if a therapy is to
progress—but also that his notion of himself was altered to
include a greater tolerance of the ambiguous sexual identification of the patient and of his own more successfully repressed
perverse impulses. This expansion of the therapist's self-image
made greater acceptance of the patient possible.

Two further examples underscore dramatic variations of
the process of the dream as an interpersonal communication in
individual therapy.

The first comes from my work with a woman whom
I saw in consultation after her female analyst had committed suicide. The patient, in grief and agitation, described her gratitude to her analyst for the major gains she
had made in her life, and her rage at her for committing
suicide. The patient's mother had died in childbirth when
the patient was 3, leaving her with a profound sense of
abandonment, which was painfully aggravated by the
trauma of her analyst's sudden death.
The patient said that although she herself had never
felt suicidal, she had a dream that struck her as oddly alien
some weeks before the therapist's suicide.

In the dream, I was driving my car. The grim reaper appeared in the rearview mirror. Looking back, I could see it clawing at the rear window of the car, its face pressed against the window.

She had reported this dream to her analyst, who had insisted that it represented death wishes of the patient despite the patient's denial.

The patient's identification with her dead analyst was profound. My work with her focused first on sorting out whether she herself had a suicidal identification with the analyst. I came to believe that this patient had introjected the analyst's determined suicidality as an identification with the analyst's self being hunted by a murderous internal object. The grim reaper in the rearview mirror was also the analyst. The patient's report led me to believe that before her death, the analyst had been pursuing and even hounding the patient, projecting her own internal situation without insight. Her analyst's deathly intent was still pursuing the patient like a foreign body lodged inside her that would not relent. I learned that on the margin of some clinical notes found near the dead analyst, the analyst had written, "I wonder if this patient knows of my plan to kill myself."

Clearly this dream represented the receiving of an unconscious message of deadly accuracy. Whereas the dream, on the one hand, stated the unconscious communication the patient had received from the analyst, on the other, it must also have been the patient's desperate, half-knowing attempt to communicate with the analyst about the state of affairs in the analysis and about the analyst's own situation. If the analyst's note in the margin was not about this analysand, then at least one other of her patients had unconsciously also perceived the depth of the analyst's despair.

The second example comes from a young analytic patient, Paul, who at one phase of analysis regularly reported dreams of a girl in whom he was interested. She refused to be romantically or sexually involved with him, but she would tell him intimate details of her life and relationships with other men. I was puzzled by Paul's detailed and insistent reporting of her dreams. It was not that my patient did not report his own dreams. He also reported many of them vividly. In an identification with me, he consciously played analyst to this girl and valued her dreams.

He reported one of her dreams in which she dreamt that a man was walking down the road. She thought the man was Destiny—not her destiny, just "Destiny." Then there was a pimp trying to push her off on a boy who was to be "the date of her lifetime." She got dolled up and as she walked to the elevator, she wondered why her hand was mangled. Now holding a dog on a leash, she met the boy. In his car, she asked him if she could kiss him. They kissed, and then she felt she had to leave. Three women were present as she left, and so was the figure of Destiny. She passed by him, ignoring him, but knowing she was not getting away. Her hand had been bloodied again, so it was twice mangled.

Paul had tried to work on the dream with the girl and told her that the dog was symbolic of her genitals, showing that she feared that if she became sexually active, she would be endangered. She had been most interested in the three women, who Paul thought stood for three parts of herself.

Paul had begun this session by discussing his use of this girl as a surrogate for himself, that in a way he had been living through her. Then he associated further to her dream himself. He identified himself as the pimp in the dream. He was in the process of breaking up with this girl. The dream was painful for him because it reminded him of a recent time when she had spent the evening with him and then spent the night with another man. He said that the girl had once told him she felt he forced her on another man.

This dream was another in the list of examples of Paul's attempting to find himself vicariously. On the one hand, his focus on someone else kept him away from his own analytic work. And on the other hand, the search in someone else did further his search for himself and his own sexual identity. Just before reporting this dream, he mentioned his decision to give up his relationship with this girl, because he thought he should focus on the psychoanalytic relationship with me and because he thought I would no longer want him to use this woman as an externalization. He felt that he was thereby taking me up on the opportunity that I offered within the treatment, rather than continuing to run from it.

I offer Paul's comments not to suggest what he should have done about the relationship with the woman or about her dream, but to illustrate that there was a chain of communication, conscious and unconscious, in which the dream played a role. When the girl told him the dream, it communicated powerful things to him, only some of which he may have understood consciously. The dream certainly functioned to maintain an emotional intimacy between them despite the sexual distance. My patient had much to say about what the dream meant about his friend, and he identified himself as a meddlesome character in her life. He was threatening her sexually, and at the same time he felt threatened by the arousing effect she had on his own sexual feelings. He was also identified with her as a girl and said, "I think she wants me to be her girlfriend." That thought was not unwelcome to him.

This dream clearly conveyed the ambiguous quality of this patient's identifications and the way in which he attempted repeatedly to find himself through others. It also conveyed a message to me in the transference, given as it were by the proxy of his friend's dream, namely, that the effect of sexual relationships is to mangle a person. The dream represented his fears about his relationship with me in which he felt he was like a girl I might mangle. This dream was part of a chain of communication to me as his object. One of the elements it conveyed most clearly was my analysand's identity confusion, the fundamental confusion about himself in which he found it easier to know who he was through identification with his objects.

DREAMS IN COUPLE ASSESSMENT

In therapy formats specifically designed to deal with the relationship between a man and a woman, dreams are also an especially useful vehicle of unconscious communication. This example comes from a couple seen in a single consultation. The therapist who was seeing them in marital therapy asked me for a consultation concerning the question of whether the wife's loss of interest in sex might respond to behavioral sex therapy methods.

> Matt, age 43, and Edie, age 36, had been married five years and had lived together for the previous five. Matt had already had one failed marriage. When his relationship with his former wife was deteriorating and they were already financially strained, she had gotten pregnant for a second time by going off birth control pills without telling him. He felt so deceived that he left soon after. Although he continued to support the two children of that marriage, he had not seen them since leaving his former wife eighteen years previously. He noted that he would make his last alimony payment in two years, when he would be 45.
>
> Both Matt and Edie were frightened of committed intimacy. In addition to the sexual issue that led them to seek consultation with me, they were facing the question of having children. Edie, who had not thought she wanted

children, now felt she did. They both thought that having a child would require commitment to each other more urgently than before. Their shared fear of commitment was embodied in Edie's loss of sexual interest and fear of arousal since the marriage. Although she had hardly ever been orgasmic, her sexual desire, level of arousal, and functioning had been satisfactory before the actual marriage. After marriage she not only lost interest, but became generally aversive to sex. As happens not uncommonly, just before the consultation they had a sexual encounter that had gone pretty well, but that had not happened in years.

The battling, alcoholic marriage of Edie's parents gave her internal reasons for fearing marital commitment. Matt's parents had held together in an unhappy marriage. That experience coupled with the hurt about the loss of the family of his first marriage increased his fear of ever making another commitment.

Toward the end of the interview, I asked the couple if they had any recent dreams. Edie initially answered my question in terms of her hopes for the future. She said that she had dreamt of a life together with children and a happy family.

Then Matt, understanding that I meant nighttime dreams, said, "But she has nightmares. In one of them her face was coming off in chunks."

"Oh, yes," Edie said. "I was losing parts of my face. Pieces of it were falling off. My therapist and I had just terminated individual therapy, so it may have had to do with that. I couldn't understand it. It made no sense."

"Could you make anything of it, Matt?" I asked.

"No, I couldn't," he answered. "She usually has chase dreams, not ones like this."

Edie said, "I often have nightmares, but this one was particularly frightening. Usually in my dreams, I'm having sex, but I'm having sex with a man without a face. Sometimes, I wake up having an orgasm. That makes me hopeful. If I can have them in my sleep, maybe I can have them someday when I'm awake."

I said, "I think it's hopeful, too." Turning to her husband, I asked, "How about your dreams, Matt?"

Matt said, "If I have an erotic dream, I'm not even looking to see who it is." He laughed as though it didn't matter. "They don't have a face, or even a head. It's just sexual contact with their body."

This couple had no understanding of the dreams, which they reported in a particularly interpersonal way. It interested me that Matt reported Edie's dreams, and only then did she elaborate. They did it together. He was interested in her dreams in her sleeping state, whereas she was interested in the life dreams of the waking state. When Matt told of his dreams, they had an interesting, if alarming, congruence with hers. Edie's dreams of faceless men in an erotic situation were matched by Matt's sexual dreams of faceless, and even headless, women. After Edie reported her dream, which she felt to be particularly alarming, of her own face coming off in chunks.

This couple was not yet able to understand their dreams in the way the Green family (discussed at the beginning of this chapter) could toward the end of successful therapy. Nevertheless, even in an assessment session with a couple not experienced in therapy together, we can still understand their dreams as communications between self and object.

Both Matt and Edie were fearful of a committed relationship, and the sexual distance had been one way of avoiding some aspects of intimacy and commitment, which then had to be found in other ways. It also avoided the question of children. Each member of this couple had a severe problem of loss of self. Edie saw herself in Matt and saw there the loss of herself. Usually her excited object was faceless, but as things got closer between them, she feared the loss of her own face. I took this to mean the loss of herself, both of her identity and of her internal cohesion. Either the self or the object would be annihilated. The precipitant was the threat of the couple's intention to move closer, toward more commitment and sexual closeness. So far, Edie had kept her self together by an hysterical conversion reaction, of the kind described by both Freud (Breuer and Freud 1895) and Fairbairn (1954). She acted as though the threatening objects, both the exciting and rejecting kind, were contained in genital interaction. By re-pressing genital sexuality and the bad part objects it contained for her, she was able to maintain relations with a good, accepting object in Matt. She substituted a way of relating for an internal problem, and her dream expressed the terror implicit in the new way of relating. She was afraid she would lose herself.

For Matt, an object with a face was also an ultimately threatening object. His exciting object had been split so thor-oughly from a whole object that it lacked both a face and a head. We can speculate that a woman with a face was a per-secuting object for him, just as a man with a face and a woman without a face were for Edie.

These dreams tell us of the congruence of the marital partners' inner states. The way the dreams are told and related to in the session tells us more about the intertwined identities of the partners. The dreams reveal how they find themselves in each other, and how they share the fear that a relationship complete with sexuality will kill them, individually and as a couple. Between them, they divide the rejecting and exciting objects through mutual projective and introjective identifica-tion. Edie takes on the qualities of the exciting and rejecting object for both of them, and Matt takes on the qualities of the withdrawn object they both seek (Guntrip 1969). Underneath this collusive division and supported by Matt's interest in Edie's dream, we can see their fundamentally shared psychic state. For each of them, and for the two of them together as a couple, a whole object containing both face and genitals threatens them with annihilation of the self.

Finally, we can note that this nightmare, in which both Matt and Edie shared, was dreamt just before the consultation interview, which was conducted as a teaching interview in front of an audience. The dream was a communication to me and to their regular therapist about their shared fear of "loss of face," of the exposed intimacy of the interview. Under these circumstances, it is no wonder that Matt had such an interest in Edie's dream. He usually relied on her for the emotional responses in their marriage, and similarly he put her dream forward as the emotional communication to me in the consultation.

Work with couples and families such as these demonstrates that a dream is the royal road to more than the individual unconscious described by Freud (1900). In the conjoint therapies, the dream is also the royal road to understanding shared unconscious communication and mutual projective and introjective identification. In Chapter 9, I consider in detail therapeutic work with the dream in ongoing couple therapy. This gives further illustration of the role of the dream in communication between spouses and between the couple and the therapist in the transference.

DREAMS IN GROUP AND INSTITUTIONAL SETTINGS

In groups and institutional settings, dreams also communicate unconscious components of the inner life of one individual, making these available for resonance with the internal object lives of members of the entire group. When a group therapy member reports a dream, it is understood by the various group members in differing ways. These differences contribute to an enlarged understanding of the dreamer, and also elucidate issues for the group. The same is true, however, in work groups. The following illustration is from a group of eight therapists meeting to study concepts of object relations family therapy in an intensive and demanding week-long institute.

The group's task also included the examination of their own process in relation to learning these concepts.

In a small group meeting, a man reported his dream of the previous night. The phone rang and his dead father was on the line. The man awoke and was momentarily convinced that his father was actually speaking to him.

This man was a psychiatrist who practiced family therapy in another city where he felt somewhat isolated from his colleagues because of his interests. He told the group that his father had been a businessman who died some years before. He had a close relationship to his father, who had stood by him and offered frequent advice. Lately, the man had felt he had moved beyond his father's own achievements in life.

A woman in the group said that this was a dream about the loss involved in growth. She, too, had been practicing family therapy of a different kind than she was learning here. She was drawn to new psychodynamic concepts, but she realized that it meant moving beyond the old precepts and away from her old teachers, the "fathers" of family therapy she revered. She wondered: Did the dream of the return of the dead father mean that the man was missing his old mentors.

Other members of the group responded that they, too, had been feeling a loss of the inner companionship of the leaders of family therapy, such figures as Jay Haley and Salvador Minuchin. Another man said that he had found himself reaching back to his old teachers and their theories for comfort against the strain of learning such a new way of working and the threat he felt to his sense of himself.

At this point the man who had shared the dream said that these comments made sense of the dream for him. In feeling overwhelmed by the new ideas and experiences of the institute, he must have been reaching back to the simpler comforting advice of his father, now dead, to offer him support and the comfort of the old ways. The group acknowledged sharing this regressive longing and returned to considering the ideas and clinical experiences that were before them.

The next example comes from an outpatient mental health clinic in the middle of a major reorganization that was taking place in the wake of the resignation of the previous director and amid accusations that the clinic management might not be competent. The staff was developing new procedures, and three clinicians were taking up new roles as leaders of therapy teams.

> At the first meeting of the newly constituted leadership group, consisting of the three newly promoted clinicians and the clinic administrator with Dr. Thomas, the new director, Sarah, the clinic administrator, entered the room laughing and said that she had a dream the night before.

> I dreamt that Bonnie (one of the team leaders) wanted to rearrange the notebooks I had put together for the new procedures. It upset me a lot. Bonnie wanted to reverse things so that the blank pages were in front and the sections I've organized were in the back.

> Having reported her dream, Sarah set out three beautifully organized binders as her administrative contribution to the reorganization. The three team leaders and the other staff burst out laughing in acknowledgment of the way she feared they would undo her work.
> Bonnie had also had a dream.

> This clinic had turned into a giant cake bakery. It was a huge operation. There were a hundred or so dump trucks, and

Dr. Thomas (the director) was overseeing it all. There were all sorts of comings and goings, a very big operation.

The group laughed harder. The reference to "the big operation" spoke to the shared sense of being disrupted and overwhelmed by the expectations of the new director, who was experienced as "dumping" the mess on the team leaders and expecting them to make cakes out of it.

Sam, another of the team leaders, said that his dream was more pointed.

Patrick Swayze of *Dirty Dancing* fame and an unidentifiable woman celebrity had somehow gotten onto our staff and were seeing patients, all by my arrangement. I realized to my horror that I had not assigned them to teams or given them any cases. It was a mess.

By now the group had given over completely to laughter at the caricature of their fears of incompetence and the hint of destructive pairing in Sam's dream. This dream, more than the previous two, seemed to pick up the fears and accusations of a wild underlife full of impropriety and craziness already being made by some staff members. Dr. Thomas said that it made him think of a part of the movie *Dirty Dancing* in which the doctor/father makes false accusations with no knowledge of what is going on among the children.

Finally, the third team leader, Janet, said,

I had a dream. But I couldn't relate mine to the clinic. It was weird and uncertain. People who might be dead were there, but they were people who aren't dead. Things were all reversed and uncertain.

Dr. Thomas noted the sense of dread that there would be deadly mistakes. He was reminded of a patient of Janet's who had recently had to be hospitalized, and he wondered if he would be called on to deal with casualties among the staff.

These dreams occurring simultaneously in an administrative group under strain expressed even in their manifest content both the shared anxieties during the clinic's transition and the personal anxieties of staff members. All four dreams represent accusation, incompetence, wildness, and threats of patient deaths. They reflected the day residue of the climate in which the reorganization occurred, where staff shared the fear that efforts to make something organized out of chaos would be undone. The laughter, joking, and elaboration of the dreams became part the group's way of acknowledging and bearing these anxieties as they promptly went on to attack the practical problems before them. Their work proceeded smoothly and resulted in a thorough reworking of the clinic procedures, an eventual enhancement of morale in staff and patients, and clinic stabilization and growth. The telling of the dreams to each other and to the new director was an act of communication and sharing from which to build structure out of unconscious chaos.

THE DREAM IN SOCIAL AND CULTURAL COMMUNICATION

The most famous example of the large-scale institutional effect of the dream is found in the Bible. Joseph's interpretations of Pharaoh's dreams incorporated the national interests of both the Egyptians and the Jews. Joseph took full advantage of the use of the unconscious of this singularly important single dreamer, because Pharaoh's individual concerns embodied the concerns of his nation and therefore were of national importance. I like to think that Joseph unconsciously assumed that the nation was inside Pharaoh's unconscious and that the dreams represented that aspect of Pharaoh's understanding that was beyond himself.

A more recent dreamer of note, of course, is Freud. He has had, for us, as broad an influence as Joseph on the Egyptians. The details of Freud's dreams and their relation to his life issues as revealed in self-analysis convinced his readers, as no amount of theorizing would have done, of the power of the unconscious. His dreams and findings about them, originally reported only in professional publications, reached the imagination of writers who transmitted them to Western culture at large, where they have altered and deepened our life experience and given us our richest tool for understanding our inner worlds. Freud's literary contribution, *The Interpretation of Dreams* (1900), is perhaps the richest and most creative example of the interpersonal effect of the dream. As W. H. Auden wrote in his eulogy "In Memory of Sigmund Freud" (1945):

> If often he was wrong and at times absurd,
>   To us he is no more a person
>   Now but a whole climate of opinion.
>
> Under whom we conduct our differing lives. . .
>   (p. 166)

And most especially, Auden wrote, it was Freud's understanding of the dream that changed the way we live.

> But he would have us remember most of all
> To be enthusiastic over the night
>   Not only for the sense of wonder
>   It alone has to offer, but also
>
> Because it needs our love: for with sad eyes
> Its delectable creatures look up and beg
>   Us dumbly to ask them to follow;
>   They are exiles who long for the future

That lies in our power. They too would rejoice
If allowed to serve enlightenment like him,
    Even to bear our cry of "Judas,"
    As he did and all must bear who serve it.

(p. 167)

We live in Freud's "climate of opinion" and with a way of thinking about personhood and development that is continually being modified, but that stems from the dreams of one man. There has never been a more striking example of the capacity of the dream to communicate from one man to others, and to influence our entire intellectual culture.

9

Dreams in Marital

Therapy

In this chapter, I focus specifically on the use of dreams in the course of marital therapy, examine the interplay between self and object in the dreams of couples, and look at the use of the dream in understanding the couple's transferential relationship to the therapist. I do this, first, by looking at dream work by two couples at an impasse in couple therapy. Coincidentally, the dreams of both these couples involve babies who represent painful aspects of themselves. Then I conclude with an example taken from a couple therapy session close to successful termination by a couple who used their interlocking dreams to confirm their confidence in their marriage and readiness to manage their issues without therapy.

CLIVE AND LILA: DECREASING DISTANCE

The first couple was struggling with their chronic inability to decrease distance between them. In couple therapy, the wife was more comfortable and more adept at using insight than her husband. This example lets us examine the use of a single dream of one partner for the progress of therapy.

Clive and Lila came because there was moderate strain in every area of their marriage. Originally, Clive had a great deal of difficulty sexually. He tended to keep his distance physically as well as emotionally. When the couple did attempt to make love, Clive usually lost his erection. As a result, he shied away from sex. Lila felt unloved and uncared for.

They were polar opposites in many ways. He was practical, she was emotional. He loved to spend an evening locked up with his computer, papers, and gadgets; she would like to spend the weekend with several other couples. She did not mind privacy, however, or time alone, despite preferring an active social life.

After a phase of sex therapy of the kind previously described (Scharff and Scharff 1991), we resumed marital work. An emotional distance remained between them, although they felt now that they had the capacity for increased physical closeness. The focus was now repeatedly on Clive's inability to talk when Lila wanted more communication, both about the everyday matters of their life and about emotional issues. Over and over again, Clive withdrew silently. Then Lila battered him, hoping for an answer, for a way in.

As we worked together weekly for approximately two years, things got better in many respects. They were increasingly able to talk to each other for extended periods. They could plan together for a mixture of social and private time with adequate time alone for each of them. But the problem remained that when Lila experienced distance between them, she attempted to correct it by moving toward Clive with an eager longing, which he handled with a wordless retreat. It was always easier for me to get Lila to talk. She was good at it and did not mind engaging. What she minded was that Clive had such a hard time with it in therapy and at home. She would say to me, "If Clive would only *talk*!" And he would shrug his shoulders and look at his belt, wordlessly retreating from her entreaties.

Lila was 37, an attractive woman who had been spectacularly successful as a public interest lawyer and had, in her young adult life, focused on her career. At that time, she had a series of relationships that were exciting but secondary to her ambitions. Then she looked toward 40 and felt lonely. She met Clive and felt safe with him. He was available and interested, and he would not impinge on her career.

Clive had been a confirmed bachelor. He was, at 43, used to his single ways and to living an independent life in which he spent a great deal of time alone both with his work as a systems analyst and with his interest in computers. He had not expected to get married. Although he was delighted to have found Lila, he frequently felt hemmed in by her.

Only recently, after sex therapy, had they raised the issue of children. Lila had always assumed she did not want to be a family woman, but recently had begun to change her mind. Clive was extremely reluctant, saying that if they had trouble finding enough time for each other now, how would they do with children. More than that, children were a bigger responsibility than he wanted.

They could turn out badly if you did not do things just right. He was not at all sure that they could manage.

The paucity of access to Clive's internal life tended to reduce our understanding to the all-too-simple. Clive's father died when he was 6, leaving Clive at the mercy of his mother and older sister, who had made life miserable for him. From early on, he felt that their demands and the clinging nature of the relationship with his mother were overwhelming. He spent his childhood alone in flight from the house. It was specifically women that he felt he had to escape. He had been a prematurely independent little boy out there, a latency boy on the run from the clutches of females who would smother him given any chance. He hardly ever remembered details of any encounters with his mother or sister, but he did recall tricks his sister would play on him, such as sending him to the store for feminine napkins and then teasing him about his conversation with the storekeeper. He had no memory of his father and virtually never talked about his death.

Lila had a fuller range of internal experience to share. She remembered her mother as clinging and invasive, too. Even now, she kept her distance from her grasping mother. Her father, a passive man who hid behind his business and his books, had seemed insignificant relative to her mother. So Lila had much sympathy for Clive's need for distance.

Although there was a considerable amount of congruence of experience with parents, in their marriage they divided up the fat and the lean of longing and withdrawal in a consistent, repetitive mutual projective identification. Lila sought and Clive retreated. I would work interpretively principally with Lila, and then find that I was drawn almost into cajoling Clive to be more available. Countertransferentially, I frequently felt I had an impoverished understanding about which issues pushed Clive so often into retreat. I felt Clive shut me out while Lila sought me out. They had divided longing and rejection in a fixed pattern, which left me often feeling stymied. I longed to ask—but I did not—why Lila stayed with Clive. I thought I knew the answer anyway, that she would be too lonely without him. So she became her mother chasing after herself as a little girl, longing for her retreating self. Meanwhile, Clive made her into his mother seeking after *his* retreating self.

They put into Clive the parts of each of them that were in retreat from the longing of the mothers. In addition, Lila, when chased by Clive, put herself in retreat into Clive, while he also retreated on behalf of the part of himself that felt threatened by her demands. In all, they joined in a mutual projective identification, which left Lila in a perpetual resentful, hungering chase, and Clive running from being devoured and tormented.

The therapy moved slowly, covering the same ground repetitively. Sessions, at best, merely chipped away at the wall between them. In some more hopeful sessions, Clive would see a small amount of light, and in others, Lila could see how she had chased him down the rabbit hole out of a sense of her own anxiety or loneliness. At these moments he could warm to her, letting them recover the many things they did share: intellectual interests, friends, and a delight in traveling.

The Session and the Dream

The following session occurred after Clive and Lila had been working in therapy for about two years.

They told me that they had a fight—in fact, several small fights over the course of the previous week. Lila had had an interview for a new job. It had gone well, but it finished early, so she was home before she expected to be. Clive was not there, and although he was at his office, she did not know that.

She said, "Why can't he ever be home before me? He makes it a point to stay out until I'm already home, and sometimes he calls to be sure I'm there, or to tell me to meet him somewhere. Just once, I'd like him to be there waiting to greet me!"

Clive said, "I was at the office working, and the computer lost an hour of my work. So I got caught up trying to get it back. I knew this was a big interview for Lila, and I meant to be home when she got back. But when I looked up, I saw I was late. Of course, then I was worried she would jump on me for not being home on time, so I was edgy I guess when I got home, and sure enough we fought. But we did get over it."

"It's true," said Lila. "He was really pretty nice and understanding, and he held me because I was crying after the little fight, and with relief from the interview."

She said that she appreciated his holding her while she cried. It was all she wanted. But he had become upset when she kept crying. Feeling frustrated, he had shaken himself off, wandered into another room, and began watching television.

He said, "Well, I held her for over an hour, and I was good to her. But after a while I began to feel that she wasn't better and I thought nothing I did would be enough. So I just left."

"But he *was* doing the right thing," she said. "He made me feel much better. By the time he felt worried about making me feel better, I was just having a good cry."

I remarked first on Clive's having felt accused by the crying and uncomfortable with its intensity and duration. He had actually managed to stand by Lila for much longer than in the past. But her original emotional accusation had been about his need to "flee the house," so I asked about that.

I began with Lila, not sure that it was the right place to start, but because it always seemed the place to start, thanks to her ease at investigating emotional causes.

Lila said, "I think his not being home reminds me of the many times my mother wasn't at home. My mother was absorbed with the store she owned from the time I was born. She had a neighbor take care of me. She was a wonderful person, but I missed my mother. When I got home from school, I would call my mother and try to get her attention. She would fob me off, saying, 'Why don't you go do such and such?' Or, 'Why don't you go down the street to the neighbor, Mrs. James?' I just wanted to be with her!"

Lila began to cry silently, and then she continued. "My mother wasn't at home till my twin sisters were born when I was 9. Before that, people would ask her how she managed with me, and she would immediately launch into the story about how the neighbor took such wonderful care of me. But it wasn't the same for me. And then, when my sisters were born and she did start spending more time at home, I resented it because she had never done it just for me."

Clive was watching Lila attentively, not exactly taken over by her tears, but not driven away either. There was more than tolerance in his attention, and I felt a warmer connection to him than usual.

With other couples, I would have asked a husband about his feelings in listening to such a story, but with Clive I had a sense we would draw a blank. He was almost never able to answer a question about feelings. He did better with thoughts, or with working on parallel lines of thought to those Lila was pursuing, ones that might indirectly indicate his responses or empathy. I was reining in my wish to go more directly for emotional content in these moments, knowing that I would be frustrated if I did. The situation called for tact and timing to respect his defenses, yet bring forth his contribution. I could feel the strain in having to think consciously about how to manage.

I sought a way of engaging Clive. So I reached back to the situation in his home that was the opposite of Lila's loss of her mother's attention.

I said, "From your side, Clive, it seems to me that the

difficulty the other night began with your pattern of avoiding being home. At least, that's the way Lila feels it."

"No," he answered. "I just had work to do. If I'd had the data at home, I could have worked there."

"But the episode does seem to echo what you've told me so often about your own situation at home growing up," I said.

"Well, yes. I've told you that I would do anything to avoid being home with my sister and my mother," he agreed. "It was the two of them, like a couple of harpies, criticizing, mad at me all the time."

"Do you remember anything specific, any issues or a scene that comes to mind just now?" I asked.

"No. Just the dinner table, but I can't remember anything specific," he said, shaking his head.

I felt shut out by his stonewalling and by the opacity of his memory. I was experiencing just what Lila was complaining about. So in this moment, I was, as was often true, identified with her in her frustration. In these interactions, I was the seeker of a frustrating object, Clive on the run from me in the therapy. But today he and I were in closer contact than usual. I felt some part of him, if not exactly reaching out to me, at least staying his retreat while he saw if it was safe to let me within hailing distance.

I said, "I think in the vagueness of your memory is hidden the things you were running from then, and many of the things you still feel are dangerous now."

He nodded his head. He could not be more specific, but he was not shutting out the effort.

I continued. "I'm thinking about the way you left the room after holding Lila. You thought she couldn't be comforted, and then you thought something nonspecific, something that cannot quite be named. But can you tell me more about it?"

He thought. "Well, it might be that 'I can't do anything for her.' So I left and went to the den."

"Then, Lila, you felt abandoned because you had felt held and helped by him, but you wanted more?"

"Yes," she responded. "I was still crying. But I felt that now I was just having a good cry. But to Clive, it meant I couldn't be helped."

I had a moment of identifying now with Clive, of a fantasy of my being in the position of trying to help my wife and feeling it wasn't enough. The accusation by someone of not being good enough was just around the corner. In fact, I thought, that isn't very different than the way I feel with Clive and Lila quite a lot of the time: I'd like to help and somehow I don't quite know how. Nothing is good enough. So then it is me accusing myself of not being good enough.

I spoke to Lila but with Clive in mind even more. "Perhaps Clive felt that sooner or later you were going to accuse him of not doing the right thing, that you would pounce!"

Clive nodded dramatically, with a confirming grimace. Lila agreed with a somber face and she teared up again.

I knew I had Clive and that I had even joined him in the accusation that Lila was going to pounce on him for doing it wrong. It was here that she became his dreaded sister and mother. But my own sense of pouncing on him had to do with the split second of triumph in getting inside his skin, in joining him in a moment of affect. Only rarely did I feel that I got it right with Clive emotionally. Except that I had done it in such a way as to leave Lila hurt. I thought she could stand it, since the hurt was not inflicted by me as much as it was identified by me to validate her experience.

Despite my triumphant feeling, I still saw no way out of their fight. I felt like a lion waiting to pounce. I had gotten the same small quarry we usually got, but still no big kill. And I felt no hope that I could get Clive to see the kind of closeness that Lila wanted. At this moment of well-known impasse, I could feel for her longing. At least I was closer to feeling Clive's fear that she would jump on him like the women of his early life.

I asked, "Clive, do Lila's demands that you comfort

her in the right way remind you of your mother and sister trapping you?"

He nodded.

I went on. "When you feel that, you can't go along with it. And don't you, Lila, feel as though he's your mother pawning you off on the neighbor lady, not caring for you himself?"

"Yes," she said, nodding.

"And the harder she pulls on you, Clive, the more you feel in danger of being trapped?"

He nodded, and Lila gave a corners-of-the-mouth-turned-down, here-we-go-again look. "What else is new?" she agreed. "This is the repetitive bind we get into. How do we get beyond this dead end?"

The Dream

I was stymied. All this work, and a better session than most! Yet I had to agree with her that we were right back to the same old place of impasse and repetition. Perhaps it was the hope of being in touch with Clive's interior that led me to ask a question.

"Have either of you had any dreams recently?"

"Sure," Clive said. "Lots. I had several this week. For instance, I had one of them last night, just after the fight."

"Tell me about it," I said.

"It was about a baby. This baby had a wound on its buttocks. A woman—I think it was the sister—was supposed to take care of it, but she wasn't doing anything for the baby. I don't know if she didn't know what to do or what. So I stepped in and took the baby from her to take care of it. That's all I remember."

"Does anything come to mind in connection with the dream?" I asked him.

"No. No thoughts particularly. Well, the color of the blood stood out. It was very dark, the way blood is before it has had a chance to mix with oxygen when you cut yourself. So it's a dark mulberry before it hits the air and turns red." He said this taking his first finger and touching his other hand as if it had been cut. "When it's that color, you know the wound is deep. So in the dream, I touched the wound, and I thought, 'This is very deep, it's more serious than it looks.'"

"And what does that situation suggest to you?" I asked.

"Nothing! Well, what just did come to mind was that car accident in New York a few years ago. I was driving along and a motorcycle passed me going very fast. By the time I got around the next bend, people were stopped. A car had gone off the road trying not to hit the cycle and smashed up against a tree. One person was thrown out, and the guy from the motorcycle was holding his broken leg, and the other person from the car had the steering wheel rammed into his chest and was grunting because he couldn't breathe. He looked like he was going to die right on the spot.

"No one was doing anything but gathering around and saying 'Isn't this horrible!' They just had their fingers in their ears. So I grabbed a couple of guys and said, 'We have to get this guy out from behind the wheel.' So we did. I gave him CPR, and I sent a couple of people off to call an ambulance. The guy lived, miraculously enough."

I could feel the pride in Clive's statement and the contempt for all the others standing there "with their fingers in their ears." While admiring him, I had an uncomfortable feeling that the contempt for the others might well be directed at me. This gave me the sense of what it must be like to be in Lila's position when he treated her with contempt.

Lila now joined in with her association to Clive's dream. "See, that's it. Clive has to do everything. He is pretty sure no one else will do any of it."

"So, who's the baby?" I asked.

"Oh," said Clive. "That could be it. The *baby!* Children! The idea of how much responsibility children can be. And my worry about having children because I'm worried that I'll have to take all the responsibility for them, that Lila won't do enough."

"That makes sense to me of your great fear of having children," I said. "If you feel everything will fall to you, that's a big worry. But the dream suggests that you also fear there will be something terribly wrong, so bad that you can't fix it. That may apply to children, but I think it also applies to taking care of Lila. When she's hurt, as she was last night, you overestimate it. You're afraid that the hurt is deeper than anyone knows, and since you're the only one who can do anything about it, the responsibility is overwhelming."

I felt a hopefulness that we had established a new territory for future exploration, that of Clive as a resource for stopping overwhelming harm. His fear of causing harm might explain his maintaining distance. I felt a relief at the opening his dream had generously offered.

"Yes," said Lila. "And then I'm in the position of being hurt and having to tell him, as he's comforting me, that it's okay. I have to reassure him that I'm okay, that what he's doing *is* enough. Even when I'm hurt and wanting something from him, I have to take care of him so I can get *any* of what I want without his feeling overwhelmed."

I said to her, "It's because he thinks it's so serious that it will be more than he can do. He identifies with you and you have just told me how much he wants to help. But he overestimates the seriousness of the hurt because he is so afraid of it, so identified with the baby, and because he feels so responsible.

"Do you have any other thoughts about the dream, Lila?" I asked.

Uncharacteristically, Lila hesitated. She looked confused—not about the question, but about thoughts that seemed to have taken her over.

There is something in her confusion, probably in the area of which of them is the baby. I'm unsure if I have said something that does not ring true for her, or if there is another area stirred up in her. It's the end of the hour, and the pressure of that may be contributing to the question of who will care for the hurt in the baby. I had made a rather long interpretation, too long to be absorbed by them, which represented a pressure inside me to take advantage of this new opening before the session ended. In retrospect, I think that I treated the couple as though I were Clive, all on my own desperately trying to pry an accident victim from behind the wheel of their overturned marriage so I could breathe some life into them.

I returned to Lila's confusion about the dream. Finally with my urging, she answered, "Well, it's the baby. Does he think I'm the baby? He has to take care of it, but. . . ."

I said, "Yes, he feels you're the baby. But he's identified with you and it's also him. Maybe it relates to your own hurt, Clive, at the loss of your father when you were young, a hurt that is so deep you can't get at and you can't get solace for it."

Clive nodded, looking less defensive than usual. "So you think I'm the baby with the wound?" he said. "Maybe so." Then he added, with a grin, "I'll have to go off and lick my wounds while I think about that."

The dream performed a function in this session of couple therapy similar to its use with individual patients. It gave therapist and patients a vivid picture of the unconscious components behind a logjam. It is as though the repeated pattern of the couple's interaction were painted on a canvas over an underlying picture, which they had never been able to see. The dream gives a kind of x-ray view of the picture underneath, forever altering the meaning of the painting on the surface. Just as a dream can illuminate the individual unconscious, here the dream gives access to the shared unconscious, to mutual projective and introjective identifications. This dream let Clive and Lila look at the way their inner worlds influenced them repetitively, illuminating not only their individual and shared inner worlds, but casting a bright light on the shadowy pathways of their mutual interaction. Clive could see, perhaps for the first time, how his lifelong fear of female entrapment was constructed on top of his infantile neediness and his childhood losses. And Lila could begin to see how his fears and perceptions of her had added to her more conscious sense of abandonment, hurt, and need, which had their own childhood origins.

In this work with the dream, as in other work from an object relations perspective, the cues to the affective movement during the session were embedded in the therapist's countertransferential reactions to the couple. Although I could not fully articulate and amplify these until after the session, they guided my responses and questions during the sessions like an automatic pilot. The reception and processing of countertransference during the flow of the session are the vehicle for the therapist to join the couple in their bind in order to work out of it together. In this case, the dream, giving a gift as it often does to therapy, gave me an experience of their shared hurt and infantile dependency hidden behind the rough self-reliance of Clive's manner.

SHIRLEY AND SAM: EXAMINING INTERLOCKING DREAMS

Shirley and Sam, she a 34-year-old clinical psychologist and he a 40-year-old lawyer, had two school-age daughters and had lost a third baby girl, who died at 1 year of age from meningitis two years earlier. They had been working with me twice weekly as a couple for about six months when they began to bring dreams into the sessions periodically. I had not asked them to do so, although I sometimes do, but Shirley had kept a journal of her dreams regularly since her own individual psychotherapy during her clinical training. She was also interested in Sam's dreams, and on one occasion she asked him to tell about a dream he had had the previous week.

Sam did not want to talk about his dreams. In his previous marriage he had had a dream about the demise of the marriage and then it had happened. He had carried away the feeling that dreams had a predictive quality, which he feared. Shirley reported Sam's dream.

It was a terrible nightmare. He was in his family house in New Mexico, but with me and our two daughters. The house was in flames. He talked more about the details. All that he offered as hope was that there was a sprinkler system, which didn't save the house, but he had the sense it might save us.

Sam and Shirley both had associations to the dream: particular houses in which relationships had gone sour; the house Shirley loved but had to leave to join Sam; the day they first moved into the house they lived in now where Sam had been unkind to Shirley for the first time; a weekend just a year before the dream during which Shirley had felt particularly neglected during a vacation; and Sam's memories of the family house of the dream when his father was drunk and flew into rages, occasionally hitting Sam and his brother. The work on this dream concerned the status of the house they currently lived in, a compromise choice that was uncomfortable for both of them and was thus connected to the way both felt threatened in the marriage.

While they worked on this dream, I felt that a chronic impasse between them had yielded just a bit. I was able to identify the projective identifications into each other of neglect and mistreatment, which occurred in their shared fear that their marriage was like a house in danger of burning to the ground.

The ongoing difficulty in this marriage was not, as with Clive and Lila, the lack of insightfulness of either husband or wife. Both were psychologically minded—

perhaps to excess, but the sense of distance and lack of understanding persisted nevertheless.

The following dream sequence occurred on a Monday two months after the dream I just described. Sam said,

My dream occurred on a piece of ground behind a house on the desert mountainside where I used to go to be by myself. It was an important place for me. The dream was comic. I was being buried and so was someone else who had a bout of depression. My burial was slapstick. I was also aware of observing the dream and of it not working. The grave wasn't deep enough and my right leg kept popping out. Then there was a scene that followed: a lot of sexual groping with a woman—the daughter of a law partner, a provocative young woman. I was co-mingled with her.

The work on this dream dealt with Sam's sense of deadness and the splitting of his identity. He was an alive but passive observer to the burial of a part of himself that longed for an old comfortable place. The dream led from the grave to the bed, to a sexual longing, which was mingled with his own confused identity. Most of this work was focused on Sam, with Shirley as an occasional commentator.

In the next session on Thursday, Shirley asked Sam to tell me about another dream of the night before.

Sam said, "It's a companion to the dream of my own burial. Shirley died. No, she was killed. The dream begins with me witnessing this."

Shirley asked, "Do you only remember the death scene?"

"A lot follows," Sam continued.

There was a man who was very dangerous. It starts with him killing another woman. Then he killed Shirley with a sword while I watched. I went to a convent or religious place where your body had been taken. I was able to see the remains. It was a body, but it was only a little thing—almost nothing really—covered with a white cloth.

As Sam continued I thought of their baby who had died two years earlier, and whom they had only partly mourned. I suddenly saw an image of the baby lodged like shriveled remains between them. They had not dealt with this loss, although Shirley had emphasized it when they first came to see me.

Sam continued, "I was distraught. I tried to talk about it to people who were there, but none of them wanted to talk about Shirley or what had happened. I couldn't communicate to them that I was also the one who had killed her. I was divided like in my dream Sunday night where I was being buried and was an observer." He leaned forward, his hands covering his face. "There was something awful about what I saw."

"What's upsetting you now that you're talking about it?" I asked.

"I saw Amelia, our baby. Because it was so little, almost nothing of the remains. The dream told me more clearly than anything how much I've hurt Shirley. When I woke in the middle of the night horror-stricken, I think I didn't yet understand that I had done it. I am the dangerous person who has hurt Shirley! My association with Amelia is upsetting, too."

"Do you have any thoughts about Sam's dream?" I asked Shirley.

"I remember something Sam forgot. When Sam told me the dream, it began with us walking up a staircase in a store, and I felt a terrible danger. I wanted him to go with me, to leave, and he kept on going. Then this happened. So in his dream I felt I was in danger, he refused to help, and I ended up dead. That *is* how I feel these days. So since he told me this dream this morning, I've been feeling pained that his dream captures how I feel. I do feel like the dead person, like I'm being destroyed by Sam. But what's new is that he describes it as a companion to the dream of his own burial. I think that his feeling dead is part of what makes me feel dead." She paused. "By the way, I had a dream, too."

I said, "You both feel dead in this relationship. You've talked often enough about how you feel threatened by each other, but this helps us understand. These dreams of Sam's and your reactions say something to you about how the sense of loss and deadness in Sam makes Shirley feel killed off."

I was still relating these feelings of being dead to their dead feelings about the dead baby, an unmourned object still stuck in and between them. Although I felt almost as if the dead baby were lodged inside me during the session, I did not yet say something about my association. Although I felt a weighty sadness from this image seeming to have entered me, I preferred to bear it instead of hurling it back at them, which is what I felt I would be doing if I mentioned it too quickly. Since Shirley had announced her readiness to follow Sam's dream with one of her own, the sequence might offer a new opportunity for working together and sharing vulnerabilities. I sat with the dead baby as I listened.

"What's your dream, Shirley?" I asked.

"I woke with my name being misspelled. It was Ceryl Anika."

"That sounds Hungarian or Czech," said Sam.

She continued.

I was at a church service to honor artists. I was an artist, too. A famous woman artist was there. My art was being recognized: liturgical art panels like tapestries. I have vivid memories of it, a cross between medieval tapestry in color and texture, and Chagall windows. There were bios of the artists, and my bio had been submitted by my parents. Everything in it was incorrect. There was a photo accompanying it, and no one could tell me who took the picture. At the end of the ceremony, a priest was telling all the people that we must dare to be what we dream. But he couldn't convey it in words, and people were leaving impatiently. Sam was there now, and I was listening. Then I was left alone, willing to listen. Then the priest left. My mother came over to me—I love this!—to finish the song they had been singing. The verse she wanted me to know was "The dying must be able to choose their own death." Then I woke up.

Sam quickly interjected. "I'd like to point out that I stayed longer than anyone else, right?"

Shirley asked, "Do you want credit?"

"Yes, I do," said Sam.

"What thoughts have you had about the dream?" I asked Shirley.

"This is one of the most vivid dreams I can remember," she said. "I was struck by the idea of an artist having something to offer that is recognized by others. I was admiring but jealous of the famous artist, yet I had something worthy of recognition, too. But my identity was distorted. The artist was recognized by the world, but my parents couldn't get my name or bio right. It was an occasion set in a sacred spot, and the priest was trying to give a message, which others paid no attention to. But I was staying to the bitter end.

"It was a positive thing that Sam was there and stayed, because he hasn't been in my dreams for a while, but he still left before the end. My mother finished the message I had stayed to hear, which was about death. It seemed like a surprise ending to a short story. I hadn't seen the dream leading to that. I can see the religious themes, the confusion of my identity, and death—but I'm stymied."

I said, "You both have been creating a series of dreams, living tapestries, which like a Chagall window might let some light into the crypt. The themes are interwoven—feeling neglected or mistreated by your parents and by each other, confusion in your identities, shared fear of death while already feeling dead. The overlap in themes is important."

Sam said, "In Shirley's dream I can see her search for an identity and for faith. Her parents are part of what vexes her. They've let her down at some pretty crucial times, just the way she feels I have. The story reminds me of the times they've said to her, 'Do it this way or else.' "

I said, "Shirley, your parents don't know who you are. They spelled your name wrong. These days you feel it's Sam who doesn't understand you, doesn't know who you are. You might as well be a foreigner."

Sam added, "We've said that Shirley spent years making herself who her parents wanted her to be. I don't want to be a parental figure. If part of what you are doing is to lay that on me about defining what you're supposed to be, I don't want to do that."

I said, "Partly you feel accused of bending Shirley's identity to your wishes, but I think that where the two of you are stuck is not only there but in the notion of death. I have been thinking of your dead child. Amelia is still lodged in each of you, alive in her deadness, beckoning you. That's in your dream of seduction in your death, Sam, seduced by a daughter into the grave. And it's in this dream of death being the surprise ending for you, Shirley. This is the church with the ceremony for Amelia, a ceremony you've never had that would recognize her death. The priest and your mother are trying to help you let her die, which might let you live. Neither of you has been able to get past the loss, and you each feel the other is trying to remove your love and devotion for the dead baby from you, to force you into life when your identity is tied up with your dead daughter."

Shirley began to sob, wordlessly collapsed into her hands in a way reminiscent of the way Sam had covered his face earlier in despair. Sam moved to the couch next to her and held her.

*Their mourning had begun. I noticed that I no longer felt
the dead baby inside myself. Had I been able to pass the baby back
to them gently enough that they could hold the dead baby, look
at her, touch her, feel her loss, and eventually let go instead of
feeling her buried inside themselves?*

Over the next weeks, without specific mention of the
lost baby again, Sam and Shirley found a new capacity for
responding to each other and for working with my comments. It seemed clear to me that they had finally begun to
bury their lost child and to take back the lost parts of
themselves they had lodged inside her.

DON AND MAGGIE: INTERLOCKING DREAMS OF A COUPLE READY FOR TERMINATION

Don and Maggie had resolved their disagreements
over the management of Don's children from a previous
marriage and had worked in considerable depth on Maggie's low self-esteem and depression in relationship to
Don. In this session just before they realized that they
were doing well on their own, Don reported a dream.

I dreamt I wanted to make love to Maggie. At first she
seemed uninterested, but then was dressed in her robe beckoning and accommodating. We were visitors in a large house,
perhaps my aunt and uncle's house, which was the center of my
extended family's network in a neighboring town when I grew
up, only more Victorian. I had to chase a man out of our room
who wanted to loiter, then lock many doors to surrounding
rooms and porches. The upstairs doors had glass, which meant
I had to lock off much of the second floor to keep him out. I saw
a child's room, which came off a sitting room and our bedroom.
Just as I got the doors locked and we were about to begin
making love, a team of housemaids came to clean our room,

protesting that they had to and could not be dissuaded. Our lovemaking seemed doomed.

In association, Don thought of his aunt's house, the center of the family, the place he had met and largely wooed his previous wife. Maggie thought the idea of a family network seemed to stand for many people from his current job having to be at their house now, where they peered into their private life and interfered with marital intimacy. This left Maggie at times resentful of the invasion.

Maggie also had a dream.

I was on a raft, whale-watching. We were seeing the blue-striped whale. It had blue and white markings such that when it was coming toward you, it rippled so as to seem to be going away. Then I realized that also when it seemed to be going away, it would be coming toward you. I thought, "We aren't safe! We're not supposed to be watching the whales from a raft, but on a big boat." Then I realized it was a shark that might attack me.

Maggie thought the whale-shark reminded her of Don, a pun on their last name, Wells, and a cartoon of his large and somewhat overweight body overwhelming her in intercourse, consuming her with his needs and his work. They had seen whales the previous week off the coast of California, and the guide had said that the whales swimming side by side was an unusual sighting. It had looked like intercourse. Maggie said ruefully that when she thought she wanted something from Don like lovemaking, he might leave her to pay attention to others' needs and when she wanted a respite, he would be at her, asking for sex.

Together the two dreams on the same night confronted Don's wishes for more, his energetic and sometimes seemingly incessant longing, which was interfered with by his own efforts. Maggie was admiringly drawn to his size and markings, his energy and immediacy, which, however, could overwhelm her just at the moment he wanted more from her. The couple laughed about the fit of the two dreams and agreed they could do better in watching for their own needs both for intimacy and privacy, and for distance from the consequences of Don's ebullience. However, they liked the lifestyle they had evolved of making their own house the center of a network that was a symbolic heir to Don's aunt's house as the center of a warm extended family. They discussed the liabilities of this pattern and agreed to provide time for the two of them and for Maggie's need for some space for herself.

In this case the dreams described patterns of personality and neediness that were familiar to both members of the couple. The conflict described by the juxtaposition of the two dreams on the same night provided recognition of the way they were prone to let their own excesses interfere with giving to and receiving from each other. The result was rather like the effect of a picture that is worth a thousand words, or a cartoon that cuts to the core of an issue and produces a laugh of relief.

This couple could respect each others wishes, fears, and differences. They could develop their own interpretation of events, own their individual contributions, and maintain a healthy perspective, lightened with humor. The therapist found that he was responding with a remarkably undisturbed countertransference and that the couple did not require active intervention. A month later, it was no surprise when the couple set a termination date after a few more sessions.

When dreams are available in therapy with couples, they offer a unique opportunity for work on the communication between self and object at several levels. They inform the couple about each spouse's internal self-and-object relations, and they give important clues about the way each spouse uses the other as an external object. Whereas a session in which one partner shares a dream may only inform about the object relations of one spouse, it can also lead to an exploration of comparable issues in both partners. This was true in the session with Clive and Lila.

When both partners can offer dreams, we may be able to match and contrast pictures of inner object relations as if two X-rays were superimposed and compared. Sam and Shirley were able to do this, giving moving clues about how each of them had introjectively identified with their dead baby and had then tried to rid themselves by projecting the deadness into each other, and later into me in the therapy. Maggie and Don were able to use their dreams to examine the excesses of an object relations fit in which each felt the other reflected back adequately on his or her self, but in which there was some fine-tuning needed.

Finally, dreams in couple therapy are useful clues about the couple's shared contextual transference. This was true in all three couples. Clive and Lila experienced an uncomfortable longing and sense of impingement with their therapist, which was spoken for in the dream of the wounded baby. Sam and Shirley's dreams of death and misrecognition echoed with the painful deadness and feeling of being misunderstood in the therapy. And Maggie and Don, in their state of growth, were beginning to feel that their intimacy was now starting to be impinged on by the continuing therapy.

Dreams have a special place in psychotherapy. Therapists often sense that Freud's aphorism that "dreams are the royal road to the unconscious" is still true, even though the insights possible through the analysis of dreams can also be achieved in other ways. The same holds true for dream work with couples. It is not necessary for couples to bring in dreams to accomplish a great deal, but there remains an ineffable quality to the work with couples' dreams that can resonate with a depth of under-standing in the relationship between self and object.

10

Dreams in Therapy of
Families with Adolescents

Adolescence is a particularly fluid period of development. During this time of "second separation-individuation" (Blos 1967) and of identity consolidation (Erikson 1959), adolescents are particularly focused on the relationship to their objects. The family members who have contributed the original experience out of which the adolescent's internal objects were made are still usually there, still involved with the adolescent, and still able to contribute to the formation of the adolescent's evolving self. Unresolved object relations issues are carried by the parents and other family members and continue to influence the adolescent.

In turn, the growth of the adolescent influences the object relations of the parents. Parents hope to repair old deficits in self and object relations through relationship with their children, and they hope to validate what they have received from their parental objects by passing loving object relations on to their children. Difficulties with child object relations, therefore, have profound implications for the selves of parents. In the context of the continuing cycle of renewal of self and object relations, family therapy has a unique role in fostering mutual differentiation and repair to object relations for parents and adolescents alike.

In therapy with adolescents, the struggle of the teenager to differentiate the self from his or her objects has particular energy and poignancy. It is often as if adolescents will wrench their own identities from their families "over the dead bodies" of their parents, leaving them with a self in isolation from its actual parental objects and likely to repeat self-defeating struggles with new objects.

Dreams have a unique ability to contribute to this adolescent struggle between self and object. We have seen how dreams stand on the boundary between conscious and unconscious aspects of self and communicate aspects of the relationship of the self to its objects within the individual and between people in primary relationships. In the flux of adolescence, the dream offers a particularly fluid medium for communication and recombination of the elements of self and object.

This chapter gives examples of the therapeutic use of dreams in two families, allowing us to examine the formation of self in interplay with objects in contrasting adolescent girls. The first case demonstrates the use of a dream to add to a shaky alliance between self and object, between adolescent and parent, and between family and therapist. This girl was seen with her parents because she refused treatment on her own and, in the absence of any alliance with her, family treatment seemed the only alternative to residential treatment. In the second case, an adolescent girl who was fully cooperative and invested in treatment was seen individually on a regular basis immediately following the weekly family sessions. The dream she volunteered was catalytic both in the family session and in her own following session.

THE RELUCTANT DRAG-IN

Tanya Matthews was a middle class black girl who came to therapy at 15 because she had been expelled from boarding school during her freshman year for drug and alcohol use. Her divorced parents, both college teachers, related amicably around her care, but Tanya had managed to exploit their shared laissez-faire attitude to pursue a downward trend even before going away to school. By the time I saw her, she acknowledged that she had no motivation for schoolwork, no career ambitions, and no life hopes. She drank and used any drugs that were available because there was no reason not to. Her apathy was a thin cover for a dense depression. As therapy progressed, she began to notice the impact of loss due to her parents' divorce four years earlier. In self-defense, she quickly returned to the refuge of her "I don't care" stance.

I began therapy, meeting with Tanya and both parents. I was surprised by the ability of these divorced people to work in therapy together, support Tanya, and confront their shared history of turning a blind eye on her increasing drug use and acting out. I convened a family-wide meeting, which included Tanya's three sisters when they returned from college. They had also used drugs and alcohol in high school—and presumably still did—but were on smoother courses nevertheless. They confronted both Tanya and their parents—and then promptly left town for their own activities.

The first couple of individual meetings with Tanya were friendly enough, but our sessions soon lapsed into a resentful silence in which she claimed she simply had

nothing to say. At first, I prodded her a bit. If I even tried
to keep the conversation going, she moved to angry
retorts. She was only there at her parents' insistence and
did not intend to use the session. After working unsuc-
cessfully with this negativistic defense, I recommended
that therapy should consist of twice-weekly conjoint sessions, some in which Tanya met with each parent separately and some in which she met with both father and
mother.

I was again pleasantly surprised that the therapy
went fairly well, even though Tanya never admitted any
interest in it or in the educational plan that evolved. She
was accepted at St. Thomas, a local Catholic school that
had an interest in children with emotional difficulty. She
began with a steady effort and did well, all the while
protesting vigorously. She said she hated all the kids at
the school, but made friends steadily. She protested
energetically and regularly about having to come to therapy. She often began sessions by refusing to speak and
left the talking to be done somewhat painfully and labo-
riously by her parents. Then regularly—if reluctantly—she
responded to them.

In saying that I was surprised at the benefits of this
treatment and at her progress, my intention is to convey
the idea that I was dubious about Tanya's effective treatment as an outpatient at all. I had consulted two educational psychologist colleagues about referring Tanya to a
residential school before adopting this therapy plan on a
trial basis. In addition, her consistent negativism and the
regularity with which she dismissed my offerings—a dis-
missiveness that echoed her attacks on her parents when
they began to set limits or impose conditions—left me
feeling chronically unappreciated in a way that is familiar
to any parent of a surly adolescent, or perhaps parents of
most adolescents.

Nonetheless, I felt buoyed by a growing alliance with
her parents. The father said that as the noncustodial

parent, he just did not have a good feel for what was needed and left it to Tanya's mother. He, too, had been thrown out of school for alcohol use as a teenager. Although he identified with Tanya's plight, he had found therapy useful in making sense of what he wanted out of life. He knew that Tanya needed more structure and was willing to help in a more active way. Mrs. Matthews said that she felt guilty whenever she said no to Tanya, because her own mother had set such firm and forbidding limits on her. Out of fear of being like her own mother whom she had resented, she had been lax about limits with Tanya.

I found myself working therapeutically with the parents on the themes that interfered with their capacity to parent and set limits, even while Tanya sat there watching me helping them gain the capacity to cooperate in setting limits. I have never before conducted a therapy quite like it, and so was beset with constant doubts. However, Tanya's school and social life continued to improve.

The session with the dream that I present here occurred after about eight months of work. Tanya and Mrs. Matthews arrived ten minutes late for an appointment that they had asked me to begin early.

Tanya began with a renewed protest. "There isn't anything to talk about. I don't have anything to say. And I don't think you should have to talk, Mom, just to fill up the time." She shrugged her shoulders and grimaced sarcastically at her mother, with an angry glance at me.

Mrs. Matthews said, "By the way, Dr. Scharff, Tanya's father will be out of town all next week. Could we meet only once? I don't want to come three times in a row with Tanya by myself."

I felt pulled. I was sympathetic to her wish for relief from having to provide all the energy for the session, but I did not agree that Tanya should come only once a week. My ambivalence was heightened both from my own experience dealing with Tanya's reluctance and because the request suited my convenience. Pressed by a crowded schedule the following week, I opted to let the request stand for the moment. But I was aware that it set a theme of reluctance for the session, echoing Tanya's statement that there was nothing to say. I felt not yet up to confronting the pair about their resistance, fed from my own sense of how much I also had to struggle to keep things going.

Mrs. Matthews now tried to talk about Tanya's philosophy.

"Tanya, you insist that life is just fate, that there's no point in worrying. It's hard to get you to do things on your own behalf. But life just isn't that way."

Tanya wasn't having any of this. "See! You're just talking to fill up the time."

Mrs. Matthews said, "I know you don't want to talk. I think that's why Dr. Scharff asked your father and me to come in with you to these sessions to raise issues. There are things to discuss, and there's certainly work to do."

"I don't really think it's any of your business anyway what I want to do with my life," said Tanya. "I should be able to do what I want. It's a free country."

The discussion turned, again at the mother's initiative, to where Tanya would go to school the next year. It was January, and Tanya would have to be thinking of a new school or else would have to stay at the current school, which she still said she hated.

"I don't even have to go to school next year. I'll be 16, and you can't make me."

Mrs. Matthews forced the issue. "You *are* going to school."

"I hate St. Thomas! I'll go to school if you make me, but I just want to go somewhere else."

"Like where?" asked Mrs. Matthews. "You haven't developed any options."

Tanya mocked her mother. "I know. I can 'develop my options.' "

I felt Tanya's hardening but engaged negativism. As her

mother pushed, Tanya seemed to be coming out of her lair. I suddenly thought of her as a dragon practically breathing fire. I could feel the tension rising, and I could sense Mrs. Matthews wanting to retreat from Tanya's awakened anger.

"Do you feel like retreating, Mrs. Matthews?" I asked.

"Sure, I do," she said. "As soon as I start to discuss the realities, she gets nasty. But it's true that if she doesn't pursue the question of applying to other schools now, the options will be closed. And she says she hates St. Thomas. I feel in a bind, and there are lots of times I wish I could just get away from it."

"Well, I'll be 16. And you can't make me go to school," Tanya repeated.

"It's not in the realm of possibility!" said her mother, seeming strengthened by my question. "Look what happened to Michael. That's the kind of thing I worry about with you."

Michael was Tanya's reputed boyfriend, another 15-year-old who had also been dismissed from the same school for drug use a few months earlier than Tanya. Michael was now enrolled in a residential treatment school in New England and had run away from it. There had been recent phone calls from Michael to Tanya, and then from Michael's mother trying to locate him.

I took Tanya's choice of boyfriend as another sign of the poverty of her self-image. Michael seemed to be an even more troubled version of herself, as were several of her friends, according to the description she gave of them. I felt heartened to hear her mother's reference to Michael in this way, because until now the parents had not monitored Tanya's interactions with this sort of friend, allowing her a large loophole for acting out.

I understood the session so far as representing their shared feeling of hopelessness. I was thinking of Tanya's opening comments about there being "nothing to say" and of Mrs. Matthews' wish to cancel a session. This discussion about Michael spurred me to intervene.

"This session really has been about the inability to talk that the two of you share," I said. "This discussion about refusing to go to school represents the bottom line threat that Tanya is big enough to make it impossible for you, Mrs. Matthews, and for her father to do anything. It's true that if Tanya forced things as Michael has done, you and her father would have to decide what your own bottom line is, as Michael's parents have. Short of that, I believe you're saying, 'This is the situation. There's no discussing it. You have to go to school.' Perhaps what is not being directly discussed in this kind of non-discussion is that Tanya prefers it when the two of you are firmer. She may be afraid that if you don't put your foot down, she'll end up in the kind of desperate position Michael has been in, alone, on the loose, and destitute with no capacity to take care of herself."

Mrs. Matthews looked upset. "It's just like my dream," she said. "I dreamt that a girl named Amy was in the school where Michael is, which was like a prison. Amy is a troubled girl my older daughter Shandra knew, a girl who has been in a treatment school. Shandra had talked about dropping out of school sometimes, too, although she has managed to graduate from college and is doing fine. But she frequently threatened to drop out when she was Tanya's age. That's all there was to the dream." She began to cry and wiped her eyes with a tissue from her purse. "It makes me feel that to control Tanya, I'll have to send her to a prison like the school I think of when I think of Michael or Amy."

Now the full story about Michael came out. His situation had deteriorated so that he finally called Tanya to ask for her credit card—or her mother's—so that he could buy a plane ticket home. Failing to get that, he turned to his parents, who said they wouldn't talk to him about anything until he was back at school. After some time elapsed in which no one knew where he was, he showed up back in the residential school, where he had remained.

I said, "This dream tells us where the conflict is between your mother and yourself, Tanya. It's like what she fears about Michael. In the past your mother has been reluctant to set limits on you for fear you'll hate her, but now she is afraid that failing to do so will leave you alone and lost. She fears your anger. She worries that insisting on school for you will be like sentencing you to jail, but she fears for your safety and well-being if she doesn't."

Still in tears, Mrs. Matthews said, "It's true. You have to understand that I'm so scared for you. I don't know if you can use anything I can give you, and I'm scared if you can't. But when I try and you're so mad at me, I feel you hate me as I hated my mother when I used to think she kept me in prison and made me do so many things I hated. I swore I would never do that to you or your sisters, but now I think that you all needed me to insist on more things. You've all had trouble because I was scared to insist on things. I know that now. Believe me, Tanya, I want you to have a life, and I'm scared about what will happen to you. Michael could be dead by now, and you run so many risks with yourself. And I know I won't always be able to stop you. But I do want to do everything I can. I *will* do all I can, but it's not easy."

Tanya was silent, but now seemed to listen without her habit of shrugging her shoulders and grimacing.

I said, "I think Tanya, you're afraid that your parents won't be able to see how frightened you are underneath your anger and refusal. It's crucial for them to know that you will also be relieved when they can insist on things you need to do and on limits you need. It's not important that you like your parents right now, but it is important they survive your anger and stand up to you without being scared by your dragon threats to breathe fire.

"I also can say now that we all agreed to cancel one of next week's sessions because of the shared fear of words and the painful process of trying to talk. But these things have to be dealt with. I think we should meet twice next week as we had planned."

"I can see what you mean," Mrs. Matthews said. "I think I can face it."

Tanya did not exactly thank me on her way out, but she seemed at least less reluctant.

This vignette illustrates a specific aspect of the dependence of the self on the object in adolescence. The young child is overtly dependent on the external object for definition of her self. The adolescent is often involved in rejecting the external family objects in order to strengthen her internal objects, her identity, or sense of self, and to build new peer relations that validate and test this newly emerging self. Tanya had lost her sense of self in a premature separation due to the divorce and even more so because of her parents' failure to be the appropriate limit-setting objects she required to keep up her development of a central self positioned between excessively need exciting and rejecting objects.

Mrs. Matthews' dream let us understand together that her fear of being a persecuting and rejecting object for Tanya had left the teenager at the disorganizing mercy of exciting internal and external objects, alone, lost, and sedated instead of limited and defined. Her depressed apathy was a sign of the repression of her longing for an object to encounter her. It saved her from the pain of this position much of the time, but when it threatened, she became an angry dragon turning to attack others rather than feel the pain of the loss of herself, the loss that Guntrip (1969) has told us is the ultimate tragedy of the schizoid position—the loss of self experienced when there is no object to meet the hidden longing of the libidinal self.

The dream let Mrs. Matthews see that she abandoned Tanya in this way because of her own fear of aggression. She could only understand limit-setting as an imprisoning attack on her child. She saw it as imprisoning not only because of how she felt in her mother's care and control, but also because in her own inner loneliness, she wanted to keep Tanya so close to her that it might damage her as she felt damaged by similar issues of her own mother. That set of issues remained to be worked on. Meanwhile, the dream let Mrs. Matthews contain Tanya's anxieties about being lost without a holding object. Over the next few months of therapy I noted Tanya's increasing definition of an evolvingly active and constructive self.

"MY PARENTS WEREN'T LOOKING WHILE I GREW UP!"

Sally Bly, aged 15 and the middle child of three, was brought to treatment by her parents. Her mother was a nurse and her father a county administrator. They told me they had been devastated when Sally told them she had become sexually active and wanted to go to the gynecologist for the pill. They could not support this idea and had grounded her until she agreed not to have any more sexual activity. When they first saw me, they were adamant on this point. There was, at this moment, no other way they could see things. It was their only complaint, for Sally was a model student and class leader, and although not much of an athlete, was well liked and, if anything, overinvolved in extracurricular activities. Her academic dedication and her activities had been a relief to them after the troublesome learning disabilities of her 18-year-old brother, Zach, who was now, however, settled into a modestly successful college career. She also had a younger brother, Burt, aged 7, who, they said, was energetic and lovable.

When I saw Sally, I found her to be an extremely appealing girl. She was bright, funny, and thoughtful. I was not, however, unsympathetic to her parents' concerns that she might be prematurely involved in a sexual life. Still, she seemed to have a more flexible and thoughtful point of view than theirs. She said that her parents had always said to her that she should turn to them with problems, even if she thought they would disagree with her. She knew that they would not approve of the sex, but everything she had learned had led her to believe it was better to tell them and to get proper birth control than to be at risk. She felt she loved her boyfriend and was going to be involved with him sexually, so she concluded that she had acted responsibly.

But she felt the problems really were more general. She said, "They don't understand that I have grown up. They weren't looking my way, and I just grew up. I think they were too busy fighting. I miss them—my parents. But I have another problem. I don't know a single girl who has managed to stay on good terms with her mother, and I worry this will happen to my mother and me. She doesn't get along with her mother, and my mom's sister and my cousin don't speak. So I figure that since Mom and I don't get along too well now, with all of this, we don't have much of a chance. It's not helped any by the fact that Mom and Dad don't get along well. In a way, I've turned to my boyfriend to get away from home."

I was quite taken by Sally, a girl who seemed wise beyond her years. I knew that her view, infinitely more interesting than her parents', could not be the whole story either, but its precocious charm was appealing.

During several months of meetings with Sally and her parents, in which I maintained a neutral position about her sexual activity and their grounding her, we worked on the distance between Sally and her parents and the frightening model of relationships she drew from their bickering. Mr. and Mrs. Bly softened their position about the grounding, and the three began to talk about the fears Sally had about the years of distance between herself and her parents.

I also met with Sally individually, partly because she was unwilling to offer personal revelation in the family setting because of the expectation that her parents would

ground her. In the individual sessions, she worked hard
and began to see the ways in which she, too, fended off
her parents and repetitively chose boys who were emotionally negligent and even abusive. She was reevaluating
her view of her parents' relationship. She unconsciously
felt there was no alternative to it, and yet she hoped
desperately to change it. As she worked on these matters,
she realized not only that she was trying to solve her
depression, but that despite her outward academic success, she actually constantly undermined her considerable
ambition and seldom maintained her best performance.

The following family session occurred after about a
year of treatment. By now, the sessions included her
brothers, the younger Burt because the Blys realized that
their chronic distress had affected his peer relationships
and was causing him anxiety. Since Zach, the older
brother, was home from college, he was there, too.

The session began with some uncharacteristically
outrageous behavior by Burt. There had been a ceremony
at his school at which he had received an award for
spelling. Burt said to his father that he shouldn't talk about
it in front of Zach, who was somewhat uncomfortable in
the family sessions because he attended only when home
from college. Burt then began to attack his father physically in a way that he said was a combination of "hugging
and bugging." He pretended to choke his father, but he
really applied a fair amount of pressure. In the end, Mr.
Bly had to hold Burt's arms tightly to stop him so that they
were then locked in an embrace. Burt kept up the activity
despite the rest of the family's objections and threats of
discipline. It dominated the first few minutes of the
session. Meanwhile Sally snuggled up against her mother,
who was trying to say how well Burt was doing at school.

No sense could be made of Burt's behavior, nor
would he stop. Each of the others commented on how
much Burt wanted attention.

Zach said, "Do I have to come home from college for this?"

Sally said, "Look at how Burt turns a silly objection into the center of attention."

Mr. Bly said, "Well, I have a theory that he's uncomfortable with success."

"Perhaps," said Mrs. Bly, "he thinks this means he'll have to keep it up, have to keep doing well when he'd rather be playing baseball."

"But none of you thinks you can really make much sense of his disruptiveness," I said.

"Be quiet, Dr. Scharff," said Burt. "This isn't any of your business." He was being uncharacteristically rude. He was an outspoken boy but not usually unfriendly.

Mr. Bly spoke up from his position of holding Burt firmly. "I've not been behaving very well with the family either. I've been rude and kind of my Napoleon self. In fact, my wife thinks Burt's been like this because I have been pretty difficult this week. My father died a year ago yesterday. I've been missing him a lot. Realizing that this was the anniversary of his death let me feel less tense and more able to treat people better."

"Oh, he was quite a bear this week," Mrs. Bly said. "Saturday I cooked a special meal and he was such a grouch I felt like throwing it at him. But since we realized the connection to his father's death, he's calmed down."

So far I had been riveted on Burt's physical acting up. The energy behind his tenacious grasp on his father's attention had looked murderous, but at the same time paradoxically playful, close, and loving. It had made no sense until this moment of explanation of the loss of his father's. That also made sense of the physical fondness between Sally and mother in their huddle, as if defending each other from loss and disruption.

I said to Mr. Bly, "Identifying that you have been angry while unknowingly struggling with the loss of your father makes sense of Burt's looking like he wanted to kill you while also getting all that loving closeness. It also says something about Sally and Mom cuddling to have each other."

Mr. Bly turned to Sally. "Do you want to tell Dr. Scharff your dream? It meant a lot to me because it was that dream that helped me realize that I was struggling with my father's death."

"Okay," said Sally. "I dreamt I was at my grandparents' house, the one they used to live in before they moved away from Washington when I was little. In the dream, they were moving away, loading up a moving van. I was struck that it was from United Moving Van Lines. They got in the van and my grandfather started to drive. But he headed right for me in the van and was going to run me over. Then I woke up."

I noticed that Burt had now stopped moving around and was sitting comfortably and quietly held by his father. His quieting down led to a change in tenor of the whole family, which indicated that we were now approaching the emotional material that underlay his struggle.

"Any thoughts about the dream?" I asked Sally.

"Well, I think the van is really my father's car, which is a big red van. In fact, sometimes I think of him like a van because he's bigger than I am and thinks he can run people over. So I guess it's like he runs me over. I think that was the feeling in the dream, that he was running over me by moving away."

"Do you think your parents are united in moving away from you?" I asked.

"Well, not this week," she said, "but they are more together lately and I miss the closeness I've been developing with Mom now they're getting along better. And I used to have something of a special relationship with Dad at some of the times he and Mom would be fighting the most. So I guess I'd have to say yes. When they are more united, I feel they've moved away from me."

"Whose parents are the grandparents of Sally's dream, and did they move away?" I asked the family, looking for additional object relations history of this dream and current family constellations.

Mrs. Bly said, "These are my husband's parents. They lived here until Sally was 7. At that time Pops retired and they moved to Florida. Sally had been real close to them. She'd see them after school when I was on shifts at the hospital. I was pregnant with Burt when they left and delivered soon after, so then I became preoccupied with him as soon as they were gone. Sally used to tell me how much she missed them when I was nursing Burt, and she always did remember them fondly. She continued to have a pretty special relationship to them, although she always had a hard time understanding why they moved and left her."

"This is the grandfather whom Sally lost when she was 7 and whom Dad lost last year," I said. "That loss is attacking Sally right now through Dad's behavior."

"Yeah. I think that's right," said Mrs. Bly. "It's like a ghost is living in my husband and attacking Sally—and the whole family—through him. He's so preoccupied with his father's death, he can't tune in on the rest of us."

"She's right," Mr. Bly nodded. "I haven't been able to stop obsessing about what I missed having with him and now will never have. He was a distant man. We never managed to have the close relationship both of us would have liked. Actually, we did speak of it some in the past few years, but we didn't quite make up for it. So I guess it's fair to say I'm haunted by the sense of deprivation, by his moving away from me for my whole life. Maybe I felt it most when I was Sally's age and had some trouble in school. It was the only time I ever failed any course and I needed help. He couldn't understand. I think my problem bothered him and he withdrew, probably feeling he had let me down."

"I didn't know you had ever failed a course, Dad," said Zach, who had been completely quiet.

"Well, I had a girlfriend who was throwing me over, and I was so devastated I couldn't even think about school," Mr. Bly continued. "But Pops was upset that I would do so badly when I had been an A student."

"Dad, maybe you were turning to your girlfriend because you felt lonely with your parents, too," said Sally.

"Maybe so, Sally," he acknowledged. "Anyway, your dream really hit me hard this week. It was a favor, really. It let me see what I was doing to you and the family, and it helped me pull together. Do you agree that I've been better since we talked on Tuesday?"

"Yeah, I do," she said. "You've been not bad for a father. Before that, I think Mom and I had been getting close by talking about how difficult you were being."

Burt had remained quietly folded in his father's arms for all of this time. Now he said, "See, and that left me on my own. Dad was mad at everyone, and Mom and Sally had each other."

"Well, Burt," I said, "in the beginning of the hour, I think maybe you thought I was driving a moving van headed right for your family and you were trying to protect them from me because you were afraid I was going to stir up trouble."

"Maybe," he said, not necessarily convinced.

I continued, "But I also think you've been trying to do a *Ghostbusters* on your dad. You've been trying to save the family from the ghost of your grandfather by making your dad so mad—trying to strangle the bad father who left your dad and you, and get your good dad back. In a way it's worked today. I can see you got your good dad back."

"Yeah," Burt grinned. "Good Daddy." And he turned and put his arms around him with an energetic bear hug as Mr. Bly mimed at gasping for breath.

THE DREAM IN SALLY'S INDIVIDUAL SESSION

"We'll meet you at home, honey. Drive carefully!" called Mrs. Bly as she closed my office door and left Sally for her individual weekly session.

Sally took off her shoes and curled up on the love seat, relaxing into the "real thing" where she could let her hair down and tell me the things she did not say with the family there—the things her friends told her, the parties she had been to, occasionally sexual matters.

"I'm worried about the way I keep messing things up for myself," she said. "That's what I'm figuring out here, right? Like now, I have this new boy I like, Max. He's really a decent guy. He understands me. He doesn't pressure me and he's a lot of fun."

"So you're finding such a good guy kind of a puzzling experience?" I asked.

"Right! You got it!" she said. "He's nice and fun and I can't like him like I used to like Craig, who really conned me and used me. And I knew down deep he was using me. Like, Max invited me to his prom. He goes to a different school. I do want to go, but I haven't invited him to my school's prom because I keep thinking he won't know my friends, but I know he would get along with them fine.

"Let me tell you this story. Max and I were supposed to have a date Saturday night. I was trying out for cheerleaders and the meeting went a long time. Then I had lost my car keys and my mom had to come get me, so by that time instead of showing up at his house at 9 o'clock, I show up at midnight. I'm telling him I'm really sorry and he won't ever want to see me again, and Max says, 'No problem.' He just laughs about it and says okay, but we have to go out to get a coke. And he takes me to the American Diner where we sat and laughed and had a great time for an hour. But I felt guilty and said I had to pay the bill 'tho I didn't really have the money. He said, 'There's no need for this. I want to do it.' But I felt I had to make it up to him."

"We've been talking about you maybe being drawn to slightly abusive relationships with guys," I said. "And now we're seeing something that goes with that. You're actually uncomfortable with a guy who wants to treat you well. Your thinking you don't belong in a good relationship might relate to the dream we were just discussing with your family."

"Hmm," she mused. "Well, maybe it's hard for me to think about a relationship being interesting if there isn't some fighting and pushing each other around. That's all I've known with my parents all these years. I mean they don't hit each other or anything. They're just a bit nasty and quarrel a lot."

"How about losing your grandparents?" I asked. "I hadn't known they were so important to you when you were little."

"I hadn't thought much about it for a long time, you know," she said. "They've lived away for 7 or 8 years, and they were kind of old and crotchety. We went to visit after Pops died and Mums was picky about keeping her apartment clean, something Burt absolutely cannot do! But I remember now how Pops used to bounce me on his knee and Mums fed me brownies when Mom was working. And then they left and Burt was born. And Zach always used to get attention from Mom and Dad because of his learning troubles. So, yeah, I think I missed them then like Dad missed Pops when he died. That must have been a hard time for me, but I don't think I knew it."

"I've been thinking about what you said when you and I started meeting. That you didn't think it was possible for girls to grow up and have good relationships with their moms. You must have felt you lost the chance of a good relationship with her when you were little and had to turn to your grandparents. I think you held that against her for years. But today there you were, snuggled up with your mom."

"It's true," she said. "We've been getting along real well. Kind of joking about Dad, but mainly we've been pretty good friends for a while now. Mom can have some bad days, but they don't seem to set us back much. And even when I get in trouble or something goes wrong like I get behind at school, Mom doesn't really land on me."

"So it's become a different thing than last year?" I asked.

"Yeah. I think maybe we'll do okay," she said. "But you know, when you said that about my missing Mom when I was little, I was remembering that at some point she was sick and in the hospital. And I was little. They sent me to Aunt Betsy's. She is one pretty difficult lady, off-putting and bitchy when anyone is feeling they need things. I think it must have been a time I felt all alone. I can only remember it a little."

"So Aunt Betsy is like the mom you thought you had when you first came here," I said, "the bitchy woman who wouldn't stand for people needing something from her. That seems to have started when your mom had to send you away for a little while, and maybe you felt then that it was her moving away from you, too."

"Maybe so," she agreed. "I'm remembering some other things. I don't know why. Like being in my crib, which I stayed in until I could talk at about three. I wanted my parents to come in and read me a story. They wouldn't, and I cried all night by myself. And I remember a time when Mom took me to school and I didn't want her to leave me and she left anyway. I think that's like the way I felt she gave all her attention to Burt when he was born."

"These are the events that fit with your dream," I said. "The loss you felt when you couldn't have your mom at these times. Because you probably handled some of the loneliness by turning to your dad and some by going to your grandparents. Then when they left at about the time Burt was born, you must have felt there'd be no one to turn to. Sometimes grandparents are an ideal substitute for parents. And you thought your grandparents got along well, unlike the bickering of your parents. I think when they left, you felt life might not be safe anymore, that the 'united' parents were gone and you had the ones who weren't safe because they were divided."

"Score one for you!" she said, making a "high five" sign in the air. "You know, when I don't get my home-work in and feel so badly treated, I think it's because I'm feeling sorry for myself and that no one cares for me. Like it's then I want my parents to take care of me like I was a little girl."

"Then, if they don't or can't, you're disappointed and down?" I asked.

"Yes. And I think then I want a boyfriend who has troubles so I can help him do better. Someone like Craig so I can help fix him up. But the trouble is, he doesn't necessarily want to be fixed up. So I end up feeling he's pushing me around, kind of like he's the one driving a van over me. But really, I get myself into it in the first place. I kind of hire the van and put him in the driver's seat. Maybe I'm kind of like my dad after all, except I find a boy to do it for me. It's like I'm the moving company, and I go out and find people who aren't good drivers and act like I can teach them. Then, when they really don't want to learn and they mow me down, I act like I had nothing to do with it. But I hired them! I do it to myself! Oh, wow!"

This vignette from family and individual psychotherapy illus-trates Fairbairn's concept of the internal saboteur, this time discovered in the shared work on Sally's dream. The family and Sally herself were clearly working well in the therapeutic setting, open to discover repressed and denied parts of them-selves, and like the Green family, described in Chapter 8, each able to look at themselves as well as each other.

The dream here was actually a "moving vehicle" for the exploration of loss that had been transformed into anger and rejecting object relations within several family members and between them. The lost good grandparents, the parents of the father, carried forward in identifications as rejecting and persecuting objects, could be seen to be affecting the selves of the parents.

To begin with, the dream can be understood as a description of the "endopsychic situation" of the dreamer (Fairbairn 1952). The internal object relations view presented in the dream is not literally the family situation, but the constellation that the dreamer carries inside. Here, Sally dreamt not only of a rejecting father but of her antilibidinal ego or "internal saboteur" in relationship to it. The structure also illustrated the rejecting parental pair, who were, in the dream, united in leaving her and aiming their "United Moving Van" at her murderously. In cuddling with her mother while telling the dream, Sally tries to recreate an exciting object pair for herself to compensate for the rejection she feels. Her central ego or self is the dreamer and reporter of the dream, whereas an ideal object is only present in this dream by the implication of the kind of loving and accepting object she feels is moving away from her.

However, the more interesting view of the dream is supplied by the associations of Sally's family to the grandparents' move away from Washington at the time of Burt's birth. The family is united in their experience of loss of parents then and more recently with the death of Mr. Bly's father. Identifying the rejecting objects that have been voiced or enacted in various ways—through the father's embodiment of persecution, through Burt's attack on the father—allows the family to see how they as a group have been haunted by and tied to persecuting objects. They long for the united parents, but feel they cannot hope to have them safely embodied inside the family. They cannot imagine that Mr. and Mrs. Bly will be able to constitute a united and loving couple, who can be loving parents as well. Consequently, they set up substitute couples, who try to compensate the family for the sense of ongoing loss: Burt and Father, Mother and Sally, Sally and her boyfriend. With work on Sally's dream, the pattern can be explored and changed.

Through this session, Burt at first has the role of protecting the family from the intrusion of the therapist, who seems to be driving a moving van into their midst. He threatens to move the family toward the experience of loss and pain. When the dream is shared, the therapist becomes no longer a persecuting object to the group, but a helpful agent of family and individual movement. Then the self and object relations of each family member and of the family as a group can be explored and understood, and the family resumes its own process of development. And, as members refind their lost objects, they begin the process of reclaiming their selves.

PART FOUR

SELF AND OBJECT FROM THE VANTAGE OF THE FAMILY

11

Oedipus Revisited in

His Family

The Oedipus situation is not just a stage in the individual's psychosexual development. It is a collaboration between the child and the family. Freud first described the Oedipus complex as a natural consequence of the 3- and 4-year-old's drives, stemming from the in-built pattern of the child that inevitably had to unfold (1905b). When we examine it from the standpoint of the constant interaction of self and object, the picture is one of mutual influence between child and parent, self and external object, and self and internal object.

The Oedipus complex was Freud's contribution to an object relations formulation of development. He described the way that children incorporate and modify aspects of their relationships to objects as they order their internal worlds. Later, Freud (1923) described the direct consequences of oedipal organization for internal structure in the formation of the superego.

Fairbairn (1944) added considerably to our understanding of the oedipal situation. The child grows up, he noted, with one ambivalent relationship with the mother, who is perceived as exciting or rejecting as well as good. During the oedipal period, the child imposes that ambivalence upon a triangular situation and tries to resolve two independently ambivalent relationships with mother and father by splitting exciting and rejecting objects along sexual lines and assigning all of the excitement to one object and all the rejection to the other. Thus in the ordinary oedipal situation for the boy, the mother becomes the good, exciting object, and the father provides the model for the bad, rejecting object. The opposite situation pertains to the girl. For her, the father is the good and exciting object, whereas the mother is associated with the bad, rejecting object.

I have previously described four forms of inventiveness exercised by the infant and growing child in development, which together ultimately result in the oedipal splitting first described by Fairbairn (Scharff and Scharff 1987). Here I briefly review them as a foundation integrating oedipal development for the individual and the family as an interplay between self and object.

THE INFANT'S INVENTION OF THE FAMILY

The Child Finds What Is There

First, extending Winnicott's description of the child's experience of "inventing" the mother's breast (1971a), I suggest that infants have to discover already existing aspects of family life for themselves. These are aspects of life that they suddenly become able to discover at certain points in their growth. They are new for the child, but they were there before because the family put them there. The parents' relationship is such a discovery waiting to be made.

The Child's Growth Alters the Family

Second, each child's presence and growth alter the family, and this reshaping creates changing forms for everyone. The family's new-found instability during the baby's growth creates room for a shared illusion that the baby is almost intentionally causing them all to change.

Regressive Invention

Third, infants see the family in ways that they invent as they go along. From the standpoint of other members of the family, these ways of viewing the family are idiosyncratic because they are based on the infants' limited ability to think and formulate, as determined by the age and stage of development at which they make each new observation. They are also influenced by the issues that energize the infants at the time of each observation—for instance, on the heightening of separation and autonomy at age 2, and on the heightening of genital sexuality at 3 and 4.

In each new phase, children are suddenly faced with issues that are new to them in terms of their previous developmental stage and their previous object relations. For the infants, it is like trying to understand calculus with only a knowledge of algebra, and sometimes even by falling back on the more limiting mathematics of geometry or simple arithmetic. Although these earliest disciplines may give a vocabulary with which to approach the new, the language does not fit. The concepts have to be distorted to fit the new system, and the growing children do just that. In their attempts to understand their own growth in archaic terms, the children distort each new step. This is the first way in which they actively invent the meaning of events. Really, they *reinvent* them regressively and explain new events to themselves as though they were variations of old situations. So the explanations are inventions, although they are based on familiar principles, and children seriously distort things in this process. But this distortion tends to get split off, to be repressed and remain unmodified. It continues to exert itself, first because it is repressed and also because it came first and has the tenaciousness of early models.

This early thinking is close to body thinking—that is, to the bodily ways of organizing experience that precede thinking. These early explanations are shot through with the young child's experience of the body as immediate and unrefined by complex thought and verbalization.

Thus one little girl said to her mother, "My vagina is like an alligator." In this situation, her vulva and her discovery of it were read in the regressive terms of oral biting. She read a new awareness of her body as though it were a version of the old. This regressive inventiveness also applies to the child's distortion of the external world by the imposition of existing internal object relations onto new situations. Here the internal version of the world is used as an approximation in responding to new circumstances the child is meeting. This use of internal world models carries with it a conservative factor in the understanding of new experience. The tendency to thus conserve meaning by understanding events in terms of previous experience is crucial to growth, but it also carries an inevitable tendency for distortion of the historical accuracy of new external events that will not, at times, be recognized as being fully different from prior experience.

Development Imposes New Ways of Seeing

Fourth and finally, development brings in new ways of seeing. As the child is able to see things with advancing cognition and the progress of development, he or she rereads old history and rewrites it in the process. The idea that splitting occurs along sexual lines in the oedipal phase is my major case in point. This is the opposite point of the one described above where things are understood in the light of old ways of thinking. Here, old events are rewritten in the light of the child's new understanding. Old events are reinvented. This helps to justify Melanie Klein's (1932, 1945, 1961) controversial claims from her analyses of 2½- and 3-year-olds that the oedipal situation had been active during the first year of life, when the parents' relationship had been fantasized by the child as consisting of unendingly gratifying oral intercourse. Her theory was based on what she saw through the eyes of the relatively advanced 3-year-old, who, in my view, was already reporting rewritten history. Understanding of triangular situations from earlier ages revealed in Klein's 3-year-old analysands' play had been infused with sexuality in the same way that the 3-year-olds themselves had newly become sexualized. Recent contributions have described the sexualization of development during the phallic and genital phases at 2½ to 3 years of age, which brings children to see things in sexual terms that previously they have not (Edgcumbe and Burgner 1975).

Klein's description of the oedipal situation occurring at the age of 1 year was inaccurate because it was distorted by its reprocessing by the 3-year-olds she heard it from. Children do understand triangular situations as soon as 8 months of age (Abelin 1971, 1975). But they do not read triangular relationships in specifically sexual terms until the developmental sexualization of the phallic period.

Fairbairn notes that "the child really constitutes the Oedipus situation for himself" (1944, p. 124). Children make up or invent the oedipal situation by the use of splitting to deal with their newly sexualized interest in the triangular situation with the parents. This occurs when they have sexualized not only the relationships with their parents, but all relationships, because of an internal developmental push.

The oedipal situation then can be defined, first, as the genital sexualization of triangular relationships, and second, as the attempt to solve the conflicts involved through splitting good and bad, exciting and rejecting qualities between the parental objects.

Thus, as noted earlier, for the boy, the father becomes the bad, threatening object and the mother becomes the good and exciting object. There is also the minor theme of the negative Oedipus situation in which the father is the good and exciting object, and the mother the bad and rejecting object for the boy. For some children, depending on many factors including family influence, this becomes the dominant and conscious pattern, resulting in various forms of homosexuality or perversion.

These four principles of the child's reinvention of the family together contribute to one final way in which a child distorts its image of others and then influences the family on the basis of these distortions. It is a tenet of object relations theory, and of all psychodynamic models, that previous experience teaches the child to look at life in the light of that experience. The child develops internal models that operate through the structure of internal object relations themselves. As these structures are elaborated within the child, they exert an independent influence on the reading of external reality. In psychoanalysis, this principle is the basis of transference. The pervasive influence of internal life on the external world is so well known that I do not dwell on it further except where it adds to other points concerning the way in which child and family influence each other.

THE INTERNAL COUPLE

Within this situation, an important role is also played by the child's internalization of the couple's relationship itself. Children take in not only images of the individual parents, of mother and father, but of mother and father together in a relationship, both in its nonsexual and sexual aspects. It is at the oedipal period that interest becomes most heightened in this area and most sexualized. Various images are taken in of a loving couple and of a fighting or spoiling couple, and, in each case, of the infant in relationship to the couple.

All that is described to this point is from the child's point of view. In *Object Relations Family Therapy* (1987), Jill Scharff and I also described the equal and prior contribution of the couple to the growth of the family. The father and mother, and the two of them together as a couple, have fantasies that invent the child they would want, the child they fear, and the family that will ensue. These might be called their internal child and their internal family. The actual pregnancy and the child who is born modify these fantasies of their internal child and family through the interaction each of the parents has with the actual child. For instance, the child who is more or less active temperamentally, more or less responsive, who is a positive or negative reactor to new stimuli, presents different challenges and persuasions to the developing family and to each of the parents. The child who is a boy when they had expected a girl challenges assumptions about omnipotence in getting what is wanted and about the values of the two sexes.

In turn, the child is interested in the parental couple very early, at least from 8 months of age. In fact, it is the couple's relationship itself that constitutes the chief rival to the child's having a competitively more intense relationship with only mother or father.

OEDIPUS' FAMILY

All of this makes for an extremely complicated situation. To extend my thinking, I use Sophocles' play, *Oedipus Rex*, and the two other plays that form his Oedipus Cycle, as the chief illustration. I then follow with a clinical illustration.

When I first studied *Oedipus Rex* in high school, I learned that it was understood by the Greeks to be about man's

confrontation with his fate. Man must accept what has happened as being intrinsic to him despite the contradictory belief
in the influence of fate and predestination. This is underscored
by the role of Teiresias, who, because of his special relationship
with the gods, knows the truth without being told.

As an adolescent, I was uncomfortable with the idea of
tragedy as an acceptance of fate and predestination. As an
adult, I have come to think of the abiding influence of the
internal family as the modern equivalent of predestination. In
this interpretation, *Oedipus Rex* becomes an allegory of family
process. A more recent book is *What's Bred in the Bone*, by
Robertson Davies (1985); the completed phrase used in the title
is "What's bred in the bone will out in the flesh." The book is
a marvelous fictional case illustration of the way early experience is expressed throughout an ensuing life, reading in part
like a "whodunnit" and in part like a literary case history.

Despite being modified by each subsequent step, early
experience with primary objects—the parents—is most of what
is "bred in the bone." Even though much of that early experience is not consciously known, it continues to determine
personality and personal development.

As far as I know, Fairbairn (1954) was the first analyst to
point out clearly that Oedipus' story is mainly one of the
consequences of preoedipal development.

It is a remarkable fact that psychoanalytical interest in the
classical story of Oedipus should have been concentrated so prepon-
derantly upon the final stages of the drama, and that the earliest stage
should have been so largely ignored; for it seems to me a fundamental
principle of psychological, no less than of literary, interpretation that
a drama should be considered as a unity deriving its significance as
much from the first act as from the last. In the light of this principle,
it becomes important to recognize that the same Oedipus who
eventually killed his father and married his mother began life by
being exposed upon a mountain, and thus being deprived of maternal
care in all its aspects at a stage at which his mother constituted his
exclusive object. [p. 116]

I turn now to the play *Oedipus Rex*. In it, we find that Laïos fears the prediction that his son will kill him.[1] It is Iocastê who says,

> An oracle was reported to Laïos once . . .
> That his doom would be death at the hands
>   of his own son—
> His son, born of his flesh and of mine!
>
> (*Oedipus Rex*, p. 36)

To prevent this, he sent the infant to die.

> . . . his child had not been three days in
>   this world . . .
> Before the King had pierced the baby's
>   ankles.
> And had him left to die on a lonely
>   mountain.
>
> (p. 37)

When Iocastê tells Oedipus this, he responds,

> How strange a shadowy memory crossed
>   my mind.
> Just now while you were speaking; it
>   chilled my heart.
>
> (p. 37)

The first point is that Oedipus was rejected by his parents in a profound and thorough way. He was sent to die with his ankles pierced and bound. Infanticide was apparently fairly

---

[1]The usual spelling of these names is Laïus and Jocasta. However, I follow the spelling used in the Fitts and Fitzgerald (1956) translation of Sophocles' *Oedipus Cycle* from which I have drawn, that is, "Laïos" and "Iocastê."

common in ancient Greece, as it has been in some underdeveloped countries even recently. Perhaps this act was culturally sanctioned. Even so, it is the parents who are the conveyors of the culture. It was the parents themselves who took the decision and who committed the act, but there is no indication that they suffered remorse for their act, which seems to have deprived them of their only child.

When we turn to the rejected Oedipus himself, we can recall that early rejection leads to severe alteration of personality. In Oedipus' "strange shadowy memory," which crosses his heart as Iocastê tells him the story, I hear an allusion to the vague stirring to consciousness of unconscious recognition that frequently accompanies patients' emerging early memories in psychoanalysis.

In this modern reading, the play *Oedipus Rex* tells of a baby subjected to abuse by having his ankles pierced and bound, sent away to die, saved through the intercession of two pitying shepherds who fill the role of foster care workers, and eventually adopted wordlessly by Polybos and Meropê, the "good parents." Supposedly, Oedipus knows nothing of this. But modern family theory and psychoanalytic experience have taught that early events are carried unconsciously, even while not being consciously known. Further, psychoanalytic exploration and family therapy often demonstrate the effects on the individual and family of what is carried in the shared family unconscious as well as the unconscious of the individual members of that family.

Finally, it is almost inconceivable that a king and queen could adopt a child when the queen had been childless and presumably not pregnant without the whole populace being aware of the situation. When we consider this ordinary fact, Oedipus' lack of knowledge about his adoption and the failure of his adoptive parents to tell him the truth look more like shared denial of reality. There would have been talk, and Oedipus would surely have heard some of it. Might not this denial of reality have contributed to his anxiety, to his restless search for oracular truth about his origins and fate, just as modern adoptive children hope to find aspects of themselves in finding their biological parents?

With this in mind, let me propose a family and object relations-based understanding of the story of Oedipus.

Let us consider that the oracular prediction that his son would kill him represents the unconscious fear of Laïos. There is some supporting material for this hypothesis, for Iocastê says,

> An oracle was reported to Laïos once.

Then she adds the crucial disqualifier;

> *I will not say from Phoibus himself,*
> *But from his appointed ministers at any rate.*

(p. 36; My italics)

And then she gives the prophecy,

> That his doom would be death at the
>   hands of his own son.
> His son, of his flesh and of mine.

(p. 36)

Might we not consider this second-hand oracle to constitute Laïos' paranoid fantasy—a common one in fathers? This is to say, Oedipus' story actually begins with Laïos' fear of being bested and killed by his own son—revealed by an oracle. This apparently fit well enough with his own fantasy that he did not bother to check out the oracle firsthand, nor is there any note of his protest. I note further that Iocastê does not report trying to keep Laïos from acting. By her silence on this point, she seems to be a passive, compliant actor—like contemporary mothers whose silence facilitates child abuse and neglect. We would, in these days of family dynamics, see her as collusive in the rejection of her son. Else, where is the passion over her loss as the mother of their only son?

From this point, the action proceeds on two tracks in two distant families. The development of Oedipus occurs in a "good" family with his foster parents, Polybos and Meropê. He grows up "chief among the men of Corinth" (p. 40), but is disturbed when

> At a feast, a drunken man maundering in
>   his cups,
> Cries out that I am not my father's son!
>
> (p. 40)

With "anger and a sinking heart," the next day he questions his parents, who deny the rumor, calling it "the slanderous rant of a fool" (p. 40).

Oedipus says,

> This relieved me. Yet the suspicion,
> Remained always aching in my mind;
> I know there was talk. I could not rest;
> And finally, saying nothing to my
>   parents,
> I went to the shrine at Delphi.
>
> (p. 40)

The god dismissed Oedipus' question about his parentage, but predicted dire events.

> As that I should lie with my own
>   mother, breed
> Children from whom all men would turn
>   their eyes;
> And that I should be my father's
>   murderer.
>
> (p. 41)

To avoid these events, Oedipus flees and wanders far from Corinth. But in the following dramatic episode, seeming almost to occur the next day, he meets and kills Laïos, his bad, rejecting, and abusive biological father.

This encounter is also interesting from the point of view of Laïos' psychology—for the only provocation to Laïos is that Oedipus is physically present at the crossroads. Laïos attacks after forcing his unrecognized son off the road merely for being in the way. Symbolically, Oedipus is once again in Laïos' way, just as he was at his birth.

Laïos' personality is of interest. I have not seen any commentary on the fact that in the two brief descriptions we have of him, he appears as a brutal, self-centered, and raging despot. He would seem to fit modern criteria for a narcissistic personality, full of self-justifying fury. Oedipus is also quick to anger. After being struck, Oedipus immediately proceeds to kill Laïos and all but one of his party. And although this is so, the subsequent unraveling of the tale does not mention that it was actually the father who struck the son first.

What we appear to have is a narcissistic father who, from the time of the birth of his son, was fearful of him as a rival to his uncontested power over his kingdom and sexual exclusiveness with his wife. How often we see clinical situations in which a parent sees an unborn child as a rival for attention— and an embryonic sexual rival as well. These fantasized rivalries do not wait for the child to become developmentally sexualized at age 3. They often begin even before the child is born.

Like his father Laïos, Oedipus is a narcissistic character. He is self-centered, self-righteous, and full of narcissistic fury. Never does Iocastê protest this. His doom, his blindness, and his self-pronounced exile stem from his narcissistic righteousness, rage, and impulsivity. No one in the play can stop him in his narcissistic determination. He is his father's son, and to the brief family history the play gives us, we can add our modern understanding of the way in which infantile rejection promotes the formation of a narcissistic character, just as surely as does the experience of living with parents who are themselves narcissistically flawed. Oedipus turns his rage and self-righteousness on everyone near him, on his brother-in-law Creon, on Teiresias, on the citizenry embodied in the chorus of Theban elders. And finally he turns it on himself. We can also understand Iocastê projecting her own murderousness into her two husbands, even while being fully subservient and apparently worshipping them.

The fate that befalls this entire family can be understood as a contemporary psychological drama—firmly and poetically drawn. It is the drama of a narcissistic family. A father projects his own murderousness onto his son and attempts to exterminate the son as a threatening object and to get rid of the projected murderous part of himself, at the same time expressing it with disastrous consequences for his son. Whereas the father is active in rejecting the son and ordering his death, the mother accedes without protest. The son is rescued. Both the couple and the child live with the knowledge of the murderous rejection—the couple consciously and the child unconsciously. I am proposing that the child unconsciously understands the rejection by his biological parents, and because of the unexplained injury to his feet, he would grow up with at least a fantasy of parental harm, perhaps one he would imagine had been done by his adoptive parents, perhaps by his unknown biological parents.

Meanwhile, Laïos remains a difficult king—probably an arbitrary and angry tyrant. This may perhaps be represented by the plague that visits the country under the Sphinx's grip. As in the subsequent reign of Oedipus, a sick king rules a sick country. It occurs to me that there is an additional meaning to the Sphinx's riddle, "What walks on four legs in the morning, two at noon, and three at night?" It is a riddle specifically aimed at the problems in human development in Laïos' family and kingdom. Men are not free to grow and develop through the life cycle, to walk on four legs, then two, then three, under his despotic rule. The theme of development as the capacity to walk echoes with the sentence that Laïos added to Oedipus' death sentence. He ordered that the infant Oedipus be crippled so that he would not have been able to walk at all! This gratuitous added cruelty makes no particular sense on the surface, but it makes great sense as an unconscious act to stifle his development. It also points to the need for double measures to ensure against the possibility that he might survive the murder and return—like the return of the repressed bad object—to kill his father and possess his mother.

Oedipus does survive. He bests and kills his father. He can solve the riddle of development posed by the Sphinx because he has been saved by the split-off good parents. And he can walk. But his narcissistic core is ultimately no better suited for ruling than his father's. In his reign as well as in his father's, Thebes is "riddled" with the effects of unconscious and unacknowledged loss, deprivation, and abuse. The city reflects the consequences of Oedipus' inner object relations set and that of his family.

Oedipus Rex can be seen as a paradigm of the possibility of insight in psychotherapy. But the revelations of truth uncovered during the play serve better as painful parody of a misguided treatment. Increased understanding results in accelerating destructiveness, not in mercy or tolerance. The one candidate as a possible therapist is Teiresias, who has experienced much and knows much. Oedipus reviles and threatens him. Under threat, Teiresias, too, reverts to narcissistic rage. Oedipus has projectively identified with Teiresias, who becomes like him. This play and the entire cycle of plays that describe Oedipus' death in *Oedipus at Colonus* and the fate of his children and brother-in-law in *Antigone* represent the perpetuation of suffering and the transgenerational transmission of object relations. Through the next generation, a cycle continues of pervasive, familywide narcissism and rejection. In *Oedipus at Colonus*, Oedipus is led in his blind old age by his daughter, Antigone, whose own procreative adulthood is in turn sacrificed to her father. Although Oedipus is revered and sanctified, he continues to act in the same self-justifying and raging manner, threatening everyone who stands in his way. And in a final act of vengeance, he refuses to forgive one of his sons, who vies for the throne with the other.

This fatherly meanness of spirit affects the next scene of the drama. No sooner is Oedipus dead than the two brothers strike each other down. But even that is not the end of pathological grief in this most doomed of families. The action of the third play of the cycle, *Antigone*, is usually presented as the confrontation of the order of the state by the moral imperatives of the individual. For instance, *Antigone* was rewritten by the French playwright Jean Anouilh in 1942 to symbolize this kind of moral conflict in the Nazi era.

But there is another, more immediate reading in the vein we are mining. Antigone leaves her father upon his death and immediately seizes on the edict of her mother's brother, Creon, that her own brother must not be buried. In support of her protest, she commits suicide herself and is followed in death by her fiancé, who is Creon's son. Unable to mourn her unrelenting father, she in essence destroys herself to sanctify the son whom Oedipus had refused to bless. In so doing, she even rebels against Oedipus, dying as witness to her brother's right to the kind of sacrament that Oedipus had denied him. And she completes the cycle of destruction in the house of Laïos and Iocastê. In this light, the play *Antigone* becomes a psychological tragedy about the passing of the destructiveness of narcissistic character from one generation to another. Antigone, with her passionate heritage of self-destruction, cannot mourn her father and survive to have a life of her own with her own husband. Rather, she seizes on Creon's decree to justify her own self-destruction and takes her fiancé, Creon's son, with her in the process.

In *Oedipus Rex*, the oedipal situation results from family-wide action that begins before Oedipus' birth and continues throughout his life. Oedipus' "oedipal situation" itself is mostly determined by early trauma to him, determined by the parents' dynamics. Finally, in turn, the issues of Oedipus and Iocastê exert a similarly fatal influence on the thoroughly angry and tragic history of all three of their children.

THE WHEELER FAMILY

A clinical case vignette can further illustrate my contention that the whole family influences the oedipal constellation. This example comes from therapy with the Wheeler family, a case I used to illustrate the child's role in inventing the oedipal situation in a previous book (Scharff and Scharff 1987). The same case here allows us to explore the family's contribution to oedipal development and pathology. In the course of work over several years, I saw Max and Ginger Wheeler for marital and sex therapy and for individual psychodynamic psychotherapy. Later, I saw them with their daughter, Laura, in family therapy.

Mr. Wheeler

Mr. Wheeler had been adopted, and his adoptive father was reported to have died in sexually suggestive circumstances when the boy was 5. He was idolized by his overbearing mother, who remarried when he was a teenager. His feeling about both of his mother's marriages was that she had ruled and mistreated her husbands. Now married himself, Max experienced anxiety in his marital relationship. He suffered from premature ejaculation and had engaged in numerous affairs.

Mrs. Wheeler

Ginger Wheeler had two symptoms. She was completely uninterested in sex, and she was fearful that her 3-year-old daughter Laura would replace her in her husband's affections. Ginger had a picture of her parents common to many hysterics. She felt that her father preferred her and did not love her mother, whom she had been allowed to denigrate and partly replace. She was shocked—and eventually relieved—to find that her par-

ents' relationship was actually a good deal better than she
had believed.

The Couple

Max and Ginger met in an affair while Max was
married. After their marriage, when Ginger was pregnant,
Max unconsciously expected that he would be excluded by
the mother–child pair. When Laura was born, Ginger
feared that Max and Laura would exclude her, as she and
her father had excluded her mother. Ginger experienced
her fear consciously at the level of worrying that Laura
would push her out of the way. She contributed to her
fear by not maintaining her sexual relationship with Max.
Max did not experience his fear, but created compensatory
pairings for himself in the form of affairs.

The fear of relationship that this couple brought to
their marriage was considerable. Max used splintering and
splitting of relationships to avoid domination. He longed
for and feared dependent relationships. He used oedipal
splitting to keep the bad object at bay. Ginger also used
splitting and repression of the bad object, projecting its
rejecting aspects into her genitals where it was repressed,
substituting a bodily state—the absence of sexual desire—
for a problem in relationship (Fairbairn 1954). She projected the exciting aspect of the object into her daughter
where it was feared. The anxieties that Max and Ginger
shared were also felt between them in the loss of a
cooperative relationship around the issues of parenting
Laura.

Laura

I saw Laura when she was 4. She had reacted to the
threats held in oedipal triangular issues by regressing to
her earlier concerns about the relationship with her

mother. She and her mother had great difficulty separating from each other. When I asked her to draw a family,
Laura drew an "empty picture" (Figure 11-1), saying that
a dog and cat might live in the picture, but they might
fight if they were together. She was unable to locate
people in her stories or pictures. Her picture of a family
was therefore empty. Oedipal development could not
proceed because of her fear of the pair, seen as orally
aggressive, not as genitally sexual. Her parents' early fears
for their own relationship could be seen to have borne
painful fruit in her development. She, too, feared sexual
relatedness at her own developmental stage.

I next saw Laura two years later when she was 6. She
greeted me warmly and without fear. Her parents were
much better now, after individual, couple, and sex therapy, which had brought them together and given them a
normal sexual relationship. When Laura touched my hand
to show how warm it was from the clay she was playing
with, she immediately looked to the door and asked if
anyone could come in — a clear reference to fearing her
mother might intrude on our oedipal scene. In drawing a
picture of her family (Figure 11-2), she began with sky and
ground as if drawing a frame around the emptiness of the
picture she had drawn two years earlier. But this picture
she then filled in with oedipal themes. A line of smoke
connected a phallic house to a sky, which at first was
drawn in the shape of two ample breasts and was then
filled in. There was a family of three birds on one side of
the house and of four octopuses on the other. A sister had
been born in the interval and Laura was playing, or
struggling, with her place in the family. The parents'
progress had paralleled Laura's own growth in their
tolerance of warmth, intimacy, and sexuality. I thought
the spur to Laura's improvement had come not only from
her two years of maturation, but also from the growth in
each of her parents and in their relationship. But Laura
was still phobic and fearful of abandonment.

Figure 11–1.   Laura's picture drawn at age 4

When I convened a family meeting, many of these issues could be seen, although the family related in a generally warm way throughout the session. The 2-year-old sister was a focus of shared good feeling. Laura was

Figure 11-2. Laura's first family picture, drawn in an individual session at age 6

able to please both her mother and father through her concern about and caretaking of her little sister. The birth of the sister had been a spur to improved relationships throughout the family and had been part of the support to an improved oedipal constellation. I thought the overall family pattern was beneficially influencing Laura's development.

I asked each family member to draw a picture of the family. Because the parents' pictures were highly idealized (Figures 11-3 and 11-4), I asked them to make a second drawing (Figures 11-5 and 11-6), while Laura finished the one she contributed (Figure 11-7). The baby sister's drawing, of course, consisted of a few scribbles (Figure 11-8)— just what one would expect of a 2-year-old.

Figure 11-3. Max Wheeler's first family picture

Mr. Wheeler's first drawing (Figure 11-3) depicted an exciting and sexualized view of his relationship to the family. It showed a narcissistic focus on himself as a sly seductive Indian looking out of the corner of his eyes at his three tepees, each said to have a squaw inside. In a second drawing (Figure 11-5), he drew the family house. In this version, Laura stared out into the night in fright while everyone else slept. It seemed a clear statement of the way that Laura, now the identified patient, had absorbed all of the family anxiety as if to let everyone else sleep.

Mrs. Wheeler's first picture (Figure 11-4) was an idealized, faceless drawing of a happy family on a vacation picnic. Her second picture (Figure 11-6) showed an embattled family breakfast and focused on the difficulty between her and Laura. Father and baby sister flanked Laura and Mother, who were frowning at each other. Mrs.

Figure 11-4. Ginger Wheeler's first family picture

Wheeler's two pictures of family meals illustrated her use of food to organize the splitting between an image of an idyllic family situation in her first picture and a rejecting situation in the second picture. We see below that this idiom joined Laura and her mother in another drawing they constructed together (Figure 11-9).

As mentioned, Laura's original picture from this period showed a phallic house connected to a buxom sky (Figure 11-2). In this session she drew another family picture (Figure 11-7), which demonstrated a sexualized and phallic appeal to both parents. She drew herself with one arm distorted to look like a penis. She was positioned between her parents, and they were far apart. She said that they were sitting around a swimming pool, but, to

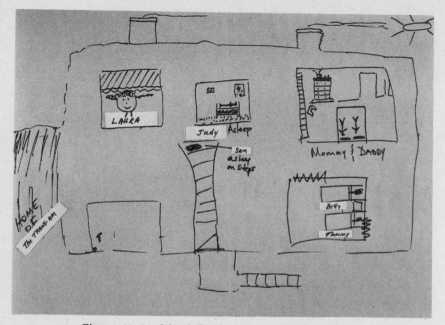

Figure 11–5.   Max Wheeler's second family picture

me, the pool also resembled a bed. The picture balanced Laura's interest in the parents as a couple, neither of whom she wanted to offend, with her individual sexualized relationship to each parent. It seemed to me to be a clearly oedipal statement.

Finally, I asked the family to share in drawing a picture (Figure 11–9). In the process, Max supported Laura in trying to work out her relationship with her mother. This occurred now on the basis of a much improved relationship between husband and wife, and of improved internalized object relationships for each of them. But Ginger still had difficulty in relating to Laura.

Laura took the lead in drawing the picture (Figure 11–9). It was of the dog asking for a snack, an animal dramatization of Laura's own wishes for afterschool snacks. In the session, Laura tried to get her mother to

Figure 11-6.   Ginger Wheeler's second family picture

draw the dog an afternoon snack in the family kitchen. Mother responded that Laura knew she herself was supposed to have fruit and vegetables after school, not candy. She then overlooked Laura's attempt at conciliation when Laura drew a banana, the kind of fruit she would prefer to the carrot sticks and celery offered by Mother. Father had been filling in the kitchen background and not interfering, providing the tolerance and containment for the process.

Following the diagnostic family interview, Laura worked in therapy individually and in sessions with her mother on her fears of the bad "witch mother" and of abandonment, fears relating both to Laura's projecting aggression against her mother and to the internalization of

Figure 11–7. Laura's family picture, drawn during the family session

her mother's aggression relating to Laura. Most of the internal persecuting and abandoning object was projected onto her mother, but discussion revealed that her father could also be experienced as disappointing. Much of Laura's anxiety stemmed from the quite reasonable fear that the marital relationship would fail, depriving Laura of her parents as a pair.

Laura's frightening internal image of a couple was shown in a picture in which a bad witch and kidnapping monster were paired (Figure 11–10). Her oedipal constellation and the fears that expressed it derived both from her parents' projections into her and from her own developmental experience. Laura feared that she would be left entirely alone, as shown in a picture that portrayed the experience of fear at being left (Figure 11–11). This fear of abandonment was built on her earlier experience of hostile mothering and exciting, inconsistent fathering. Her fear

Figure 11–8.   Laura's sister's scribbles

also embodied the fears and fantasies her parents carried with them into their marriage—the fragile, threatened narcissistic wishes of her father, and the sexualized, threatened special status of her mother, who feared rejection as a vulnerable child and as a woman. Laura's symptoms gave expression to these projections from her parents and to her realistic fear for the safety of their marriage. These fears and projections had been there through all of Laura's early life, but as Laura reached the oedipal phase, she reorganized her understanding of these difficulties in genital and oedipal terms.

Laura, her mother, and her father all needed help with several levels of object-related issues at the oedipal level. They each

Figure 11-9. The Wheelers' family picture done together

split positive and negative elements of the maternal object along sexual lines. Each of them projected fear and rejection onto maternal objects and excitement onto fathers. They handled preoedipal fears of abandonment and inadequate attachment through an oedipal disguise and a search for an exciting father. All three shared a concern about the adequacy of the self when deprived of the parental pair, which each of them understood to be a result of the attacks they had made as children on their parents as a pair.

Early in Laura's growth, these fears had delayed oedipal development. Later, the fears organized for her a way of understanding family experience and the harm Laura feared her new sexual interest would do to her parents in destroying them as a couple. Each of her parents had gone through a similar process many years earlier.

Figure 11–10. Laura's "witch-mother and monster"

Figure 11–11. Laura's picture of fear and abandonment

Finally, we can see that just as the couple's fantasies determined their treatment of Laura, so her growth and her personality influenced their experience and the experience of the whole family. Just as in *Oedipus Rex*, the oedipal situation was a shared family matter.

The oedipal situation, in the plays of Sophocles, in life, and in therapy is a family affair—with complex determinants from before the birth of the child, from the child, from the parents, from the previous generations, and even from the culture itself. It constitutes the combined attempt of child and family, as with Oedipus and his family, to correct and modify problems in earlier development and in earlier relationships. The family influences the child, who in turn influences the family before, during, and after the oedipal period. Family and child influence each other in a never-ending cycle.

12

Role Relationships of Children and Adults in the Family

Like children, adults also need the family as an institution, even though many adults survive without literally living in a family household. I do not consider here the situation of the adult who is single by choice or default. I focus in this chapter on the majority who choose to live in family situations and then find that they are in as much need of that family as the children they are raising.

The family is a crucial setting for both the child and

the adult. Both of them build their internal organization from a combination of experiences drawn from the family they live in and from their internal family. Adults and children are alike in needing relationships and family, but their functions within the family and the manifestations of their needs are fundamentally different. This is so obvious it hardly needs stating. Yet it has not been focused upon sufficiently. An exploration of the differences between the child and the adult in relation to the family highlights features of the reciprocal relationship between children and adults and enhances our understanding of the formation of psychic structure throughout the life cycle.

In this exploration, my first principle is the paradox of unequal influence in a relationship of reciprocity.

First, the mother-infant relationship: The mother and baby are in an equal relationship—centered on each other, speaking to each other, looking at and into each other, and holding each other. If the relationship is not mutual in these regards, it misfires. When either partner has vulnerabilities and areas of deficient functioning, as seen, for instance, if the baby or mother is blind, they can both work to use and build compensatory pathways to get over this handicap. They work to achieve a broadly based fit between themselves. Over the period of early interaction, they find areas of mutual interest, learn how best to cue and respond, to enjoy, and to find each other's limits.

But in another way, they are not equals. It is the mother or other primary caretaker's responsibility to lead in many ways. The baby is formed or "pre-wired" to be able to interact in these ways. Constitutional givens of temperament, rhythm, receptiveness, and responsiveness notwithstanding, there is still a quality of being an open vessel waiting to be filled and characterized by the interaction with the mother. The specific content of the baby is taken in from the mother and father, from the interactions with them and with the two of them together.

The mother (or father), in contrast, is already a psychologically structured person, waiting for experience with the baby to fill in a relatively small potential character space and to redefine her inner world. The baby does that, and the process modifies the mother's identity and her self. But it is a new version of her old self that is created, not the stuff of her whole self being built from scratch.

In the beginning, the baby is much more developed than has been thought until recently. Yet he or she is also an empty vessel that will amount to nothing without the mother or parents. The findings of the last twenty years of infant research have shown us that the baby reacts to his or her environment from the beginning in ways that fundamentally alter that environment, and yet that the baby is a vast receptacle for what is put inside it (Brazelton 1982, Brazelton et al. 1974, 1979, Lichtenberg 1983, Sameroff and Emde 1989, Stern 1985).

On the other side, parents are crucially influenced by having the child. With the first child, a woman becomes a mother and a man a father, and with subsequent children important and everlasting aspects of their identity are altered. The specifics of each child build something different into a mother. A kind of rhythm and responsiveness sets the pace for each relationship. She will be more jangled when a baby has a faster or more irritable temperament, and more lulled by a slower or more laconic baby. At one end of the spectrum, the mother will feel that a slow baby is unresponsive and rejecting, and at the other, she will feel the irritable or jerky baby to be demanding and unappreciative. The mother may feel despairing in the face of persistent crying by the baby, or overwhelmed with love and satisfaction as the baby feeds contentedly at the breast.

Responses by the baby lead to important new responses in the parents. Adults as parents accommodate to these influences in terms of their own well-established internal structure and the fantasies generated from it about their fetus. The baby may or may not be gratifying, but the *context* in which the parents experience their child is primarily that of their own preexisting *fantasy hopes and fears*. A mother, for instance, who wanted a girl and has a boy may find that her strongly alert, temperamentally active boy frightens her. She wonders if she can satisfy his imagined voraciousness. Or a father wants an exuberant boy to feed the embryonic fantasy that this boy will become the athlete the father fancied himself to have been. Another father may feel insanely jealous or put out by the baby's nighttime demands on his wife and preference for her and her breast. Biological and typological shifts in the adult are brought on by the infant's arrival and presentation of needs: hormonal shifts in the mother with accompanying emotionality, the breast as a source of food as well as pleasure sometimes accompanied by discomfort, the galvanizing effect of the infant's cry on the parent, and the accommodations required to preserve the sexual relationship during conception, birth, and the exhaustion of caring for a young child.

The parent interprets even the infant's basic, nonspecific responses in terms of the parent's own relatively elaborated specific fantasies. The baby's originally nonspecific response is shaped by the parents' interpretations of it, founded in their conscious and unconscious fantasies. The baby does or does not satisfy these and becomes thus the projection screen for hopes and dissatisfactions carried forward from previous generations. The baby is a new object of love that is accepted or rejected, a test of the mother's or father's capacities to be a parent, and at the same time in a resonating way, feels internally loved or not loved as a child by his or her own parents and by the developing internal objects. The parents' experience of the baby is, then, complex and multidimensional.

In the early phase of interaction between parent and infant, the infant's general responses can modify these relatively specific fantasies in the adult. As the baby is alert and responsive, or sleepy and dull, or irritable and demanding, smiling and satisfied, the first fantasies are modulated, replaced by an internalization of the child's actual beginning personality. Increasing communication between child and parents modifies the parents' first unopposed fantasies.

The earliest phases of finding a self in the presence of the mother have been described by Stern (1985) as the slow, steady emergence of a self, and by Ogden (1989) as the use of the mother's presence and accompanying shapes in the inanimate world as a form against which the infant molds its self. Klein (1975a,b) and Fairbairn (1952) noted how the anxiety the infant faces spurs the development of techniques for handling it. These techniques (described in Chapter 3) can be summarized as mental mechanisms that consist of introjecting the experience with mother and splitting off satisfying relationships from frustrating ones. The mother gets it right or she does not, and the baby to some extent can make it right or fail to do so. The baby gives the mother many chances, molds to what she can manage, uses her most effective channels of communication to compensate for her weak suits, and transforms what she offers. The baby, given a mother who is "good enough" at her job, will transform a good enough job into one that is wonderful enough of the time to feel satisfied and loved, and to develop the crucial capacity to tolerate frustration because of the knowledge that satisfaction will return (Winnicott 1960b).

There is, then, similarity and difference between the adult and the baby. For the adult, the baby offers the material for a new and importantly *modifying* internal experience. But for the baby, although it brings its own preformed ego to the situation ready for intricate interaction, it requires experience with adults to provide the stuff of *whole new* psychological internal structures.

To be more specific about the nature of some of the interactions between children and parents, let us look at what is going on between child and adult in three infant–mother experiments.

PARTNERS-OF-THE-MOMENT

In the first of the three interactions between child and adult, the split-screen conversation (Tronick et al. 1978), the mother and infant engage in a "conversation." Normally cameras show

us how the baby initiates conversation and the mother recip-
rocates. When this goes well, we note an exquisitely attuned
interaction. It uses many channels of signaling: eyes, voice,
muscular posturing, and position sense. Skin touch and perhaps temperature also play a role in conveying care and
comfort to the baby. Some babies begin with a narrow array of
cueing mechanisms that subsequently broaden to include a
larger array later on. In these interactions, the baby sets the
pace. The average interval of signal and response lasts about
seven seconds, after which the baby averts its gaze while the
attuned mother lets this happen without anxiety and then
responds when the baby is ready for the interaction to begin
again.

When the researcher asks the mother to hold still for three
minutes, maintaining an impassive facial expression, the baby
responds in a way that reminds us of adult clinical depression.
Watching such interactions in the lab or on videotape makes
most observers feel violated and depressed. A well-put-
together baby will keep trying to induce a response in the
mother, but will eventually look away dejectedly. In the home
situation, a well-put-together mother cannot resist her baby's
efforts so long as she is not preoccupied or otherwise upset.
The dramatic effect on the baby of a three-minute episode of
maternal impassivity in the laboratory illustrates the devas-
tating effect of the prolonged nonresponsiveness of a depressed mother at home. The researcher also filmed a mother
who was unresponsive to her baby because of her pervasive
depression. The baby subsequently developed poorly despite
attempts at intervention. When it is the baby who fails to
respond in an appropriately lively manner in interactions at
home or in the laboratory, mothers will typically report feeling
devastated by the baby's lack of responsiveness.

The influence is mutual. The major differentiating feature
is the mother's expectation and capacity for verbal character-
ization of the meaning of the infant's communication. She can
also anticipate and carry over the memory of a satisfying infant
when she is feeling oppressed or rejected. If she has a willing

partner in the business of child rearing, she can turn to the partner for reinforcement, for emotional and physical relief.

The adult has already formed an internal world full of internal objects, fantasies of relationships, hopes, and fears, and the capacity to delay, to remember, and to share through other relationships, especially with a husband, a mother of her own, or another child. The mature adult in this respect is quite different from her child.

So the experiment of recording the interchange between mother and baby reveals the relative equality between the two, but it also shows the fundamental difference between them. Both adult and child contribute a response that comes from everything they have inside. They are equal in what we could call being "emotional partners-of-the-moment." But for the infant the contribution is largely biological and stereotypic— preformed physiologically and even temperamentally, but un- formed in terms of content. The content—including the meaning that will accrue over time for the parent–infant pair— is largely formed by the internal history of the adult. In sum, whereas the infant influences the adult strongly, the adult internalizes the experience in terms of the adult's pre-existing internal world. The adult then relates to the child from this expanding but stable base and provides the stuff of the infant's evolving internal world, which the infant sorts into primitive categories of experience that form the object upon which the psychic structure of the self is built.

THE CHILD AS AN INCOMPLETE ENTITY

In the experimental "Strange Situation" designed by Mary Ainsworth and her colleagues (Ainsworth and Wittig 1969, Ainsworth et al. 1978) to test the security of attachment, the child relates to a strange environment and to a strange person in the presence and absence of the mother. The securely attached 12-month-old will be more likely to approach the stranger if the mother is there. This capacity may transfer to a comfort with the stranger even in the mother's absence. When the infant has an insecure or anxious attachment, the child will be too anxious to leave the mother to approach the stranger. But at the poorest level of attachment, which Bowlby (1969) calls *detachment*, the child pays little attention to its own mother and heads for the stranger, somewhat promiscuously looking for something better and perhaps more secure. Then, in the most crucial phase, the child shows in the reunion with the mother whether the brief separation has been a strain, either by clinging to the mother or, if the pair is less securely attached, by turning away from her.

This experimental situation demonstrates how the well-put-together child is still an incomplete entity. The child who ventures out on his or her own prematurely has solidified an incompleteness, whereas the appropriately developing child carries a capacity to be more complete when with its parent. Capabilities will be augmented through an open template with the parent, and the parent, in this unequal partnership, donates capacities of judgment, of binding anxiety, and of attachment.

THE PARENT AS THE LEADER

The visual cliff experiment was developed by Emde and his colleagues to demonstrate the phenomenon of social referencing (Campos and Stenberg 1980, Emde and Sorce 1983, Emde et al. 1978, Klinnert et al. 1983). The situation is one of visual ambiguity during which the infant references or checks with the mother to decide what action and emotion are appropriate to the situation. The experimenter places the junior toddler at one end of a glass platform facing mother who is at the opposite end. Underneath the glass, the ground appears to drop sharply away, although the path to the mother actually lies safely across the solid plate glass platform. In this experimental situation, children can be seen looking at their mothers, signaling intense anxiety about the path. If the mother encourages a child to come to her across the platform, smiling and confident, the baby proceeds slowly and cautiously. The baby traverses the glass toward the mother, perhaps going feet first and scooting, feeling its way. But if the mother looks horrified when the child checks with her, if she signals concern and danger, the baby bursts into tears and retreats, not daring to cross the threatening visual cliff.

This experimental situation adds to our view of the baby as incomplete without the parent. But note that the baby lets the parent know what it needs! The baby signals not only the need for a specific cue, but the need for leadership. This experimental situation underscores the effect that the mother has on the direction the child will take. The child and mother are seen to negotiate, however, on what the child can manage.

These exchanges between toddlers and mothers underscore the more mature reading of the surrounding world that mother and child both assign to the adult role. Onto the substrate of essentially equal person-to-person initial interactions is grafted the notion of leadership in encounters with the surrounding world. Both the child and the ordinary parent take these for granted.

CHILDREN AND ADULTS: SIMILARITIES AND DIFFERENCES

Following is a summary of some of the principal similarities and differences of children and adults in the context of the family and in the treatment setting when families are seen together.

The Main Similarities

1. Both adults and children need others to form mutually centered and holding relationships. Both need affective

partnerships-of-the-moment—when they are together and share the experience of being seen *into* and being seen *by* the other. These are the times when they are each other's objects, and in being so, help each other to define their selves.

2. Both children and adults need two aspects of primary relationships: the context within which to find themselves and the centered relationship with the object.

3. Adults and children need families for attachment. They need support from others, and they need a family to give them internal working models or images of the relationships and roles in the family (Bowlby 1969).

4. Children and adults both have the capacity to donate their own understanding to the family experience, both in everyday life and in a therapeutic setting. The perspective of each family member, young and old, is needed in a daily way to inform the rest of the family. Even infants have full responsibility to let others know about their situation.

5. Children and adults both have continuous needs to move toward growth in their capacity for sublimating and transforming internal needs.

This foundation of the broadly human similarities frames our examination of the differences that are based on developmental needs and roles determined by different maturational levels.

The Main Differences

1. There are obvious differences between adult and child in maturity and ability to understand cognitively. With these discrepancies come differing levels of responsibility for the relationship.

2. Ordinarily, in a given family, children remain more dependent than their parents well into the adulthood

of the children. Through life this early direction tends to become a permanent, expected psychological feature that exercises continuing influence, often until the aging of the parents finally reverses the trend late in the life of the family.

3. Adults should have a secure reliance on their internal objects, instead of the reliance on external objects that is characteristic of children (Bowlby 1988). Children remain more dependent on their actual objects than adults well into adolescence. Even then, children are dependent on peers as a bridge toward later, more active dependence on inner objects. Unlike children, adults can live alone without a daily need for a family of external objects. Parents who have previously lived alone are likely to have confidence in relying on their internal objects.

4. The predominance of responsibility rests with the parent. The adult shoulders responsibility *for* others, whereas the growing child is held to have responsibility *to* others.

5. The adult is concerned with the complexity of relationships in the family, whereas the normally self-centered child responds to the urgency of simple internal needs and external stimuli.

The complexity of the family is more comprehensible for the adult than for the child. From the child's perspective, as from the adult's, there are several important relationships, admittedly, but for the child under age 3, each aspect is thought of as though it does not have any particular implication for the others. The child's capacity to think is less developed because the cognitive apparatus is immature and because many developmental events have not yet occurred.

The child and the adult differ in their experience of triangular relationships. As we noted in Chapter 11, before the age of 7–8 months, triangular relationships are probably not understood by the child. Children from the age of 7 or 8 months exhibit interest in the parents' relationship and in other sets of relationships, like those between siblings and its parents (Abelin 1971). But it is not until shortly before age 3 that these take center stage. When this happens, the triangle is newly understood in sexual terms, an imposed core of oedipal rivalry, and the source of conflict over love and hate, sexuality and dependency.

In contrast, the adult in the family is constantly concerned with the effect one relationship has on others. The father who is jealous of the child's ownership of his wife nevertheless wants the child to have her full devotion. The mother who is absorbed with her infant keeps her husband's needs in mind nevertheless. The adult in the triangle considers the implications of each relationship for the family as a whole group, not in terms of their sexual implications alone, but in more comprehensive, varied, and flexible ways.

THE CHILD AS CONTAINER INSTEAD OF CONTAINED

This background of shared human similarities and of developmental differences normally found between children and adults in families prepares us for an examination of the way the resulting role relationships function in treatment settings.

1. In treatment, children and adults show differences in developmental levels in all the areas discussed above and in the use of objects. In terms of psychosexual development, they are also different in the relative channeling of expressions of sex and aggression.
2. Therapists expect different language and conceptual levels as well as different modes of communication. For example, adults ordinarily communicate best verbally, whereas children communicate better through play.

3. In family treatment or when a family brings a child for individual therapy, we expect a family's adults to take the lead in arranging the therapy, formulating the reasons for therapy, and setting the goals. But we do not expect them to take the lead in expression of individual points of view. That is to say, the child and each member of a family must still speak for himself or herself. In disturbed families, maturational differences are not sufficiently pronounced and require correcting. One goal of treatment, whether in the family or individual setting, is the restoration of an appropriate difference in levels of maturation and responsibility.

In the family, child and adult are alike in being able to share observations both from inside the self and from their roles in the family interaction. They have similar needs for intimate contact and contained support from each other.

The discrepancy in maturational level and corresponding responsibility diminishes over time as the child grows. Nevertheless, the adult is the senior partner so long as the child is still a child, and usually well into the period in which both are fully functioning adults. In troubled families, we often see a breakdown in this arrangement. In the family literature, this is referred to as the family with a *parentified child* (Whitaker and Keith 1981). This reversal of roles in violation of the natural differences in maturation has not been extensively discussed in the psychodynamic or child therapy fields, although it is frequently mentioned clinically. Bion's (1967) discussion of the container and the contained gives us a language that allows us to think about the internal ramifications of this kind of reversal for the developing self. It is the parents' role to be the container of anxieties in the family. Family and individual pathology occurs when children are called on to be containers instead of being allowed to be contained (Muir 1989). Ordinarily, the growth of the capacity to provide holding to oneself is fostered by the parental model. The reversal of this pattern in children who understand that they must take over this area for the psychological survival of their parents, and therefore of the family, leaves a residue of premature development, resentment, and anxiety.

Summary

Adults come to family interaction with well-formed identities, even though their identity as parent is modified dramatically in interaction with their children and spouses. But children take on their identities almost wholly in the interaction with their mothers and fathers. It is not merely an image of the object—of mother, father, sibling, and so on—that is introjected, but of the interaction itself—of the relationship—that is internalized. Children's subjective experiences of themselves in relationships become the building blocks for psychological structure and identity.

Even when the child develops an identity that is a bulwark against parental influence, the building blocks of psychic structure are provided by experience with the parents. The struggle against the parent or parents gives an aggressive tone to internal objects derived from it. In every case, there is an element of struggle to identify with and against the parent. The resolution determines the nature of the internal object and self. It follows from our earlier discussion of the inextricable relationship between self and object that the choice of a new external object is an aspect of identification. The significant other person is a good or poor recipient of the projections and trial projective identifications that are the stuff of every intimate relationship.

When the child first moves out of the family to relate to peers and teachers, these identifications have a broad, sweeping quality. In adolescence, they become more closely refined and specific. When we see children in analysis, we have an opportunity to trace the way in which growing children's search for and choice of partners expresses their internal object sets. In male homosexual object choice, for instance, the child rejects some aspects of his mother as a partner but incorporates others that are often organized as a strong unconscious identification, usually with a bias against heterosexual relating. He turns against a critical. or overwhelming maternal internal object by which he feels constantly overwhelmed, but he is nevertheless strongly identified with it at the same time. Further development in adolescence may modify or cement this dynamic, leading to confirmation of a heterosexual or homosexual object choice and identity.

Although the parents identify with their children at the same time that the children identify with those parents, the parents' already existing identifications have more staying power, and the child grows in the context of these, modifying them less thoroughly than being modified by them.

THE SIMPSON FAMILY

Aspects of the Simpson family's therapy were reported in a previous volume (Scharff and Scharff 1991). The parents sought help initially because of sexual difficulty: Mrs. Simpson because she "hated sex" and Mr. Simpson for premature ejaculation. As part of their consultation they readily agreed to a family evaluation that I suggested to explore their difficulty with their middle child, a 5-year-old boy, Alex, who soiled, wet, and was broadly immature. In that evaluation, I noticed that the 3½-year-old girl, Jeanette, was also immature and overexcited, perhaps oversexualized or seductive. The older boy, Eric, seemed to be fine, solidly into latency development.

However, in reevaluation a year later, I noted in Eric internalization of aggressive objects with which he had identified. He used a Superman action figure to attack Jeanette's helpless baby dolls and proclaimed that Superman had become an evil force. I had not seen this in Eric earlier. I could not understand this on the basis of one interview, and I became concerned for the children, who I had hoped would benefit from their parents' improved relationship. The parents were in better shape since the previous year. A year's intensive psychotherapy with a colleague had allowed Mrs. Simpson to flourish; she was less frequently depressed, although she still had severe regressions, two of which were to bring brief hospitalizations in the next few months. But Mrs. Simpson had taken and maintained a part-time job. The most dramatic change was that she was now interested in sex, and the couple was no longer fighting over that aspect of their relationship. Because of Mr. Simpson's premature ejaculation and Mrs. Simpson's inability to even approach orgasm, they still required specific sex therapy, but for now we agreed that the first priority was family work.

The session I report here came after approximately eight months of weekly family work. We had not been able to meet the previous week, but in the session two weeks earlier, I had investigated the central role of the mother's depression in the family and had been able to understand with them the role of each of the other family members in relation to it.

Today, two weeks after that session, they came in, the children leading eagerly as usual. Eric began by showing me pictures of transformer robots he had drawn. These were called Demolishicons, the most powerful of which was Demolishicor. He then began to build with the collection of colored blocks that all three children liked to use and for which they often vied. Alex began to draw. Father suggested he draw Donald Duck. When Alex said he could not, Father said, "He can *be* Donald Duck, but he can't draw it."

Jeanette was eating candy from a packet, and Alex drew a Mickey Mouse face. They were all whispering. I asked about the candy and the whispering. Was there a secret? They said there was no secret. They had arrived a half hour early and Mother bought candy because her mouth was dry from the antidepressant medication. The discussion of her medication brought into the room memories of her hospitalization and the panic that led to it. As she talked, Alex handed her the picture he had been drawing of Monstro the whale, which Alex said had swallowed Geppetto, Pinocchio's puppet-maker father. Jeanette handed her mother a picture, which she said were the primary colors. She named them for me.

So far I felt that the activity in the room was avoidant, although not unusually so for the opening part of a session after a previous emotional one and a missed session.

Eric was now constructing a small building, which he said was a museum. It was the same sort of structure he had built the last time, and he told me the same sort of thing was going on there: "Nothing!" Eric wanted more cars and blocks to complete his design. Father and Alex tried to help him think how he might do so with what was available and without taking something from Alex.

Mother said, "Eric, if you can't have it the way you want, it would be nice to try to have it another way." Eric rejected her advice and began to pout noticeably.

The museum was loaded with toy soldiers with rifles, and all the guns were pointed straight at me. Laughingly I said, "You say there's nothing going on there, but I see all those guns and I see where they are aimed!" The family laughed, too. "Why am I the enemy? What awful thing am I about to do?" I asked.

Eric now took an action figure of the Incredible Hulk, a great, green, unfriendly figure, and waved it menacingly at me. It was coming to fight. I thought silently about the way the Hulk figure had previously provided an analogy for anger in the family. In a recent session we had talked about the way Mother felt that she was an uncontrollable Hulk who wreaked damage on the family when she meant to work for the good.

As I was searching among the toys for a figure with

which to engage the Hulk in dialogue, Mrs. Simpson handed me a baby doll, saying, "Babies have been known to be vicious."

I felt Mrs. Simpson's offer indicated her identification with the way Eric was treating me and projective identification with Eric's angry transference to me. So I handed the doll back to her so that the origins of this transference could be examined in the family and said, "Maybe the baby can find out what I've done wrong."

She obligingly took the baby and through it said to the Hulk, "Okay, Hulk, what have I done?"

Eric said for the Hulk, "I'm mad because you won't let me rule."

Mother said, "You can't always have your way, and pinching won't help." The doll and the Hulk wrestled.

Alex, who was watching this interaction, came over to the play struggle to interject, "The baby lost her diaper and she's going to poop all over the floor." He stepped in to fight playfully with the Hulk himself.

Thinking of Alex's lifelong struggle with soiling, I said, "Alex said that when the Hulk attacked the baby, she would lose control of her poops. Is it hard for people to control their poops when they're fighting?"

Alex did not answer me. A minute later he stopped the fight, picked up a car, and knocked over the museum Eric had built.

Eric was furious and hurt. "Alex! Why did you have to do that?" he said. He dropped the Hulk and began to rebuild the museum.

I said, "When Alex got between the Hulk and the baby, he talked about people loosing control of their poops. But instead of losing control of his own poops like a baby this time, he destroyed the museum. Then Eric got mad. How does this relate to what usually happens in the family?"

Mother said, "Eric acts aggressive, but if you return it

in kind, he doesn't like it. He thinks what he does is fine, but if someone else does it to him, it's wrong."

Lightly touching Eric's shoulder for support because I felt this discussion would be hard for him, I said, "So you're saying, Mom, that Eric expects that he can play like the Hulk without objection. And he's surprised if someone else gets mad."

I felt rebuffed when Eric said, "Please don't touch me, Dr. Scharff. I have a sunburn." I realized that he was not experiencing what I said as sympathetic. He wanted me to lay off.

Eric continued rebuilding the museum. Alex now put a family of small dolls in a car and drove over to visit the museum. Eric made Demolishicor attack the family.

Father said, "Jeanette and Alex can't stop Eric. He ignores it when they try to defend themselves, and he overwhelms them."

Mother had now turned red, and she spat out, "I'm livid. When he does this, I get so mad. Right now, I just want to leave the room!"

I said, "Tell me about it instead."

She said, "I can't discuss my anger yet. I feel he's so stubborn, even after you point it out to him. It causes everyone else to be unhappy. He monopolizes things like the blocks. I just want to knock over that museum." And she leaned over and scattered the blocks of the museum with the back of her hand. I felt stunned.

I turned to Eric, with whom I was feeling identified. "Eric, how do you feel right now? Does this happen at home?"

Eric nodded slowly, painfully close to tears.

Father said, "Usually things break down when my wife is feeling like this. Eric, now come on! Give some of the blocks to Alex and Jeanette."

Mother said, "Eventually we intervene. Then he's upset we've forced his hand."

Father said, "Then Eric feels we favor Alex and Jeanette."

"Is that true?" I asked Eric.

He nodded sorrowfully, putting his head down on a table, becoming inert.

Looking for the object relations history of this moment, I asked, "Is there something in your own growing up that echoes with this situation, Mrs. Simpson?"

"It's like my father," she said. "We would dread the time he came home when he would line us up and yell at us, looking for someone who did something wrong. Then if one of us admitted something, he would yell at that child. It was awful. He had to be in charge. He made the rules, and no one else mattered. And my mother didn't protect us from him. Just like I can't protect Jeanette and Alex."

"So you feel that Eric is like your father, who you felt was so destructive?" I asked.

She nodded, beginning to sob. "And when I feel that and I get so mad at him, then I feel that I'm like my father, too, like when I knock over his building. I hate that worse than anything in the world. I hated that man, and now I'm just like him. And then I hate Eric worse for making me feel that way."

I felt a great sadness as I watched and waited with the family. Seeing Eric now slumping over the table, Father said to him, "Come here, son." Eric got up slowly and accepted a loving hug from his father. He lay draped across his father's chest while his father stroked his arm and back. It looked comforting, and at the same time it did not get in the way of the work.

I felt grateful to Father for comforting Eric in a way that let Mother keep speaking. He was managing to hold the family in holding Eric. It let me keep my attention on Mother. In this way, Father was providing holding not only to a single family member in distress, but through his intervention with Eric, was holding all of them and was augmenting my own capacity for therapeutic holding, contributing as surely to the therapy as if he had been speaking. His action led to a chain of repair. Jeanette now went to her mother. Climbing onto Mother's lap, Jeanette comforted her. While she did so, Alex played among the remains of the museum, making a simpler building to house the family car he had been using.

While seeing this train of events out of the corner of my eye, I said to Mother, "When you feel you're bad like your own father, you hate Eric, but you also hate yourself."

"Yes," she sobbed. "And I feel I've damaged him just the way I felt my father hurt me. And I can't undo it. There isn't any way out."

It was painful in the room. I wondered what despair I had wrought. And at the same time, I felt almost exhilarated that the family was managing to hold a steady course through the straits of this despair.

Thinking of Father's intervention a moment earlier, I wanted to try to enlarge the object relations field of this moment to include him. Mr. Simpson could hardly ever remember anything about his childhood, but it seemed clear to me that he was fully emotionally involved at this moment. So I turned to him and asked, "Does this have any echoes for you?"

He said, "My childhood wasn't so dramatic. At least I don't remember any events like that. Sometimes we'd be spanked with a belt for doing something wrong. I can't remember anything more."

I realized that even as he said he could remember so little, he was actually giving just a bit more than he ever had before: he remembered spankings. I said, "Not being able to remember is one of the things you struggle with. What would you be spanked for?"

"I only remember one time," he said. "I was spanked for going over to a little girlfriend's house when I was about Eric's age. My father womped me with his belt. It hurt! I can relate to Eric's sulking now when I think about it."

"Did you know about your dad's being spanked with a belt?" I asked Eric. He shook his head.

Over the next couple of minutes, we established that in Father's recollection, what he had been punished for was a sexual event. He had been strapped at least partly because it was a girl he disappeared with. Given the sexual symptomatology of the family's original request for help a year and a half earlier, the continuing sexual dysfunction of the parents, and the sexualization of Jeanette's development, I thought this was an important contribution. I did not know yet what more to make of it. Putting it in place as a small piece of the family's inhibition of Father's adolescent sexual identity formation would have to wait until several months after this session.

I now said to them, "Mrs. Simpson, you get so mad at Eric because he makes you feel this way. He reminds you of your father, then you feel you're like your angry father yourself when you get so mad. And Eric feels destructive and is hopeless about how to get your love. Through all of this, Mr. Simpson lives through you, also hating the angry father like the one who strapped him for an innocent visit to a girl, and hating you as an angry father in whom sexual interest will invoke rage. That's the time the two of you have a similar struggle, when sexual matters are at issue.

"But in the setting with the children, it is often Eric who brings in the bad father when he wants something for himself. He feels bad about it and he becomes Demolishicor—the destructive robot controlled by someone else. But he also does it in a paradoxical way to keep you, Mrs. Simpson, from feeling that you are the Hulk or the Demolishicor yourself."

Mother said, "Yes, you're right. And I want to bust up his museum because I don't want him to be so high and mighty. Then I feel awful."

At this moment, Alex took the car and broke down the last remains of the museum. I noted to myself his enactment of the destructive forces we were discussing.

I said, "And it is at those times—just like now—that Alex takes on Eric for you, Mrs. Simpson. It is part of the reason that Alex's impulsive destructiveness is so hard to stop."

Jeanette climbed down from her mother's lap and began to play sweetly among the ruins.

Father was rubbing Eric's head. I asked Mr. Simpson, "Can you add anything?"

Father said, "Eric's hurt. He has a hard time when his mother's so unhappy with him. He wants to do better, but he doesn't know how to change."

I asked Eric, "Is that right?"

He nodded.

Mother said, "He probably hates me back."

I said, "So you're afraid he'll hate you like you've hated your father?" I felt I was taking a chance when I added, "But is there anything else you feel for Eric?"

She answered, "I love him! Really I do! He's a wonderful kid. I feel hopeless, like all the damage is done. He's already been hurt. I've done it! I hate myself!" And she began to sob again.

Alex began again to build a simpler block house for the family car.

I said to Eric, "Do you feel like crying?"

"Yes," he said. "I feel sad."

"I know you do," I said. "This has been painful for everyone, your mom included. This is what's behind so much of what goes wrong at home. It gets in the way of the loving. In your family, Mrs. Simpson, you felt your dad hated you and you hated him, but you wanted his love. It's painful being so mad at Eric and caring about him, too. He's in a situation like yours. And you envy him being so competent, getting so much—even from you— and then wanting more. It makes you remember how you felt you had so little. The image of a bad father comes out at these moments of breakdown, and it often keeps you, Mr. and Mrs. Simpson, from feeling you can be good parents. Each of you has felt that you couldn't get enough love, that there isn't enough to go around. It gets played out here. If someone wants too much, it's as though he is taking it from the rest of the family. I think this may also be operating in the sexual relationship between the two of you. But that we'll have to explore with the two of you alone. What's important for now is the way the family plays out the anger each of you has over what's missing."

In this session, some of the similarities and some of the differences between adults and children in family functioning are demonstrated. And some of the deficits that contribute to the developmental disturbances in this family are clear, too. In a way, it is clearer because this family, at a midpoint in their treatment, demonstrates the failures in expectable differentiation between adult and child functioning. And through treatment, the family begins to take responsibility for them. There is both deficit and growth, a repetition of reversal in levels of responsibility and yet the growing exercise of perspective and insight. In short, they are working things through.

REPARATION LEADS TO GROWTH AND DIFFERENTIATION

For the purpose of examining shifts in maturational levels between children and adults, I focus here mainly on the pair of Eric and his mother.

First, Eric and his mother share the need to be loved and responded to. Their need for attachment to each other is clear, and it drives everything that happens between them. They cry over their failures in achieving a loving relationship, and they share in the acknowledgment of reciprocal needs. Eric and his

mother demonstrate a moment of crucial failure when Mother
is overcome by Eric's self-centered behavior and knocks over
his building. Such moments in family treatment offer what I
have called a *core affective experience* (Scharff and Scharff 1987).
When they discover the shared needs that underlie this painful
breakdown, they reestablish a partnership-in-the-moment, in
which each sees into and is seen by the other.

Second, they reestablish each other as intimate, loving
objects, having explored some of the ways they have been each
other's bad objects. Mother realizes the way Eric has become
her "bad father," and he understands why she has had so little
tolerance for his neediness. In arriving at shared understanding, they become not only benign but loving. In such a
moment, they support each other to repair their relationship.

Third, in doing this work, they create a reparative working
model that will also apply in the future to maintain relationships that meet their needs for love and attachment, for the
effective expression of aggression, for differentiation, and for
support of each other's maturation and development.

Fourth, they each improve their capacity to gain perspective on what is happening in the family. They develop a shared
understanding of the rents and tears both in the family's
holding fabric that is the context for their family life, and in
their centered relationship, the one between object-mother and
child.

All this leads to a fifth point, the reworking of identifications. A treatment moment such as this one illustrates the
intricate interplay between internal object and self. The formation of the self is fashioned in the movement between a
relationship with an object and an identification with it. In this
session, Mother and Eric assist each other in the move toward
more benign identities, less harmful to their objects. In a cycle
of projective and introjective identifications, they put the
aggressive bad object into each other. In their life together, they
had frequently been unable to provide containment of paranoid anxieties and had resorted to splitting and repression.
Now assisted by the family's improved capacity for holding

and for mourning, the cycle becomes one of tolerating the pain and of reparation. As Mrs. Simpson modifies her projective identification of Eric so that he no longer has to house the bad object of her aggressive father, his own identification as a destructive boy is tamed and he becomes more loving and available. And as Eric sees his mother as less threatening, she feels that she becomes a better mother. Her identity, too, becomes more benign.

Finally, and here I am thinking of Alex's play and Mrs. Simpson's verbalization, the family as a group demonstrates growth in its capacity for sublimation and transformation of internal needs. Alex's encopresis—an expression of chaotic anger that can only be evacuated without form or structure—resolves as he keeps working at rebuilding the ruins of the museum. Alex has often embodied the disappointment and anger the family has been unable to master previously. In this session we see the way his inner world is slowly transformed by the family's shared therapy experience.

THE DIFFERENTIATING ELEMENTS

This family demonstrates some of the major differences between children and adults in treatment. There are the actual differences in the levels of maturity and the ability of the adults and children to understand. In their own language, often through the medium of play, the children speak for issues just as clearly as the adults. But the adults must take the lead in providing verbal understanding, just as the children take the lead with their play in expressing both the verbally defended issues and the issues from their side of the relationships.

This family had been operating as though Eric and his mother were on roughly the same level of need and maturation, but that it was only Eric who had the potential to lead the family out of the land of hopelessness. Eric was tasked with being the container for generations of disappointment. The family grows in this moment of therapy because both Mother and Father are willing to retake the lead in maturation and the provision of containing anxiety. Mother and Father have been acting as though the two of them were helpless to contain Mother's destructive rage, as if she were driven from inside with Father helpless to control her. In this they have also been acting as though Eric were responsible for her and for the family, instead of the parents for the family and Eric. They were operating as though he had just as great a responsibility to provide containment for his Mother as the parents, and especially his mother, must do for him. This pattern results from the assumption that Father is inadequate to his task. Then both parents look to Eric to make up for this male deficiency, leaving Eric responsible for taking care of his mother's anxiety. When Father reasserts his capacity to provide holding, and Mother acts again as the more mature partner in the relationship with Eric, all are relieved. She had been complaining that Eric was irresponsible, as though he were the destructive adult she grew up with. Then she feels periodically that she, herself, is that destructive adult. When her perspective is enlarged, when she becomes the one with the area of responsibility *for* Eric and herself, and now expects Eric once again to be responsible *to* her rather than *for* her, she offers an object relationship in which he is eminently more comfortable, and so is she. The parallel processes seen in the family with Father in regard to Alex and Jeanette are part of the same development.

Finally, we can elaborate further on the theme of modifying identifications. Mother and Eric move to reestablish a balance in which Mother is less dominated by persecuting and rejecting internal objects and is thereby more reliant on improved internal objects. She discovers an improving image of herself, which is more effectively bolstered by her husband. As she is less reliant on Eric to compensate for deficient internal objects, Eric can be more reliant on her to provide a better interactive life out of which he can resume building his own internal objects. In the language of Eric's play, fewer of the soldiers—his angry objects—now have to be showcased in his museum, and more good objects are given life.

In this manner, the family uses therapy to reestablish a holding environment, a context of growth not only for the children but for all five family members. The children are freed to work with modifying their own internal needs within a supportive and constructive context. Eric is freed, for instance, to acknowledge his needs instead of building a museum to preserve the remains of the old objects. Alex is freed to make contributions to the family's perspective as he matures before our eyes. The children are freed from being containers of pathological projective identifications and anxieties and can now experience the parents as containers. The family pattern of providing holding and an appropriate context for growth is restored as both parents and children resume functions appropriate to their ages and roles.

CHILD AND ADULT DIFFERENCES IN THE INTERNAL FAMILY

Experience with the actual family is the basis for internal structure for each family member, that is, of the internal family for each of them. In health, there is a difference between the relationship of child and of adult to the family-as-a-whole and therefore in the composition of their internal family. The child, even the older child, tends to look to the family group for support and sustenance. The child's attitude is one of taking from and deriving from. Mature adults, even though getting a great deal from their families, have an attitude of giving to, of letting the family derive from them. This difference between the child and the adult holds mostly for their attitude toward the external family group and its real-life current family members. Both child and adult need support and sustenance from the figures they carry within.

This leads us to a final, most important difference. Although the child is like the adult in having a several generation family, and his or her immediate internal family consists of parents and siblings, the child is unlike the adult in being the new generation. The child is at the bottom of the waterfall.

The adult with children is midway, with primary external objects that are older and younger—ones who made him or her, and ones he or she made. This dual role, being child and parent, summarizes the full complexity of the contrast between child and adult—the position of being both child and adult at the same time, in the real world. In the internal world, such an adult has older and newer internal objects contributing to a more complex psychic structure than in the child.

When Mrs. Simpson sees herself as though she were an emotional child at the bottom of the generational ladder, with Eric as only her persecuting or idealized father, he cannot grow. When she once again takes back the projective identifications she has put into Eric, she resumes her position mediating between generations, and he is freed to grow.

THE ROLE AND EMOTIONAL POSITION OF
THE THERAPIST

Whether through family or individual therapy, part of a therapist's role is to repair the ability of each person to use and support other family members. This repair can come about only through a maturation in internal object relations, leading to growth of confidence that there are enough good internal objects and that one can make one's self available to be used by others without risking irreparable loss or damage. In this manner, each person becomes not merely an object to be used or abused by others, but part of an interlocking and reciprocating system of self and object in which each is formed, informed, and modified in relation to others. The deterioration of this capacity will lead to misuse and abuse of each other in the family interactions. When each family member can only see the other family members as revolving around him- or herself, there seems to be no choice but to batter the others into the empty spaces of one's own needs.

With maturation of the capacity to use and respond to others, as led by and embodied by the family's adults until the children are developmentally complete, the family can act as a mature unit in its capacity for concern for each other, facilitation of the growth of each other, and meeting the needs of each family member and the family as a whole to be loved and understood.

What about the personal needs of the therapist? Much of the clinical literature, especially early classical psychoanalysis, was written as though he or she were a disembodied parental figure without any need for attachment and intimate relating. Of course, the therapist fully shares the human state of having human needs. The essential difference is that—at least in the therapeutic setting—therapists can and must be far more dependent on their own internal objects than they expect their patients to be. Since the patient or family they are treating is not their family, they are freed to allow individuals or families in treatment to resonate with the therapists' own internal objects and internal families, and to make their peace at this distance. Although this is an exaggeration of what I have described as the adult position, no one in their own family can or should have this kind of distance, even though parents should have more of it than children. Some of therapists' personal needs must, perforce, be met by satisfactory work with their patients or families in treatment. They need to find in their work a chance to repair their objects and challenge the potential of their selves. In this task they find support from their internal objects, including those derived from their past families, current families, colleagues, and membership in the therapeutic profession.

And just as the therapist is required to take a mature stance of responsibility like the parent of a family, so the patient—even the whole family—is temporarily freed to take and to regress—that is, to take the child's position of depending on rather than being there to be depended on, until the family has reorganized itself as a well-functioning unit with clear role relationships.

Within the common human condition, children and adults show important differences in the use of internal objects and in their relationship with external objects throughout life. These differences derive from and affect their different roles in the family and the effect of the family on them. Both individual and family therapy aim to redress the imbalances in these matters, and both rely on the ability of the therapist to contain the anxieties during the exploration and realignment of the interior of the individual and the family.

13

The Interlocking of Self and Object during Life Development

In the family, each person is a primary object for every other family member. Not only are the parents the primary objects for the children, but the children become new primary objects for each parent, potentially strengthening the marital bond because the parents share the children as objects for care and concern as well as for introjection. Just as the child introjects both the individual parents and the parental couple (Scharff and Scharff 1991), so each parent introjectively identifies not only with a child, but with a child in relation with that parent's spouse. That is, a mother takes in her daughter and identifies with her as a growing girl and a potential woman, but she also takes in the experience of her daughter in relationship with her husband, and in so doing has the opportunity to modify aspects of her internal object relationship with her own father.

Ogden (1989) has described beautifully the way in which the child's first presentation of the father is through getting to know the mother's internal object constellation, which includes her own father. That is, the child's first experience of an oedipal constellation occurs through an introjective identification with the mother's self and her paternal object. Almost equally important in a family with two parents, I suggest, is the child's introjective identification from the father's projection of himself and his maternal object, and that these are communicated unconsciously to both boy and girl babies and young children.

There is another aspect of growth within the family, which I first described in a book on adolescent development and the transition from school to work (Scharff and Hill 1976). I bring this aspect into the current context because it is consistent with my present view that the development of the individual is dependent on the members of the family and others with whom the individual has primary relationships.

It is this: Psychoanalysis and the dynamic developmental psychologies have described life stages in ever-increasing detail and with increasing sophistication. But they have not as yet described the complexity of the way in which one person's developmental stage interlocks with those of others in the family. I find that interlocking occurs universally. The infant's first crucial developmental steps intertwine with those of its parents who are becoming parents through that infant's birth. Or, if this is their second or later child, they are becoming parents of a growing family and, as every parent knows, the addition of each child changes the family experience dramatically simply on account of the numbers, even before we consider the unique individual contribution from each child.

Children find that their family experience is determined

by birth order and number of siblings already in place. It is changed dramatically by the birth of subsequent siblings. The role of children as each others' primary objects has been vastly underestimated, a lack of understanding that is only now being redressed. For instance, Bank and Kahn (1982) point out that siblings often have the closest relationships within families, and at the end of the life cycle may spend more time together than at any time since childhood. Today, with divorce as a prominent factor disrupting the shaping of the family, siblings may be the only constant objects as children travel together back and forth between their two homes.

However, all these complications become part of a larger pattern in which children's developmental life transitions occur in the context of the development of the adults with whom they live. We must consider the complexity that ensues when we acknowledge and explore the adult crises of development that are going on at the same time as those of the child.

Erikson's (1950, 1959) original work on the seven developmental stages described seven groups of developmental tasks. Erikson saw that development began in childhood but continued across the life span from early childhood dependency through adolescent struggles with identity formation to the adult stages of the development of intimacy, generativity, and finally the maintenance of integrity.

What we can now add to this is the way in which the infant, child, and adolescent face these tasks at the same time that the adults who form their objects face their own adult developmental tasks. And in a complex and reciprocal way, the adults undertake their own developmental crises while the children face theirs. These processes interlock and influence each other. In many cases, the adult crises are triggered or significantly punctuated by the developmental stages of the children.

For instance, it is common enough for the attainment of intimacy by young adults to be punctured by the birth of a first child, an increase in family size, or the birth of a first child of a particular sex. The oedipal struggles and ploys of children

confront parents who are struggling with challenges of intimacy and generativity they had not expected. And in a
reciprocal way, the parental struggles for intimacy and sexual
relatedness may extend to include children in encouraging or
interfering ways. Examples extend right through the developmental epochs. Adolescents struggling for identity, including
sexual identity, may find that they have introjectively identified with their parents, who are struggling with questions of
their own capacities and worth in the midlife stage of adult
development. Such is the case in the vignettes that follow.

VIOLETTE LA FRANCE

The following case concerns a 15-year-old French girl,
the youngest of three children. She was brought by her
parents who were in their fifties. They initiated therapy
because she had asked for birth control, planning to begin
an active sexual life with a man of 23. The parents were
astounded and deeply upset. In the interview with them,
it quickly developed that their own sexual life was nonex-
istent, having stalled several years ago. Even when their
sex life was occurring, Mrs. La France had not experienced
sexual passion for her husband whom she loved and
deeply admired, because he had been chosen by her to be
a safe, nonerotic choice in her own mid-twenties. She did
so because she remained in love with the man of her
fantasies, an exciting but unreliable artist. Mr. La France,
for his part, had chosen his wife because she was beautiful
beyond his dreams and socially glittering, whereas he was
an awkward although brilliant scholar. Feeling little regard for his powers as an attractive man, he was willing to
do without an active sexual life in order to have her. Now,
twenty-five years later, having compromised their chances
for vital marital and sexual intimacy, and shortly after the
additional symbolic loss to their sexuality from Mrs. La

France's hysterectomy for fibroid growths, Mr. and Mrs. La France had both projectively identified with Violette's flowering sexuality, only to find that it was assuming proportions that alarmed them.

For her part, Violette was furious at her mother for an anti-sexual attitude. She took encouragement unconsciously from the adoring and encouraging fondness her father lavished on her and hoped to find this in the sexual relationship with an older man. Thus her urgent search for sexual intimacy was a precocious attempt to find compensation for parenting that derived from a sterile bond. Her parents found that the rift in understanding between themselves and Violette threatened their attempts to feel confirmed in their generativity. Another way of saying this uses the concepts of midlife crisis (Jacques 1965) and adult transitions (Levinson et al. 1978). Both parents were negotiating adult developmental stages as they attempted to help Violette negotiate her adolescent development, but their previous failure to establish an integrated capacity for intimacy now compromised their achievement of a sense of generativity and of a move toward the later acquisition of a sense of integrity. Their concerns for the well-being of their daughter further eroded their sense of parental competence, one component of generativity.

THE HOLMES FAMILY

The second example comes from my study of adolescent development in the transition between school and work (Scharff and Hill 1976). The Holmes family was referred by their family doctor to the Tavistock Clinic's Adolescent Department in London where I was working, because two family members were symptomatic. They had run into each other at the doctor's office, each there without knowing the other was experiencing difficulty, each surprised and alarmed.

The boy, Keith, age 16, had been sent to his doctor's office because of "shaky feelings" on the job. He had left high school after the British equivalent of junior year to move into an apprenticeship as a draughtsman, a career course that was not unusual for nonacademic students. This job provided for a day a week study at a college of further education, with the expectation of a diploma in draughtsmanship at the end of four years. He had found school difficult during his last year, and he now found the day at college difficult. He was afraid of being called on to speak in public during class, an old fear he carried from school. To his alarm, he found that the public speaking phobia spread rapidly. He suddenly found that he was afraid to use the telephone for fear he might be asked to read a letter over the phone and would be unable to do so. He began to refuse to answer the phone at work. Since his job involved frequent telephone calls, he grew increasingly afraid at work in case he would have to answer the phone or explain himself. It was for help with this fear that he went to his doctor's office, and it was then he met his father. When the doctor referred Keith to the clinic, he suggested that the whole family come with him.

Mr. Holmes, too, had gone to see the doctor for help with a symptom of anxiety, and it was also related to work. He had had a checkered business career. He did not have a university degree but had worked his way up in business until he reached a middle management position in a large printing corporation. However, he had not been promoted for a number of years now. He had been commuting long hours in order to work for this firm after it moved out of London. Feeling that the lack of credentials meant that his career growth was effectively at an end, he had recently decided to invest with his wife in a neighborhood dairy and newspaper shop, one previously owned by his wife's parents, which would be more lucrative although less professional. However, in the transition, he had become unable to sleep from the anxiety about giving up his career, and it was then he had gone to see his family doctor, meeting Keith in the waiting room.

When I saw the family, a description of the family-wide stress emerged. The family was in the middle of arranging to move into the apartment above the shop and would be living close to Mrs. Holmes's mother for the first time since the parents had been married twenty years ago. In addition, in an individual interview, Keith revealed that his family had a secret that he was not supposed to know: Mrs. Holmes's father had died of late-stage syphilis contracted in his youth. This set of grandparents had apparently not gotten on well, and the syphilis had come as a final late-life blow to the grandmother. It had added shame to her bitterness about the long-standing arguments between Keith's grandparents, and that shame had apparently been shared by Keith's mother about her father.

I saw Keith together with his mother, father, 6-year-old brother, and 18-year-old sister, who was about to get married. It became apparent that the mother bore more than her share of family burdens. She had always been the more active parent. Staying at home meant she had been the one to set limits on the children and care for them generally, whereas Mr. Holmes had been the provider. With their new investment in the dairy shop, she would also be called on to take the lead in the family's financial support. It was she who knew how to manage the dairy shop, since it had formerly been owned by her parents. She had never been able to move very far from her own family. Her inability or distaste for leaving her mother was the reason they had previously decided that Mr. Holmes would commute to work when the firm moved headquarters outside London instead of the family moving, too. The new living arrangement above the dairy shop meant they would be living just around the corner from Mrs. Holmes's mother.

The difficulty Mrs. Holmes had with separation had

affected the decisions the couple had recently made. We could see that her separation anxiety was echoed in Keith's difficulty with speaking in class. Finding his voice in public had the unconscious meaning of making the break from his family and of differentiating from the silent mass of schoolmates in class. His move into a job coincided with his father's making a transition that signaled the midlife failure of his own career, compounded by his mother's continued difficulty separating from her family.

Mr. Holmes also recounted a symptomatic aspect of his own development. In his youth, he had overcome a public speaking phobia. Unable to speak before even small groups of employees, he had worried that his career would be jeopardized by this public speaking disability. He had faced his difficulty with a self-styled desensitization program, deliberately setting out to organize religious forums at which he would speak. Only by this conscious effort had he overcome a dread similar to the one now confronting Keith. He had come from a coal mining family in the north of England and his interest in business had been viewed by his parents, particularly by his mother, as threatening because he would become too different from them. As he told us this, he wept with recognition that his parents had feared losing him through his own career advancement and had wanted to hold on to him, their only child. He then realized that his parents' marriage had been marked by many angry arguments, but that they had been united in devotion to him. When he married at 19 and moved to London with the firm he had worked for since then, the life appeared to have gone out of his parents, who had seemed depressed to him ever since. We could now see that his public speaking phobia had expressed his family's difficulty with his adolescent separation—individuation and the loss it meant for his parents—and that his self-styled cure of the phobia represented his creative work to get past the impasse in his development.

In the light of the father's story about the phobia of his youth and the way it expressed the issues of his family then, I wondered about the transmission of object relations issues in Keith's growing anxiety about work, expressed in his phobia about speaking in class and use of the telephone. As Mr. and Mrs. Holmes faced a change of career and a change of dominance in the family with mother now assuming a major leadership role in the family's financial life, a family crisis threatened that was echoed in Keith's individual crisis. Both his father's bitterness about his own stalled career and the domestic pattern of the family of "pinning all worries on Mom" were consistent with Keith's increasing anxiety about pursuing a new career that involved learning, promotion, and a progressive assumption of independence and responsibility. Like his father, Keith had pursued a nonacademic career, but one that offered social and professional advancement. He was not consciously aware of the bitterness or anxiety his father felt but had not acknowledged within the family. All Keith was aware of was his own crippling symptom, which threatened to remove him from work right at the beginning of his career.

Our exploration of the family pattern began with understanding the meaning of the parents' family histories for their adult anxieties. We related them to the father's current disappointment and bitterness, and the threat that Mrs. Holmes would become more of a manager than her husband or son could tolerate. Mrs. Holmes also feared that her difficulty with separation would alienate her husband and son as it had her father from her mother, and Mr. Holmes realized that, without knowing it, he worried that Keith's independent progress would cost him the companionship of his son at an age similar to the age at which Mr. Holmes had desperately wanted to leave his own parents behind. Keith's uncertainty about moving into the world of work and responsibility thus embodied his own adolescent anxiety about separation and independent striving, but at the same time expressed his parents' history of object relations issues.

Interlocking and reinforcing family themes emerged. Mr. Holmes was able to see that the life issues he had found crippling did not need to be passed on to Keith. He and Keith began to work together to relieve the anxiety present for both of them in the work area, and Keith quickly found himself able to use the phone, take on more difficult tasks, and move more confidently toward competence at college and at work.

At the same time the couple realized that they had been inhibited by the legacy of Mrs. Holmes's family secret. Mrs. Holmes had taken in from her mother the fear that separation, including letting Mr. Holmes pursue his career fully, might stimulate in him a promiscuous sexuality in which she and her mother imagined her father had engaged as a young man. Keith's adolescence had triggered this fear again for his mother in a way that the couple's older daughter's adolescence had not because she was a girl who had been unambitious and had remained close to her mother.

The couple's restriction of the range of their operations in the world had pushed each of them to hope that Keith would achieve a freedom of expression in the world that they had not. Yet, they were unconsciously afraid that this would include sexual activity that could expose him to risks like those Mrs. Holmes's father had run. Keith's use of the phone had more meaning than simply interfering with his ability to work. If he could not make calls, he would not reach out to establish sexual connections with girls. This inhibition protected the parents from their fears for him at the same time as it blocked the hope that he would grow beyond the restricted development imposed on him by the parents from their own object relations set.

In addition, we learned that the parents' sexual life had become more circumscribed in this period of crisis.

Partly because of the husband's anxiety about domination by his wife, he had lost his usually active interest in sex, leaving Mrs. Holmes more anxious about whether she was valued as a woman, or whether she would be appreciated only as the proprietess and manager of the dairy shop—an asexual mother to the men of the family. Now that Keith's older sister was getting married, Mrs. Holmes was the only woman at home, and she had begun to fear that everyone would depend on her without appreciating her own needs, including that of reassurance that she was still sexually appealing to her husband.

ADOLESCENT ECHOES OF PARENTAL BLOCKED DEVELOPMENT

In the two families discussed in the preceding sections, the adolescents' developmental crisis echoed the strain of the parents' midlife developmental setbacks. In the setting of an object relations understanding of the family, the adolescents' anxieties could be seen to be driven by the adult issues—both the individual ones of each parent, and by the midlife crisis in the parents as a couple. The parents were now experiencing conscious and unconscious aspects of the toll of earlier developmental compromises through the limitations imposed on themselves and on their relationship. Successful negotiation of this adult developmental stage required new personal growth. The adolescents' sexual and work identity developmental issues had a significant role in propelling the parents toward the crisis in their own lives. Violette's attempt to make a premature sexual relationship to reassure herself of her capacity for sexuality was driven partly by her individual, age-appropriate needs, and partly by internalizing her parents' unconscious hope that she would create a sexual pairing that would substitute for their lack of sexual intimacy. Her actions drew attention to her parents' need for enhanced intimacy in their midlife if they were to be able to use the holding capacity in their own relationship to let her separate from them in the manner appropriate to adolescence.

For Mr. and Mrs. Holmes, the sexual issues were triggered as their daughter was leaving for marriage and Keith was becoming self-supporting. But the area of expression for their crisis occurred primarily in the area of work. Keith's phobia of speaking in class and using the telephone embodied a family-wide failure to encapsulate and detoxify fears about the men reaching out into the wider world through career and sexuality, lest the wider world defeat competency and hopes for intimacy, both at midlife and at adolescence.

Both cases show that: (1) adult development needed to proceed to provide the context for the adolescent's development, and (2) the adolescent's development triggered new needs in the adult development of the parents.

The adolescent's self has had to embody and contain the issues of its adult objects precisely because the adults were unable to make their own developmental moves necessary for maintaining the optimum context for the adolescent's continuing growth and separation. At the same time, the adult selves had put these issues into their children precisely because they could not solve or contain them in their selves and in their relationships. They hoped unconsciously to solve these issues through the projective identifications with their children. The adolescent's failure to do so was experienced as a personal failure by the parents because of the projective identification of each parent with the adolescent. It was also felt to be the failure of the family's overall holding capacity and was carried by the family group as a shared feeling of inadequacy.

These two families demonstrate that development of each family member individually has to be understood as involving and challenging the development of the other family members and of the family as a whole in a continuously interlocking and interdependent cycle.

PART FIVE

Refinding the Self through Refound Objects

14

The Object Relations of

the Therapist

In the process of supervision of psychotherapy, we are interested in many aspects of the work from the details of technique to transference and countertransference. One of the richest areas of growth for a trainee at every stage is in the interplay between the professional's personal issues and the issues of the client. In the object relations approach to therapy, we focus our work in this area because this is where we can understand clients from inside their resonance with our own object relations. Similarly, in doing supervision, we focus on the correspondence between the trainee's issues and those of his or her client because here we find the greatest potential for making strengths and vulnerabilities of a therapist fully available for the work of therapy.

The following vignette from supervision offers an opportunity to look at an instance of this interplay that resonated between patients and therapist as it did between therapist and supervisor.

MRS. MILLS AND THE SMITH FAMILY

Mrs. Mills was a moderately experienced therapist of children and adults, who, however, had not been working professionally for the preceding five years while having children. She was reentering the field by taking a training program in object relations family therapy.

I supervised Mrs. Mills in the treatment of Mary Smith, a woman in her early twenties, and her family. Mrs. Mills met with the family regularly and saw individual members occasionally. Some years before, Mrs. Mills, then recently licensed, had seen Mary when she was a homeless adolescent, ejected by her parents for oppositional behavior. Mary kept in touch with Mrs. Mills on and off over the next few years. At the time of the supervision, Mary had been in a tumultuous marriage for the previous four years. Her husband, Mr. Smith, had an 11-year-old daughter from an earlier marriage. The Smiths now had a 3-year-old boy. But the tragedy in the Smith family centered around the death of their infant daughter less than a year before these sessions. The baby developed a rapidly malignant and horribly deforming tumor at 2 months of age and died at home at 5 months of age. The already borderline Smith family had been coming apart at the seams ever since. Mr. and Mrs. Smith railed at each other, the 11-year-old girl was angry, and the 3-year-old boy talked incessantly and dominated the family. He was, however, the only one to talk directly about the baby's illness and death.

Mrs. Mills was often anxious about this family, who could not discuss the death. They became more chaotic with each reminder. She often wished they would go away, although she felt responsible to help. At the time of the following vignette, the anger between husband and wife had reached a boiling point, and Mr. Smith's anger seemed particularly threatening to Mrs. Mills. When Mrs. Mills thought the husband might be violent, she presented the case to classmates in the family training program's group supervision in such a manner that they were all convinced that he was likely to go out of control and hurt not his wife but Mrs. Mills. With their encouragement, Mrs. Mills arranged to move an individual session she had scheduled with Mr. Smith from her regular office to an office in the suite of a male classmate while he was also seeing patients, so that she would feel protected. In our supervisory session, I could not find anything in the material or history to justify a realistic fear, so I tried to understand her fear as countertransference — although I supported her need to protect herself meanwhile. It was clear that the therapist's fears for her own survival were impairing her capacity to provide containment for this chaotic family, and that these fears were especially prominent in this phase.

The chaos continued. Mary Smith began feeling suicidal as she had before, and on one occasion she stormed out of the house with the 3-year-old boy. A couple of days later, after both a family and a couple session, Mary came back. The couple session had allowed Mr. Smith to explore and express his rage that his wife "dumped everything on him." It began to look as though the therapist's fear for her own life when meeting with the husband represented an overidentification with the wife.

Mrs. Smith's contention that the husband would do something violent to her was, I thought, a projection of her own rage, which Mrs. Mills, in her own identification with Mrs. Smith, could not see. I asked Mrs. Mills if anything occurred to her about her own vulnerability in trying to contain this chaos, the projected rage, and the family's difficulty in mourning the baby's death.

Mrs. Mills told me that at age 17, on one day's notice, she had emergency surgery for a mass in her chest. She was convinced she was going to die. Her normally reserved father sat outside the operating room crying. Both parents stayed with her at the hospital. The mass was not malignant, but, as the surgeons could not remove all of it, they contemplated another operation. She vividly recalled being wheeled into a room "full of a hundred doctors" for a case conference.

We agreed that she was identified with the threat to life that this family could not metabolize. When Mrs. Mills first met her, Mary Smith had been 16 and abandoned by her parents. The girl's age and her sense of aloneness when her parents were crippled with fear resonated with Mrs. Mills's own anxieties during her adolescent surgical threat.

By the next week's supervision, Mrs. Mills had reflected more on her surgery and her identification with the wife. She realized that her own parents had been under enormous stress at the time of the surgery, leading to fears for their survival as a couple. During the week, Mrs. Mills had a dream.

In the dream, I am going to face my own surgery, but it is happening now. I said to the doctors, "I won't let you operate until I write letters to my children." I wrote letters to each of them, including my baby, telling them how special they are and recalling special moments I've had with them.

Mrs. Mills had commented before how hard it was for her to work with this family, because she so often thought of her own healthy young children and because this family made her think about things she would like to forget. Now she remembered being at the funeral of the Smiths' infant. The family was not then in treatment with Mrs. Mills, but Mary had been in touch with her during the baby's illness. Looking at the coffin, Mrs. Mills had had the fantasy that she could see the baby inside and could see the horrible distortion of the baby's face from the tumor. She had been overwhelmed with sorrow, whose depth had seemed to extend personally even beyond that of the Smiths' tragic situation.

I said that we had both seen that she was identified with Mrs. Smith as a frightened adolescent and as the parent of young children. She was also identified with her own mother seen in Mrs. Smith as the mother of a dead baby. I said, "You came close to death from a mass yourself as an adolescent."

Mrs. Mills wiped a few tears from the corners of her eyes.

After a few moments, I said, "I think this dream means you identify yourself with the dead baby. Maybe you couldn't face that earlier."

She said, "I don't think I ever understood how frightened I was of dying. I was just so mad at my parents for being depressed themselves that I felt like they abandoned me in the hospital. I couldn't understand their fear I would die." Then she sobbed for some minutes.

Recovering, Mrs. Mills then pursued the theme of abandonment, the feeling that had consciously dominated her own adolescent experience of surgery. She said that Mary Smith's mother had left when Mary was 4, leaving seven children. Mrs. Smith had felt terribly abandoned throughout her life, reenacting it in her adolescence by getting herself ejected by her father and stepmother. We could see that the baby girl who died had represented the patient's fantasied chance to give her daughter the love and care she herself had missed. Because it was Mary's first daughter, the baby had been more of a focus for these hopes than her son. Through the relationship with the baby girl, the patient had hoped to make up for what she never got from or gave to her mother.

I said that things seemed a bit more complex than we had understood. Mrs. Mills was identified with Mary, who was herself identified with the dead baby and who was also guiltily reacting to its death as though Mary herself were the abandoning mother she had when she was 16.

Mrs. Mills agreed and thought this might explain Mary's becoming suicidal after the death of the infant and again at its first anniversary. We could now trace the effects of this ambivalent identification of the patient with her abandoning mother. The baby's death must have reactivated this desperate bind for her.

We could also see how the whole constellation resonated with Mrs. Mills's history. Just as the two living Smith children were not getting what they needed from their depressed parents, and just as the fragile bond of the parental couple was riven by the infant's death, so Mrs. Mills had been unable to provide effective holding to the Smith family because of being unable to bear the idea of herself as a dead object and because of her identification with the mother through which she had joined them in their predicament. The Smith family had also become a dying baby to her, and here she became the parent who could not stand the loss and failure.

The identification that we fashioned together in supervision could now provide the means to understand the Smith family, and particularly Mary's dilemma. It enabled Mrs. Mills to move toward providing the holding that the family had been unable to provide for itself.

THE ROLE OF THE THERAPIST'S UNIQUE HISTORY

Mrs. Mills then asked a question of great interest to us. "But what if I hadn't had my own surgery? How would I know what had happened?"

The answer is that we each have our own unique history, our own internal objects that will resonate with our patients' situations in unique ways to provide us with the clues we need. The issue is not whether a therapist has had surgery or her own acute threat of death. It is that the specific facts of Mrs. Mills's personal situation provided her own way of joining with this family and of working with me. Her dream provided us with clues to the countertransference, clues that were consistent with other clues we could now understand.

For instance, Mrs. Mills had not wanted to think about her own vulnerability or past situation. At the same time, she had been feeling more and more dread about treating this family. In the supervision sessions, I had been trying to contain her hopelessness about the family's chaos. When I urged Mrs. Mills to stick with this family, I felt as though I was brutalizing her. I suffered increasing doubt about my faith in the therapy and in my ability to help Mrs. Mills through supervision. I agonized about whether I was exposing her to harm in questioning her judgment about the potential for violence by the husband.

Her experience of feeling threat to her personal survival while trying to help this family was triggered both by her own prior life experience and by factors particular to Mary and the Smith family. The confluence of these produced a crisis in the therapy and in the therapist's training. Mrs. Mills began to doubt that she could remain an effective mother to her own children while reentering the field of psychotherapy. Here was a resonance with the Smith family's fears for survival. Mrs. Mills doubted that she could care for her own needs and those of her children, and she thought that she might therefore have to let her professional self remain dead.

The therapist's dream was primarily an expression of her personal struggle, which she experienced as she was torn both by the family and by me in the supervision. My urging her on with this family felt to her as though I were the doctor of her own adolescence, pressing dangerous surgery upon her, surgery that threatened her existence now. When she wanted to write to her children before proceeding with the operation, she was telling me, in the supervisory transference, how endangered she felt with my prescription for her work, how our work and her work had threatened to take her away from her children. I was giving her a prescription she felt to resonate with the life-threatening surgery many years before.

For a long time I had felt, in the supervisory countertransference, how threatened Mrs. Mills was. I was threatened, too. I acknowledged my own fears for risk and my doubts concerning my supervision. The work on this dream let us both understand from various levels of countertransference how her own fears as a student resonated with the family's internal risk. It allowed us to understand the resonance of the internal experience of risk in the patients, in the therapist, and in me as the supervisor. This work gave Mrs. Mills new comfort in staying with this family and in her reentry into the field of analytic psychotherapy. And, as her supervisor, I also felt better for having worked this through.

There are threats to personal survival when any of us undertakes a new venture. Some kinds of work, however, accentuate the sense of risk dramatically. Just as a doctor reacts to the threat of the inherent risk in the gravely ill patient by an unconscious accentuation in concern for his or her personal survival, so the psychotherapist learning to deal with high risk patients must react in resonance with his or her personal vulnerability and inevitably will act self-protectively. In a similar way, parents view themselves in new ways and experience threats to their self-esteem as they see the progress and travails of their children. Personal histories of vulnerability are triggered. Those psychotherapy trainees who are the most at risk personally will be most apt to suffer crises of larger proportions. The amount of vulnerability is determined by a blend of personal vulnerability of the therapist and the extent of external stress imposed by the patient or client population.

Therapists all seek to have their identity confirmed by healing their patients. So the interaction of the therapist's object relations with the unconscious of the patient reflects this fundamental hope to repair the object and to help our dependent objects grow as an expression of our own hopes for growth and survival. It is only when the object is made "good-enough" that we can dispel our own fears of damage caused by our envy, greed, anger, and narcissism. The failure of repair of psychotherapy patients, like the death of the medical patient or the faltering of a child, threatens therapists with the evidence of their own destructiveness. This defeat of our efforts at repair also deprives us of an image of a person who can confirm our goodness in return. There is no object to help keep at bay the ever-present possibility of the return of our infantile destructiveness or helplessness against the forces of disintegration.

VULNERABILITY AND LEARNING

A psychotherapy trainee, like a medical trainee, feels his or her own survival is linked to the life-or-death issues of the patient. This situation of vulnerability is also a time of great learning potential. As supervisors and teachers of psychotherapists, we have many chances to work directly to strengthen the vulnerabilities of our students. At times we do so by teaching technical skills or examining transference. At other times, we can facilitate the examination of the relevance of the therapist's personal history to the patient or family's therapeutic situation, as I was able to do in this instance with Mrs. Mills. And at all times, we are a model for our trainee-therapists as they take in our ways of working with the unknown, with anxiety, and with the supervisory relationship.

There are complex issues of countertransference for the supervisor. I worried that I might be jeopardizing the safety of my trainee. Was I propelling her into a dangerous or hopeless situation? Yet, I also worried that unless she could develop an understanding that would let her continue with the family, I might not be able to teach her anything worth knowing. My countertransference conflict concerned the question of her safety balanced against her growth. As I struggled, I suffered my own pangs of hopelessness about her and about myself.

We all live with this situation when we supervise psycho-therapists who encounter patients at risk. When we support them to confront their internal risk, and especially when we do so by confronting our own sense of being at risk, we offer an opportunity in which it is often possible to transform old vulnerabilities into new strengths—both for our trainees and for ourselves.

15

The Object Refound and

the Self Reclaimed

SANDRA

On a Monday hour a few months before
ending her analysis, Sandra began with a dream.

I was climbing a hill with Richard, a hill in a
remote, lonely place. A woman waited for us in a little
gazebo. I said to Richard that I thought a lot of people

passed through this place, but he said, "Almost no one comes here." It had a desolate and deserted feeling to it.

As Sandra approached the end of our five years of work, her fear of loneliness and of losing me was contained in this dream walk in a desolate, lonely spot with Richard, an ex-boyfriend fifteen years older than herself, who had died a year earlier from chronic lung disease.

As I listened to this dream, I felt identified with her ex-boyfriend. A chill wind whistled through my bones. I was filled with an inner loneliness. There was an eerie, mythological quality to this dream. In keeping with her hysterical psychopathology, Sandra's dreams were usually concrete, often sexualized. This one felt oracular. Richard, she thought, stood for me. The other woman was her mother. In my mind, however, it was *my* mother in a distinctly unfriendly and disapproving mood.

Later in the hour, Sandra reported another dream from the weekend, this one directly about the two of us:

I had gotten into sexual trouble of some sort. You said to me, "Don't you know I die a little inside when you get yourself into these messes?"

I felt drawn in by this dream, which seemed to follow on from the first one. I listened to her associations, which she no longer needed my prompting to give. My thoughts hovered over her thoughts, her history, and her effect on me. Sandra's life before and in the early stages of analysis had been one long string of sexual troubles: luring boyfriends into sexual escapades in high school at times of loneliness, seeking affairs with men who mildly abused her during her marriage and afterward, and taunting me sexually in the early stages of analysis. Early in the analysis she said to me, "I never met a man I couldn't get to sleep with me. I don't see why you'll be any different."

Throughout her life, she had used sex to form relationships to men and women. Through the agency of her analysis, she had gradually and painfully moved beyond this behavior both in our analytic work and in her life. She had grown in integrity and in caring for herself and others, but she now felt deeply the loneliness she had formerly run from. In this hour her sadness was stirred and the hollow winds of the lonely hill were now inside us.

Sandra said, "How bizarre of you to say in the dream that you die a little when I get into messes." Then she became stagey in the old way. Theatrically, with a coy innocence, she asked, "Do I look like I'm the kind of person who would commit murder?"

I thought of the pun on "die" found in Elizabethan love poetry that linked death and orgasm.

> Call us what you will, we are made such by love;
>   Call her one, me another fly,
> We're tapers too, and at our own cost die.
> (John Donne, "The Canonization," lines 19–21)

And I thought of sexual longing and death as Romeo concludes his final speech by saying,

> Here's to my love! O true apothecary,
>   Thy drugs are quick. Thus with a kiss I die.
> (Shakespeare, *Romeo and Juliet*, V: 3, 119–120)

Despite the murderous "confession" and the feeling of death in both dreams, I felt sexually excited rather than killed. I had a fleeting but vivid glimpse of being in bed with Sandra. This was interrupted, however, by an immediate fantasy of being censured and "cut down" by the senior woman analyst who had supervised my work with Sandra during my analytic training. The image of her also reminded me of the "other woman" in Sandra's first dream, whom I had felt was my mother in critical form. I noted that I was not worried about my wife's feelings about my fantasy of an affair with Sandra. The frightening image was of castration by an older professional woman, a supervisor, because I had sinned by responding sexually to a patient. Without my being fully aware of it, my image of a female object had been split into a sexually seductive woman (Sandra), a harsh critical woman (the supervisor), and an understanding woman (my wife.)

A moment later Sandra said, "I solved my weekend loneliness by masturbating Saturday morning."

As soon as she said this, I felt we were on the same wavelength. I pulled back from my own fantasy, which had been a response to her repressed sexual excitement through which she had entered me and held on. I recognized I had taken it in from her without being able to identify it. When she identified it, I felt it let go of me.

Sandra referred to the fact that for most of her life she had been unable to masturbate with her hands and that instead she had used both running water and, beginning at age 12, a vibrator. The first vibrator she used was a body massager that belonged to her mother. In the analysis we had come to understand that it stood not only for her mother's exciting possession, but also for her brother's penis, which had linked him to her mother, as well as for her father's penis, which her mother controlled and for which Sandra longed. Sandra's first use of the vibrator had occurred while her family was watching television in the next room. Sandra had masturbated with her mother's vibrator after feeling shut out by them. This happened during her tumultuous twelfth year when Sandra was also deeply frightened by the fact that her mother had a hysterectomy and her father had gall bladder surgery at almost the same time.

I had this story in mind during this hour as Sandra now remembered her excitement and fear when she used her mother's vibrator. "Although I was worried about being caught, the idea of using something of hers turned me on too much to be careful."

My sexual fantasy feeling of involvement with Sandra returned, flying in the face of my own values against sexual acting out. My next thought was that if sex occurred, we could never recover the analytic work or my professional standing, not for the usual reason of the damage done to the holding environment, but for the bizarrely primitive reason that we would be caught. In my reverie, we had already been caught and it was too late for recovery. Our doom was sealed.

Part of the fantasy of doom came from my relationship with my supervisor. I felt intuitively—whether it was true or not—that she had not shared my comfort with the use of my own primitive fantasies as part of the work. This gap that I imagined existed between the supervisor and myself was part of my fantasy of her as an internal object that would condemn me.

Suddenly, it came to me. This transference and countertransference sexual reenactment in fantasy represented Sandra's fear of losing me and my own loss and impending loneliness without her as a valued patient. I was experiencing the shared loss in a mode I had taken in from her—in an identification with her way of feeling loss and threat. In my confused welter, feeling aroused and threatened, the condemnation came from a harsh aspect of a maternal superego attacking my longing just as Sandra's image of her disapproving mother had often attacked her own longing.

Sandra continued by saying that in her loneliness over the weekend, she thought she had found a vibrator in the trash like that one of her mother's long ago. It turned out to be an animal hair clipper. The idea of the vibrator had excited her, and she was disappointed to have to masturbate without it. When she was unable to reach arousal with her hands, she had used the base of an electric toothbrush. She had the fantasy of inserting the metal end of the toothbrush base into the introitus of her vagina, using it as if it were a penis cut off from a body. She next thought it would tear her vaginal mucosa. She was excited just as—she shamefully noted—she used to be by stories of torture.

I was now no longer aroused. Suddenly I felt deflated, puzzled, upset by the image of internal cutting and bleeding. A scene came to me from Ingmar Bergman's film, *Cries and Whispers,* in which a women breaks a glass inside her vagina. This led me to think of a penis being inserted into that vagina in that scene, being cut by the broken glass. I felt endangered. The image of censure by another woman now gave way to an acute sense of being directly attacked and genitally injured by Sandra.

Sandra continued. "I read a newsclipping once about a man who killed hundreds of women and then had sex with them, some after decapitating them. That's gruesome—sex with dead people." Sandra paused. "I feel angry, too, but I can't talk about being mad somehow. All that perverse sex is making me sick. It seems brutal, not the way masturbation has become—kind of caretaking of myself. Having sex with you would destroy our work. It would kill *us* off!"

I was recovering now. I felt informed by my own fantasies, which had reached the depth of splitting my internal objects not only into parts of women, but into disembodied body parts in murderous relationship. I felt together enough to say, "The dreams and the news story both combine death and sex. Your toothbrush, which you used as your mother's vibrator, is my penis cut off from me. You 'decapitated' my penis and took it for yourself."

She said, "I'd like to have one of those penises from a sex shop. That's the way I've used men—as penises. The vibrator reminds me of that. This is me trying to hurt you, cutting off your penis. I want it to myself and you won't give it to me. When I was 3, I wanted Mother to come and put in a suppository when I was in the bath. I didn't tell you that I put my finger in my anus when I masturbated Saturday. I didn't want to tell you that. I guess I was furious. I have a sense of excitement in torturing you, like I had when Daddy beat me with his belt on my behind. Castrating you, having your penis like I had Mother's suppositories, fighting with you like when Daddy beat me—then I wouldn't have to miss you."

A weight lifted in my chest. Relieved by her insight, I felt I was recovering myself, my professional life, and my connection with her as a patient who had taught me a great deal by her capacity to plumb these depths from which we had both learned to recover. I answered as best I could considering my fantasy of a narrow escape from certain professional death.

I said, "You wanted to kill me a little and then have sex with my decapitated penis. When you feel desperate, you feel that having that part of me is the only way of making up for the dreadful loneliness you think you'll feel when you can't come here any more, and for a part of you that you fear will be desperately missing. And you're more desperate when you feel I'll disapprove of you, that I won't understand your loneliness and loss."

The book's opening example is drawn from work with a man beginning his analysis at a time I was beginning my experience as an analyst. This session with Sandra came toward the end of her analytic experience and near the end of my analytic training. The session resonates with these endings, with Sandra's recovery of herself and her objects, and with the counterpart of that recovery in me.

In the beginning of her analysis, in the absence of a capacity to control herself, Sandra counted on being able to control me by getting under my skin. Not surprisingly, many of my early responses had to do with distancing myself from her, protecting myself lest she subtly invade my mind, a possibility that I found far more frightening than the sexual invasion she openly threatened. The distance I maintained was an ordinary therapeutic one. I thought about things rather than acting on them. I took time to understand when confused. And I distanced myself from her defensively. It was all I could manage.

Despite the defensive elements in my distance from Sandra, this let things grow between us to the point where new understanding slowly emerged. From Sandra's standpoint, I both took her in and put her off. I agreed to offer a relationship that would contain room for her and her concerns, but was enough on my terms that I could tolerate it within the bounds of my professional standards and my personal needs.

That got us into business. Once I had protected myself in this way, I could afford, gradually, to let Sandra in. As she told me about herself, her history, and her daily life, her strengths and her difficulties, a relationship slowly grew that got inside each of us. And just as the relationship is the basis for a mother and father's nurturing of the growth of a child, our therapeutic relationship became the basis for her growth.

Sandra began analysis at the mercy of self-destructive forces, lonely, and unfulfilled. She finished feeling that her life was substantially in her control and that although she was not always happy, she was no longer self-destructive, now capable of sustained relationships. She still suffered disappointments, and at those times, as in this session, she was drawn to the old places and the old ways. But she was different. She now had a capacity to transform those moments into new opportunities, an ability to resist the primitive ravages of her pain and disappointment, and a new use of objects that could elevate such moments from threats to destroy relationships into opportunities for closeness, understanding, and growth.

This session offered a dramatic example of Sandra's new capacity. Her dreams, fantasies, and longings recalled the history of her difficulties and of her growth. In the context of the therapeutic relationship, she and I could understand, tolerate, and transform the primitive urge to sadness and mourning. In this session, it took the two of us. But by this time, Sandra could also manage similar situations on her own outside the treatment, demonstrating repeatedly that she had taken in this kind of process and made it her own.

In this hour, things were also happening in me. It was not that Sandra could not have handled her sense of loss without me. By now, I felt confident that she could. This hour was a matter of her getting into me at firsthand what she was suffering, an experience beyond what she could have told me about in simple and descriptive words. This hour was about our experiencing it together, because the loss belonged to both of us. By allowing Sandra's experience to get inside me, I could experience what she did, understand what she felt, and then experience my own sense of loss.

This session was an intense mutual experience, full of the history of our whole therapeutic relationship, a moment alive with the story of the five years of our relationship and with the loss of each other we both anticipated.

Having been able to keep my distance from Sandra through the use of the therapeutic situation, I was, eventually, also able to let her in—even to take her in—just as she was eventually able to let me in deeply, therapeutically, instead of bending all her efforts at getting under my skin, at taking me in deceitfully. This session represented the fullness of that hard-won mutual capacity. We relived the troubles, now in more depth and resonance than when she was actually threatened by the anxieties over the many years of her growth and the first years of our work together. We exercised our capacity to be deeply in touch and deeply moved without having to enact the fears and loss. She conveyed to me the fullness of her longing and despair, and her capacity to convey these to me was our living testimony of her change and growth, even as my ability to tolerate a painful and threatening internal experience was my evidence of the growth I had experienced with her, of my transformation as her analyst, which was the counterpart of her personal growth.

In the beginning of our work, Sandra could not have told me of her primitive fantasies, nor could I have taken them in. I could have listened to primitive material, but I could not have allowed it to be in touch with my own fantasy life. Since Sandra's analysis came early in my experience, my capacity to work grew during the years we worked together. I had her to thank for a great deal. This hour was a testament to the loss that her departure meant to me, just as surely as it was a testament to her loss in leaving me.

The threat Sandra felt was not her threat alone. I, too, was approaching the part of my career when I would be going it alone, without the guidance of supervisors and teachers. Her fear had an echo in me. Eager to be on my own, I was also fearful of the dangers. Just as the dream of my first analytic patient, Adam, which opened this book, could have spoken for my fears as a beginning analyst, Sandra's dream of loneliness, fear, and longing spoke for an aspect of my fear. Our loss was shared, and the experience resonated with the mutual aspects of losses and gains for the two of us.

THE GOALS OF THERAPY

The goals of psychotherapy and psychoanalysis can be summarized as the reclaiming of parts of the self that have been lost through splitting, repression, and projective identification (Steiner 1989), the mending of those that have been damaged, and the growing of those that have atrophied or failed to develop through neglect or self-restriction. But these goals are inextricably tied to the refinding and repair of internal objects, to the maturing of internal object relations, and, inevitably, to the growth of the person's capacity for external relationships that follows.

The process of therapy involves not only the relationship between the patients and their objects, but the relationship between patient and therapist. Each of the partners in the therapeutic relationship should be able in some measure to refind themselves in each other and to reclaim themselves from each other. Parts of the self that have been lodged in each other for safekeeping and for defensive purposes alike need to be, finally, recognized for what they are. This reclaiming will involve, however, a concomitant recognition of the other as an object in his or her own right, with an independent existence but also with a function for the self that is a legitimate one, one that does not violate the object's need to be an object and a self at the same time.

This is hardly a radical statement when put in terms of the patients who have to relinquish their therapists and take the therapeutic functions into themselves, just as children leaving home must, as best they can, carry the parenting functions inside as caring internal objects.

But it is harder for us to recognize that the therapist must be able to do a comparable thing. It is not that the therapist's life is as radically altered by the departure of any particular patient as is the patient's by the process of termination. The therapist, in most circumstances, will go on being a therapist. But life with that patient is ending, and what the patient has carried for the therapist, has meant to the therapist, has to be reckoned with, mourned, internalized. This loss will be experienced in the countertransference, where the defenses against it will also be felt (Searles 1959). It is not that the loss must be equal for the therapist or that change be of equal magnitude, but what loss, change, and refinding there are should be acknowledged, studied, and understood to be an integral part of the process of growth and change in relationships.

EVE FACES TERMINATION

This last example comes from later in my experience. This patient, too, was at the end of an analysis, with major changes in her capacities for relationships and for work. I had learned a great deal from her, too, but since I was more seasoned when we began, I had perhaps changed less myself during our work. Of that, however, I cannot be entirely sure.

It's Friday. Eve, a 24-year-old law student, is getting married this month to a man she loves and feels is a good match for her. But she is anxious.

"Things feel all wrong today. I got my ring yesterday at the jeweler's. And I don't like it. I thought I liked it at the time, but when I picked it up, it was nothing, just ordinary. They have a policy that things can't be returned or exchanged, but policies are made to be given exceptions. I felt Donald's impatience when I was looking at rings, so in a way I felt pressured to get one. This one has lines like cracks on it. I really wanted one to go with my engagement ring, to fit inconspicuously beside it, but they didn't have one like it. Then yesterday I found one that did fit, but at another store. I should take the loss if they won't accept it, but I feel like arguing with them."

I felt a bit startled with a reference I thought might be to me in the phrase "Policies are made to be given exceptions," but I thought I might be personalizing things. I felt called to attention, but dared not speak.

Eve continued. "Then I parked in a fire lane at the cleaners—only for 3 minutes. And the security guard gave me a ticket for $25. The man said, 'Sorry, lady! There's nothing you can do about it!' I was mad. Only 3 minutes! It wasn't much, but I didn't feel like letting them get away with it. So I went over his head and argued with the building manager. He said, 'We have to do it. If the fire marshall comes, he'd give you a $250 ticket.' So I said, 'What about the other car that's parked there that you didn't give a ticket?' The manager said, 'He works here, so we let him do it.' But I used that against him. He had to agree that contradicted his argument, and finally he let me out of my ticket."

I'm drifting off a bit, put off by her self-righteousness. She's done two things to defeat herself in minor ways and is insisting that it's the other guy's fault for holding to the rules. Yesterday she was upset about my vacation just before her wedding, claiming angrily that I often left her at times she felt in need of me. Today my leaving her in the hour by drifting off is happening at first outside of my awareness. I gradually become aware that this drifting off is the equivalent of leaving her already.

"Then I went to where Mom had ordered the brides-maids' dresses. They came into the store in the wrong color. I said to the lady, 'This isn't the color you showed us, and we've ordered hats to match.' She said, "It's not my fault. We have to take them the way they come.' I said, 'But then you shouldn't advertise that people can pick their color. I'm paying you to get it right!' I'm just not satisfied with it."

I said, "You're upset with things not working out. Some of them you set in motion, others you didn't have a direct hand in. But the effect is to feel that things are happening to you in either case."

"I don't think it refers to you, though," she said.

"Well, I wondered," I said. "I thought perhaps the reference to 'policies being made for exceptions' referred to me."

"I don't think so," she said. "I've given up on fighting you about your policy of charging for missed appointments. I used to get mad when Dad was paying for my analysis, but even though I'm paying for it myself now, I just think, 'What the hell. It's part of coming here.' I really don't think I'm mad at you today. Maybe that's your issue, something you brought to it."

I thought she was right. I didn't feel she was out to challenge me or demand I take something back. That wasn't it, but she had been saying something important to me silently in the reference to policies.

"There is something, though, that you were trying to

say to me in your throwaway line about policies being made for exceptions. I'm thinking about you telling me a number of times that you appreciate my firmness so much. This is a shorthand between us, but I'm not sure what for."

"Maybe." She was not particularly convinced, and continued on. "Well, then a friend called, a girl I had been out of touch with for a long time. She wants to be closer. It reminded me of a mutual friend of ours who tried to pick up with me after we had a kind of falling out. We met at a wedding, and as we were leaving, she said, 'Call me. Let's catch up and forget about what happened.' I wanted to, but what I said was, 'Okay. But I don't want to forget.' It drove her away. I haven't heard from her since."

"You're upset about something you do to people. To yourself, too. And if it can be blamed on the other person, it lets you off the hook, like the bridesmaids' dresses."

"Yes, or like the ticket. It upsets me when I think that *you* wouldn't get a ticket. I have an image of you parking in illegal places and not getting tickets."

"Where does that come from?" I asked.

"Oh, there's the time I saw you speeding on the Beltway, leaving me far behind. I thought, 'You travel in the fast lane. I'm just plodding along even though I'm young and it's me that's supposed to be in the fast lane.' "

I thought of the time the previous week I had parked near a sign clearly warning me not to—and had been towed. And of the speeding ticket I had received another time on the Beltway. I thought her image of me as getting away with things did fit with a fantasy she and I both had of me—one that got me in my own brand of trouble. It certainly did not fit with reality.

"What makes you think I get away with things?" I asked.

"I suppose I really don't know," she said. "It's just an image I have of you."

"That I get away with things and you don't. Then you envy me for the fantasy idea you have of me," I said.

"Yeah. I think that's what happens," she said. "But what do I want from you? Do you think I'm worried about getting married?"

"Yes," I said, realizing that's what I thought. "I think you're worried that you'll make a bad choice, like about the ring. You want a marriage that fits with the engagement ring inconspicuously, no more complications, no cracks in it."

"You don't miss a trick, do you? How do you do that, fit things together like that? That's good, that is!"

I liked the praise, even the envy. I felt puffed up, a bit inflated. I thought I shouldn't feel so good about it, but it was a nice antidote to the days I felt I didn't understand anything, or when she said I hadn't helped much. But I wondered, why was she doing this to me?

"Yes," she continued. "I'm worried I guess. Getting married is far more complicated than when Donald and I were just living together. It was just like it was the two of us. And for a long time I didn't find this part of myself intruding, and I didn't have to worry about those kids he's got from his first marriage. Or my mother. Now it's so complicated! My mother pouts to get me to pay attention to her because, although she likes Donald, she says she doesn't know what she'll do without me. And his 4-year-old daughter is acting up something awful, probably for the same reason."

"So there are those things that are imposed on you, like the dresses coming in the wrong color. You'd like the marriage to go well, like the dresses matching the hats, with no trouble."

"And I'd like *you* to make it right!" She fairly leaped at the idea. "Things seem so right for you. I want you to make them right for me."

Now I felt this was what she had been after about the policies that called for exceptions. I should be able to make it right for her. I relaxed and realized, too, that her excessive praise of a moment ago was aimed at inflating me so that I would go to work

on her behalf, try extra hard to make things right for her. In a
way, it had worked. I had felt energized by her praise to try to
make more connections, to make more right for her.

"So you inflate your idea of me to help you feel
better. You even inflate me with praise about how good I
am at analysis, but then you find you're envious of me," I
said.

"I think you have to be pretty good to help me, so it's
reassuring at first to think you're so good. Then I find I'm
diminished. I feel so little next to you," she acknowledged.

"What you feel worst about is not just the things that
happen to you, but the times you feel you make the bad
things happen," I said.

"Like making the wrong choice of rings. Or parking
in the fire lane," she agreed.

"Or even worse, taking a slap at people. You're
worried you'll hurt people, drive them away," I said.

She was startled. She jumped in place on the couch
so that it almost looked as though I had hit her. "That
hurts to hear you say I take a slap at people."

"It's what you're most afraid of."

She said, "I do it to you, but I can hardly stand to
think of it. I guess I think other people don't do it. You
don't do it. I think of you as never getting in trouble in this
way. I know it must happen to you, too, but I want you to
make it better. Why? What am I afraid of?"

I was able now to be aware of times I did something similar
to her "taking a slap at people." It looked as though she felt I had
done it to her just now when she looked so hit by my comment.
I remembered an unkind comment to my wife, a moment I felt
ashamed of now as I remembered it. That led me to think of the
anxiety of my own that had led to it.

"You came in feeling anxious. Part of it was that
things would go wrong—in your marriage mostly at the
moment. You want me to set it right. Like with the dress
lady: 'You're paying me to get it right!' So I should be able
to! What you want set right is partly the feeling things can

go bad, but the most important things to set right are the things you do to yourself and the people you care about and need—to your friend, your fiancé, to me."

"I feel worse than when I came in. I don't want to do those things. Why do I do them?"

"It starts when you feel jangled and splintered on the inside, and you're desperate to get things to fit, like the rings and the dresses—but inside. Then you feel you have to get something special to make things fit, and that you have to get it from someone else—the dress store, Donald, me, because you're afraid you'll keep ruining things."

"I do feel I have to get it from you. And you're not going to be here when I need you. I know you have to take a vacation, but I'm worried I can't keep things going without you. How can I do it?"

"It's the feeling you yourself can't fit smoothly together, like rings with no cracks, or the dresses and hats. But inside, you're afraid you can't fit the splinters back together. So you need me so the splinters don't fly out at the people you need. So they can settle in and fit together without jabbing you from inside."

"I don't know if I can do it for myself. I just don't know," she said, now with tears. "It's not just that you're not going to be here when I get married. I'm not going to be coming here very much longer anyhow. I'm going to miss you at the wedding. I wish you could be there. But that's okay, because I know you made it possible and that you're glad. But I don't know if later, when I'm not coming here anymore, if I'll be able to keep it up. Will the splinters fly out when you're not there to help me keep them in? I thought I could manage it, but at times like this, I get frightened I can't."

She had spoken my fear, too, the fear in every termination. Would our work have been enough? Had I given enough? Had she taken in enough? But I felt that she had reached the point of concern for herself and the people she cared about that had eluded her in the anger of the first part of the hour. I felt we had moved

beyond the blaming and guilt to begin to share the loss of our work together. In that, I felt considerable reassurance.
"We still have some time to work on that," I said.

As Eve faced her marriage, we also faced the loss of each other. Neither of us was invulnerable to the loss, although it was her—and my—reward for our work. In this hour, I felt she also wanted to reassure me that I was still needed, presenting the gratifying envy of me so that I would not envy her for getting away with her new husband, leaving me behind with my loss of her. Her feeling that I would not want to let her go came from a fear of being left behind that her mother had conveyed to her. But it also had a basis in our current situation in the loss I always feel when a patient is ready to go it alone, leaving me with a twinge of feeling no longer needed.

Our work ends with loss. Our patients, who have lost parts of themselves and their objects, come to us to find them once again. To work with them we must, in turn, lose ourselves in each of our patients. If things go well—and with their help— they and we eventually find ourselves again. It is a mutual refinding.

16

Epilogue: Refinding

Our Selves through

Our Patients

At the heart of the object relations approach is a way of working that occurs in the interplay between two people, in an area of overlap that is both between them and within each of them. When the approach is effective, it is so because of the mutual involvement of both patient and therapist as complete human beings, each with a range of conscious and unconscious communication through which they can share complementary, resonating object relations systems.

And so we must also consider the object relations of the therapist—of ourselves—in this examination of the inextricable relationship between self and object. Our patients are our objects. They are a repository for split-off parts of ourselves. And at the same time, they put into us parts of themselves, some of which we take in and identify with, changing our own object relationships—for better or for worse. At times, the pleasure in our patients' growth or identification with their better qualities pulls the therapist toward growth. At other times, our object relations are affected negatively, to the consternation of our spouses and families.

I can well remember an episode—because it was not long ago—when I came home to my family with an abruptness and anger, which, although not beyond my own repertoire, had no discernible trigger in immediate family or personal events. It was not until my 12-year-old daughter asked, "What's got into you, Dad?" that I had a flash of insight that it was my last patient who had got into me. I had taken in, with a kind of glee, his previous evening's temper tantrum because I partly admired his verve and aggression in the face of family constraints.

But more often, it is the mature, resilient object relations set of the therapist that is at the leading edge of the work, available to be taken in by the patient, modified, and made the patient's own. To be sure, we projectively identify with our patients, put into them aspects of ourselves that do not belong to them. But if we can help the patient to contain and modify them, we take them back in a form that is our own, while leaving the patient free to accept the useful aspects and reject others.

This therapeutic struggle, which is the everyday stuff of our work, occurs because it is our selves that form our therapeutic instrument. Patients become our objects. Against and with them, we evaluate our selves as therapists. What we take in from them, what we provide to them, what we offer to them for their own use are all functions of our selves. And we judge and understand our selves according to how the experience with these patients reflects us. Our professional self-esteem is just as intertwined with our patient-objects as our personal self-esteem is intertwined with our families and friends.

This is not to say that therapists should not have professional distance from patients. They need distance to manage the flux of self and object inherent in psychotherapy. No other profession so deliberately teaches its practitioners to put themselves on the line in this way every day, and at the same time calls for the reflexive examination of that experience.

Ultimately, it is not the simple reflection of ourselves by the patient that determines our judgment of our professional effectiveness and contributes to our self-esteem generally. It is a complex interaction between our self-evaluation and the reflection of our objects in our patients, along with that reflected image of our selves provided by internal and external objects constituted by our peers, teachers and supervisors, parents, and other primary objects who all contribute to our object relations set in which our self resides. In the process, we must find new internal objects and we must grow new and changed parts of our selves to relate to them. We must—just as our patients must—reclaim lost and buried parts of our selves. In the therapeutic crucible with our patients, we experience a reunion with those parts of our selves, parts we had forgotten, parts we had never known directly, parts that grow new capacities with experience and age.

This is the experience that brings personal renewal. An evolving process, it goes on as long as our work goes on. Threatening and challenging, it is fundamental to our work. It is, finally, the relationship between our own selves and our own objects—patients and families—that requires renewal and yet that brings renewal throughout the life course of our work.

References

Abelin, E. (1971). The role of the father in the separation-individualization process. In *Separation-Individuation*, ed. J. B. McDevitt and C. F. Settlage, pp. 229–252. New York: International Universities Press.

———— (1975). Some further observation and comments on the earliest role of the father. *International Journal of Psycho-Analysis* 56:293–302.

Ainsworth, M., and Wittig, B. (1969). Attachment and exploratory behavior in one-year-olds in a stranger situation.

In *Determinants of Infant Behavior*, ed. B. M. Foss. 4:111–136. New York: Wiley.

Ainsworth, M., Blehar, M., Waters, E., and Wall, S. (1978). *Patterns of Attachment*. Hillsdale, NJ: Lawrence Erlbaum Associates.

Aponte, H. J., and VanDeusen, J. M. (1981). Structural Family Therapy. In *Handbook of Family Therapy*, ed. A. Gurman and D. Kniskern, pp. 310–360. New York: Brunner/Mazel.

Atwood, G., and Stolorow, R. (1984). *Structures of Subjectivity: Explorations in Psychoanalytic Phenomenology*. Hillsdale, NJ: Analytic Press.

Auden, W. H. (1945). In memory of Sigmund Freud. In *The Collected Poetry of W. H. Auden*, pp. 163–167. New York: Random House.

Balint, M. (1952). *Primary Love and Psycho-analytic Technique*. London: Tavistock, 1965.

―――― (1957). *Problems of Human Pleasure and Behaviour*. London: Hogarth Press.

―――― (1968). *The Basic Fault: Therapeutic Aspects of Regression*. London: Tavistock.

Bank, S. P., and Kahn, M. D. (1982). *The Sibling Bond*. New York: Basic Books.

Beebe, B., and Lachmann, F. M. (1988). The contribution of mother–infant mutual influence to the origins of self- and object representations. *Psychoanalytic Psychology* 5:305–337.

Bion, W. R. (1961). *Experiences in Groups and Other Papers*. London: Tavistock.

―――― (1967). *Second Thoughts*. London: Heinemann.

―――― (1970). *Attention and Interpretation: A Scientific Approach to Insight in Psycho-Analysis and Groups*. London: Tavistock.

Blos, P. (1967). The second individuation process of adolescence. *Psychoanalytic Study of the Child* 22:162–186. New York: International Universities Press.

Bollas, C. (1987). *The Shadow of the Object*. New York: Columbia University Press.

―――― (1989). *Forces of Destiny: Psychoanalysis and Human Idiom*. London: Free Association.

Bowlby, J. (1969). *Attachment and Loss, Vol. 1: Attachment*. London: Hogarth Press.

―――― (1973). *Attachment and Loss, Vol. 2: Separation: Anxiety and Anger*. London: Hogarth Press.

―――― (1980). *Attachment and Loss, Vol. 3: Loss: Sadness and Depression*. London: Hogarth Press.

_____ (1988). *A Secure Base: Parent–Child Attachment and Healthy Human Development*. New York: Basic Books.

Box, S. (1981). Introduction: space for thinking in families. In *Psychotherapy with Families: An Analytic Approach*, ed. S. Box, B. Copley, J. Magagna, and E. Moustaki, pp. 1–8. London: Routledge & Kegan Paul.

_____ (1984). *Containment and countertransference.* Paper presented at the Washington School of Psychiatry, Fifth Annual Symposium on Psychoanalytic Family Therapy, Bethesda, MD, April.

Box, S., Copley, B., Magagna, J., and Moustaki, E. (1981). *Psychotherapy with Families: An Analytic Approach*. London: Routledge & Kegan Paul.

Brazelton, T. B. (1982). Joint regulation of neonate–parent behavior. In *Social Interchange in Infancy*, ed. E. Tronick, pp. 7–22. Baltimore: University Park Press.

Brazelton, T. B., Koslowski, B., and Main, M. (1974). The origins of reciprocity: the early mother–infant interaction. In *The Effect of the Infant on Its Caregiver*, ed. M. Lewis and L. A. Rosenblum. I:49–76. New York: Wiley.

Brazelton, T. B., Yogman, M., Als, H., and Tronick, E. (1979). The infant as a focus for family reciprocity. In *The Child and Its Family*, ed. M. Lewis and L. A. Rosenblum, pp. 29–43. New York: Plenum Press.

Breuer, J., and Freud, S. (1895). Studies on hysteria. *Standard Edition* 2.

Buber, M. (1978). *I and Thou*. Trans. W. Kaufman and S. G. Smith. New York: Scribner.

Campos, J., and Stenberg, C. (1980). Perception of appraisal and emotion: the onset of social referencing. In *Infant Social Cognition*, eds. M. E. Lamb and L. Sherrod. Hillsdale, NJ: Lawrence Erlbaum Associates.

Casement, P. J. (1991). *Learning from the Patient*. New York: Guilford.

Davies, R. (1985). *What's Bred in the Bone*. Toronto: MacMillan.

Dicks, H. V. (1967). *Marital Tensions: Clinical Studies Towards a Psychoanalytic Theory of Interaction*. London: Routledge & Kegan Paul.

Donne, J. (1952). "The Canonization." In *The Complete Poetry and Selected Prose of John Donne*, ed. C. M. Coffin, pp. 13–14. New York: Modern Library.

Duncan, D. (1981). A thought on the nature of psychoanalytic theory. *International Journal of Psycho-Analysis* 62:339–349.

_____ (1989). The flow of interpretation. *International Journal of Psycho-Analysis* 70:693–700.

_____ (1990). The feel of the session. *Psychoanalysis and Contemporary Thought* 13:3–22.

_____ (1991). *What analytic therapy does.* Paper presented at the Washington School of Psychiatry Object Relations Theory Conference, Washington DC, May 5, 1991.

Edgcumbe, R., and Burgner, M. (1975). The phallic-narcissistic phase: a differentiation between pre-oedipal and oedipal aspects of phallic development. *Psychoanalytic Study of the Child* 30:160–180. New Haven: Yale University Press.

Emde, R. N. (1988a). Development terminable and interminable: I. Innate and motivational factors from infancy. *International Journal of Psycho-Analysis* 69:23–42.

_____ (1988b). Development terminable and interminable: II. Recent psychoanalytic theory and therapeutic considerations. *International Journal of Psycho-Analysis* 69:283–296.

Emde, R. N., Klingman, D. H., Reich, J. H., and Wade, J. D. (1978). Emotional expression in infancy: I. Initial studies of social signaling and an emergent model. In *The Development of Affect*, ed. M. Lewis and L. Rosenblum, pp. 125–148. New York: Plenum Press.

Emde, R. N., and Sorce, J. F. (1983). The rewards of infancy: emotional availability and maternal referencing. In *Frontiers of Infant Psychiatry, vol. 1,* ed. J. D. Call, E. Galenson, and R. Tyson, pp. 17–30. New York: Basic Books.

Erikson, E. H. (1950). *Childhood and Society.* Rev. ed. New York: Norton, 1963.

_____ (1959). *Identity and the Life Cycle. Psychological Issues,* Monograph 1. New York: International Universities Press.

Ezriel, H. (1950). A psychoanalytic approach to group treatment. *British Journal of Medical Psychology* 23:59–74.

_____ (1952). Notes on psychoanalytic group therapy II: interpretation and research. *Psychiatry* 15:119–126.

Fairbairn, W. R. D. (1940). Schizoid factors in the personality. In *Psychoanalytic Studies of the Personality,* pp. 3–27. London: Routledge & Kegan Paul, 1952.

_____ (1941). A revised psychopathology of the psychoses and psychoneuroses. In *Psychoanalytic Studies of the Personality,* pp. 28–58. London: Routledge & Kegan Paul, 1952.

_____ (1943). The repression and the return of bad objects (with special reference to the war neuroses). In *Psychoanalytic Studies of the Personality,* pp. 59–81. London: Routledge & Kegan Paul, 1952.

_____ (1944). Endopsychic structure considered in terms of object relationships. In *Psychoanalytic Studies of the Personality,* pp. 82–136. London: Routledge & Kegan Paul, 1952.

_____ (1951). A synopsis of the development of the author's views regarding the structure of the personality. In *Psychoanalytic Studies of the Personality,* pp. 162–179. London: Routledge & Kegan Paul, 1952.

_____ (1952). *Psychoanalytic Studies of the Personality.* London: Routledge & Kegan Paul.

_____ (1954). Observations on the nature of hysterical states. *British Journal of Medical Psychology* 27:105–125.

_____ (1958). The nature and aims of psycho-analytical treatment. *International Journal of Psycho-Analysis* 39:374–385.

_____ (1963). Synopsis of an object-relations theory of the personality. *International Journal of Psycho-Analysis* 44:224–225.

Freud, S. (1895). The psychotherapy of hysteria. *Standard Edition* 2: 255–305.

_____ (1900). The interpretation of dreams. *Standard Edition* 4/5.

_____ (1905a). Fragment of an analysis of a case of hysteria. *Standard Edition* 7:7–122.

_____ (1905b). Three essays on the theory of sexuality. *Standard Edition* 7:135–243.

_____ (1909). Notes upon a case of obsessional neurosis. *Standard Edition* 10:153–318.

_____ (1910). Future prospects of psycho-analytic therapy. *Standard Edition* 11:141–151.

_____ (1912a). The dynamics of transference. *Standard Edition* 12: 97–108.

_____ (1912b). Recommendations to physicians practicing psycho-analysis. *Standard Edition* 12:111–120.

_____ (1914). Remembering, repeating, and working through. *Standard Edition* 12:147–156.

_____ (1915). Observations on transference love. *Standard Edition* 12:159–171.

_____ (1917). Mourning and melancholia. *Standard Edition* 14:243–258.

_____ (1918). From the history of an infantile neurosis. *Standard Edition* 17:7–122.

_____ (1923). The ego and the id. *Standard Edition* 19:3–63.

_____ (1926). Inhibitions, symptoms, and anxiety. *Standard Edition* 20:87–174.

_____ (1937). Analysis terminable and interminable. *Standard Edition* 23:216–253.

Gill, M. (1984). Psychoanalysis and psychotherapy: a revision. *International Review of Psycho-Analysis* 11:161–169.

Gill, M., and Muslin, H. (1976). Early interpretation of transference. *Journal of the American Psychoanalytic Association* 24:779–794.

Greenberg, J. R., and Mitchell, S. A. (1983). *Object Relations in Psychoanalytic Theory.* Cambridge, MA: Harvard University Press.

Greenson, R. (1967). *The Technique and Practice of Psychoanalysis,* Vol. I. New York: International Universities Press.

Guntrip, H. (1961). *Personality Structure and Human Interaction: The Developing Synthesis of Psychodynamic Theory.* London: Hogarth Press.

_____ (1969). *Schizoid Phenomena, Object Relations and the Self.* New York: International Universities Press.

Hamilton, N. G. (1988). *Self and Others: Object Relations Theory in Practice.* Northvale, NJ: Jason Aronson.

Heimann, P. (1950). On counter-transference. *International Journal of Psycho-Analysis* 31:81–84.

Hughes, J. M. (1989). *Reshaping the Psychoanalytic Domain: The Work of Melanie Klein, W. R. D. Fairbairn, & D. W. Winnicott.* Berkeley, CA: University of California Press.

Jacobs, T. J. (1991). *The Use of the Self.* Madison, CT: International Universities Press.

Jacques, E. (1965). Death and the mid-life crisis. *International Journal of Psycho-Analysis* 46:502–514.

Jones, E. (1952). Foreword to W. R. D. Fairbairn's *Psychoanalytic Studies of the Personality.* London: Routledge & Kegan Paul.

Joseph, B. (1989). *Psychic Equilibrium and Psychic Change: The Selected Papers of Betty Joseph,* ed. E. B. Spillius and M. Feldman. London: Routledge, Chapman Hall.

Kernberg, O. (1975). *Borderline Conditions and Pathological Narcissism.* New York: Jason Aronson.

_____ (1976). *Object Relations Theory and Clinical Psychoanalysis.* New York: Jason Aronson.

_____ (1980). *Internal World and External Reality: Object Relations Theory Applied.* New York: Jason Aronson.

_____ (1984). *Severe Personality Disorders: Psychotherapeutic Strategies.* New Haven: Yale University Press.

Khan, M. M. R. (1963). The concept of cumulative trauma. *The Psychoanalytic Study of the Child* 18:286–306. New York: International Universities Press.

_____ (1974). *The Privacy of the Self.* London: Hogarth Press.

_____ (1979). *Alienation in Perversions.* New York: International Universities Press.

Klein, M. (1928). Early stages of the Oedipus conflict. In *Love, Guilt and Reparation and Other Works, 1921–45,* pp. 186–198. London: Hogarth Press.

_____ (1932). *The Psycho-Analysis of Children.* Trans. A. Strachey, Rev. A. Strachey and H. A. Thorner. London: Hogarth Press.

_____ (1935). A contribution to the psychogenesis of manic-depressive states. *International Journal of Psycho-Analysis* 16, pp. 145–174.

_____ (1940). Mourning and its relation to manic-depressive states. *International Journal of Psycho-Analysis* 21:125–153.

_____ (1945). The Oedipus complex in the light of early anxieties. *International Journal of Psycho-Analysis* 26:11–33.

_____ (1946). Notes on some schizoid mechanisms. *International Journal of Psycho-Analysis* 27:99–110.

_____ (1948). *Contributions to Psychoanalysis, 1921–45.* London: Hogarth Press.

_____ (1957). *Envy and Gratitude.* London: Tavistock.

_____ (1961). *Narrative of a Child Analysis.* London: Hogarth Press.

_____ (1975a). *Love, Guilt and Reparation, 1921–45.* New York: Delacorte Press.

_____ (1975b). *Envy and Gratitude and Other Works, 1946–1963.* London: Hogarth Press.

Klinnert, M. D., Campos, J. J., Sorce, J. F., et al. (1983). Emotions as behavior regulators: social referencing in infancy. In *Emotion: Theory, Research and Experience,* vol. 2, ed. R. Plutchik and H. Kellerman, pp. 57–86. New York: Academic Press.

Kohut, H. (1977). *The Restoration of the Self.* New York: International

Universities Press.

_____ (1984). *How Does Analysis Cure?* Ed. A. Goldberg. Chicago: University of Chicago Press.

Levenson, E. (1983). *The Ambiguity of Change: An Inquiry into the Nature of Psychoanalytic Reality.* New York: Basic Books.

Levinson, D. J., Darrow, C. N., Klein, E. B., et al. (1978). *The Seasons of a Man's Life.* New York: Knopf.

Lichtenberg, J. (1983). *Psychoanalysis and Infant Research.* Hillsdale, NJ: Analytic Press.

_____ (1989). *Psychoanalysis and Human Motivation.* Hillsdale, NJ: Analytic Press.

Lichtenstein, H. (1961). Identity and sexuality: a study of their inter-relationship in man. *Journal of the American Psychoanalytic Association* 9:179–260.

Loewald, H. W. (1960). On the therapeutic action of psychoanalysis. *International Journal of Psycho-Analysis* 41:16–33.

_____ (1980). *Papers on Psychoanalysis.* New Haven: Yale University Press.

McDougall, J. (1970). Homosexuality in women. In *Female Sexuality: New Psychoanalytic Views,* ed. J. Chasseguet-Smirgel, pp. 94–134. Ann Arbor, MI: University of Michigan Press.

_____ (1985). *Theaters of the Mind: Illusion and Truth on the Psychoanalytic Stage.* New York: Basic Books.

_____ (1986). Identification, neoneeds, and neosexualities. *International Journal of Psycho-Analysis* 67:19–33.

_____ (1989). *Theaters of the Body.* New York: Norton.

Meltzer, D. (1975). Adhesive identification. *Contemporary Psychoanalysis* 11:289–310.

Mitchell, S. A. (1988). *Relational Concepts in Psychoanalysis: An Integration.* Cambridge, MA: Harvard University Press.

Modell, A. (1984). *Psychoanalysis in a New Context.* Madison, CT: International Universities Press.

Money-Kyrle, R. (1956). Normal countertransference and some of its deviations. *International Journal of Psycho-Analysis* 37:360–366.

_____ (1971). The aim of psychoanalysis. *International Journal of Psycho-Analysis* 52:103–106.

_____ (1978). *The Collected Papers of Roger Money-Kyrle.* Ed. D. Meltzer and E. O'Shaughnessy. Strath Tay, Scotland: Clunie Press.

Muir, R. (1989). Fatherhood from the perspective of object relations theory and relational systems theory. Paper presented at Washington School of Psychiatry's Annual Symposium on Psychoanalytic Object Relations Family Therapy, Bethesda, MD, March 18, 1989.

Ogden, T. H. (1982). *Projective Identification and Psychotherapeutic Technique.* New York: Jason Aronson.

_____ (1986). *The Matrix of the Mind.* Northvale, NJ: Jason Aronson.

_____ (1989). *The Primitive Edge of Experience.* Northvale, NJ: Jason Aronson.

Palombo, S. R. (1978). *Dreaming and Memory: A New Information-Processing Model.* New York: Basic Books.

Racker, H. (1968). *Transference and Countertransference.* New York: International Universities Press.

Reiss, D. (1981). *The Family's Construction of Reality.* Cambridge, MA: Harvard University Press.

Sameroff, A. J., and Emde, R. N., eds. (1989). *Relationship Disturbances in Early Childhood: A Developmental Approach.* New York: Basic Books.

Sandler, J. (1976). Actualization and object relationships. *The Journal of the Philadelphia Association for Psychoanalysis* 3:59–70.

Scharff, D. E. (1982). *The Sexual Relationship: An Object Relations View of Sex and the Family.* Boston: Routledge & Kegan Paul.

_____ (1987). The infant's reinvention of the family. In *Object Relations Family Therapy,* by D. E. Scharff and J. S. Scharff, pp. 101–126. Northvale, NJ: Jason Aronson.

Scharff, D. E., and Hill, J. M. M. (1976). *Between Two Worlds: Aspects of the Transition from School to Work.* London: Careers Consultants.

Scharff, D. E., and Scharff, J. S. (1987). *Object Relations Family Therapy.* Northvale, NJ: Jason Aronson.

_____ (1991). *Object Relations Couple Therapy.* Northvale, NJ: Jason Aronson.

Scharff, J. S. (1989). Play: an aspect of the therapist's holding capacity. In *Foundations of Object Relations Therapy,* ed. J. S. Scharff, pp. 447–461. Northvale, NJ: Jason Aronson.

_____ (1992). *Projective and Introjective Identification and the Use of the Therapist's Self.* Northvale, NJ: Jason Aronson.

Searles, H. F. (1959). Oedipal love in the countertransference. *International Journal of Psycho-Analysis* 40:180–90.

_____ (1963). The place of neutral therapist-responses in psychotherapy with the schizophrenic patient. In *Collected Papers on Schizophrenia and Related Subjects,* pp. 626–653. New York: International Universities Press, 1965.

_____ (1965). *Collected Papers on Schizophrenia and Related Subjects.* New York: International Universities Press.

_____ (1979). *Countertransference and Related Subjects: Selected Papers.* New York: International Universities Press.

_____ (1986). *My Work with Borderline Patients.* Northvale, NJ: Jason Aronson.

Segal, H. (1973). *Introduction to the Work of Melanie Klein.* London: Hogarth Press.

_____ (1981). *The Work of Hanna Segal.* New York: Jason Aronson.

_____ (1991). *Dream, Phantasy and Art.* London: Routledge, Chapman Hall.

Shakespeare, W. H. (1954). *The Tragedy of Romeo and Juliet.* Ed. R. Hosley. Yale Shakespeare ed. New Haven: Yale University Press.

Shapiro, R. L. (1979). Family dynamics and object-relations theory: an analytic, group-interpretive approach to family therapy. In *Adolescent Psychiatry: Developmental and Clinical Studies,* ed. S. C. Feinstein and P. L. Giovacchini, 7:118–135. Chicago: University of Chicago Press.

Slipp, S. (1984). *Object Relations: A Dynamic Bridge between Individual and Family Therapy.* New York: Jason Aronson.

Socarides, C. W. (1978). *Homosexuality.* New York: Jason Aronson.

Sophocles. (1956). *Oedipus Rex.* In *The Oedipus Cycle of Sophocles, An English Version,* English version by Dudley Fitts and Robert Fitzgerald. New York: Harvest Books.

_____ (1956). *Oedipus at Colonus.* In *The Oedipus Cycle of Sophocles, An English Version,* English version by Dudley Fitts and Robert Fitzgerald. New York: Harvest Books.

_____ (1956). *Antigone.* In *The Oedipus Cycle of Sophocles, An English Version,* English version by Dudley Fitts and Robert Fitzgerald. New York: Harvest Books.

Steiner, J. (1987). The interplay between pathological organizations and the paranoid-schizoid and depressive positions. *International Journal of Psycho-Analysis* 68:69–80.

_____ (1989). *Projective identification and the aims of psychoanalytic psychotherapy.* Paper presented at the Washington School of Psychiatry Object Relations Theory Conference, Washington, DC, November 12, 1989.

Stern, D. (1977). *The First Relationship: Infant and Mother.* Cambridge, MA: Harvard University Press.

_____ (1985). *The Interpersonal World of the Infant: A View from Psychoanalysis and Developmental Psychology.* New York: Basic Books.

Stolorow, R. D. (1991). The intersubjective context of intrapsychic experience: a decade of psychoanalytic inquiry. *Psychoanalytic Inquiry* 11:171–184.

Stolorow, R. D., Brandchaft, B., and Atwood, G. E. (1987). *Psychoanalytic Treatment: An Intersubjective Approach.* Hillsdale, NJ: Analytic Press.

Sullivan, H. S. (1953a). *Conceptions of Modern Psychiatry: The First William Alanson White Memorial Lectures.* New York: Norton.

_____ (1953b). *The Interpersonal Theory of Psychiatry.* New York: Norton.

_____ (1962). *Schizophrenia as a Human Process.* New York: Norton.

Sutherland, J. D. (1963). Object relations theory and the conceptual model of psychoanalysis. *British Journal of Medical Psychology* 36:109–124.

_____ (1980). The British object relations theorists: Balint, Winnicott, Fairbairn, Guntrip. *Journal of the American Psychoanalytic Association* 28:829–860.

_____ (1985). *The object relations approach.* Paper presented at the Washington School of Psychiatry, Sixth Annual Symposium on Psychoanalytic Family Therapy, Bethesda, MD, April 1985.

_____ (1989). *Fairbairn's Journey to the Interior.* London: Free Association.

Terr, L. C. (1991). Childhood trauma: an Outline and Overview. *American Journal of Psychiatry* 148:10–20.

Tower, L. (1956). Countertransference. *Journal of the American Psychoanalytic Association* 4:224–255.

Tronick, E., Als, H., Adamson, L., et al. (1978). The infant's response to entrapment between contradictory messages in face-to-face interaction. *Journal of the American Academy of Child Psychiatry* 17:1–13.

Tustin, F. (1986). *Autistic Barriers in Neurotic Patients.* London: Karnac.

_____ (1990). *The Protective Shell in Children and Adults*. London: Karnac.

Virag, R., Frydman, D. I., Legman, M., and Virag, H. (1984). Intracavernous injection of papaverine as a diagnostic and therapeutic method in erectile failure. *Angiology* 35:79–83.

Volkan, V. D. (1976). *Primitive Internalized Object Relations*. New York: International Universities Press.

_____ (1987). *Six Steps in the Treatment of Borderline Personality Organization*. Northvale, NJ: Jason Aronson.

Whitaker, C. A., and Keith, D. V. (1981). Symbolic-experiential family therapy. In *Handbook of Family Therapy*, ed. A. S. Gurman & D. P. Kniskern, pp. 187–225. New York: Brunner/Mazel.

Williams, A. H. (1981). The micro environment. In *Psychotherapy with Families: An Analytic Approach*, ed. S. Box, B. Copley, J. Magagna, and E. Moustaki, pp. 105–119. London: Routledge & Kegan Paul.

Winnicott, D. W. (1947). Hate in the countertransference. In *Collected Papers: Through Paediatrics to Psycho-Analysis*, pp. 194–203. London: Tavistock, 1958.

_____ (1951). Transitional objects and transitional phenomena. In *Collected Papers: Through Paediatrics to Psycho-Analysis*, pp. 229–242. London: Tavistock, 1958.

_____ (1956). Primary maternal preoccupation. In *Maturational Processes and the Facilitating Environment: Studies on the Theory of Emotional Development*, pp. 300–305. London: Hogarth Press, 1965.

_____ (1958). *Collected Papers: Through Paediatrics to Psycho-Analysis*. London: Tavistock.

_____ (1960a). The theory of the parent–infant relationship. *International Journal of Psycho-Analysis* 41:585–595.

_____ (1960b). Ego distortion in terms of true and false self. In *The Maturational Processes and the Facilitating Environment: Studies on the Theory of Emotional Development*, pp. 140–152. London: Hogarth Press, 1965.

_____ (1963a). Communicating and not communicating leading to a study of certain opposites. In *The Maturational Processes and the Facilitating Environment: Studies on the Theory of Emotional Development*, pp. 179–192. London: Hogarth Press, 1965.

_____ (1963b). The development of the capacity for concern. In *The Maturational Processes and the Facilitating Environment: Studies in the Theory of Emotional Development,* pp. 73–82. London: Hogarth Press, 1965.

_____ (1965). *The Maturational Processes and the Facilitating Environment: Studies on the Theory of Emotional Development.* London: Hogarth Press.

_____ (1968). The use of an object and relating through cross-identification. In *Playing and Reality,* pp. 86–94. New York: Basic Books, 1971.

_____ (1971a). *Playing and Reality.* London: Tavistock.

_____ (1971b). The location of cultural experience. *Playing and Reality,* pp. 95–103. London: Tavistock.

Wright, K. (1991). *Vision and Separation between Mother and Baby.* Northvale, NJ: Jason Aronson.

Yogman, M. (1982). Observations on the father–infant relationship. In *Father and Child: Developmental and Clinical Perspectives,* ed. S. H. Cath, A. R. Gurwitt, and J. M. Ross, pp. 101–122. Boston: Little, Brown.

Zetzel, E. (1958). Therapeutic alliance in the analysis of hysteria. In *The Capacity for Emotional Growth,* pp. 182–196. New York: International Universities Press.

Zinner, J., and Shapiro, R. L. (1972). Projective identification as a mode of perception and behavior in families of adolescents. *International Journal of Psycho-Analysis* 53:523–530.

Index

Abelin, E., 237, 274
Abuse
    memory and, 123–124
    Oedipus and, 242
Adolescence
    changing internal object rela-
        tions in, 95–119. *See also*
        Internal object relations
    dream analysis, 207–229. *See
        also* Dream analysis (in

family therapy with
    adolescents)
life development perspective
    case example of family,
        299–305
    parental blocked develop-
        ment and, 305–306
memory and, 129–130
Adulthood, memory and,
    130–133

Age level, family role
    relationships and, 273-274
Ainsworth, M., 269
Anouilh, J., 248
Antilibido system, object
    relations theory and, 32-34
Aponte, H. J., 53
Arms-around mother context
    maternal-infant relationship,
    44-45
    self recovery (in therapy), 136
Atwood, G., 13
Auden, W. H., 181
Autistic contiguous position,
    26, 35, 39

Balint, M., 12
Bank, S. P., 297
Beebe, B., 12
Bion, W. R., 12, 15, 20, 29, 30,
    41, 42, 43, 47-49, 52, 275
Birth order, life development
    perspective and, 296-297
Blos, P., 207
Bollas, C., 12, 43, 52, 147
Bowlby, J., 12, 31, 270, 272, 273
Box, S., 12
Brazelton, T. B., 265
Breuer, J., 10, 50, 175
Buber, M., 45
Burgner, M., 237

Campos, J., 270
Casement, P. J., 53
Childhood, memory and,
    127-129
Communication, dream as
    communication, 157-182.
    See also Dream as
    communication

Conjoint therapy, transference
    and countertransference
    and, 58-59
Container/contained
    phenomena
    family role relationships
    and, 274-276
    self recovery (in therapy),
    136-137
    transitional space reconciled
    with, 47-49
Contextual transference,
    described, 54-57
Countertransference. See also
    Transference and
    countertransference;
    Transference and
    countertransference use
    dream as communication
    and, 167-168
    therapist's object relations
    and, 317-318. See also
    Therapist's object
    relations
Couple assessment, dream as
    communication, 172-176
Culture, sociocultural
    communication, dream as,
    180-182

Davies, R., 240
Depressive positions,
    transference and
    countertransference, 37-39
Developmental factors
    drive theory and, 14
    infant's invention of family,
    234-238
    interpersonal relationships
    and, 14

inventiveness concept and,
     234
life development perspective
     and, 296
object relations theory and, 36
paranoid/schizoid and
     depressive positions
     (Klein), 37–39
schizophrenia and, 24
Dicks, H. V., 43, 165
Dream analysis
analyst and, 6–8
psychoanalysis and, 181–182
transference and, 4–5, 60–61
Dream analysis (in family
     therapy with adolescents),
     207–229
case example of reluctant
     drag-in, 209–217
case example of sexual
     activity
     described, 217–223
     dream analysis, 223–229
overview of, 207–208
Dream analysis (in marital
     therapy), 183–206
distance reduction, 184–196
interlocking dream analysis,
     196–206
interlocking dream analysis
     in continuing therapy,
     196–203
interlocking dream analysis
     in terminating therapy,
     203–206
overview of, 183–184
Dream as communication,
     157–182
couple assessment, 172–176
family object relations,
     164–165

group and institutional
     settings, 176–180
individual therapy and
     interpersonal
     communication, 166–172
interpersonal
     communications,
     163–164
overview of, 157–161
projective identification and
     unconscious
     communication, 165
sociocultural communication,
     180–182
structure of self and object
     depiction (Fairbairn),
     161–162
transference meanings, 166
Drive theory, development
     and, 14, 15
Duncan, D., 53

Edgcumbe, R., 237
Ego
introjective identification
     and, 41
object relations theory and,
     32–33
self-contrasted, 35
Emde, R. N., 12, 265, 270
Envy, transference and coun-
     tertransference use, 84–93
Erikson, E. H., 207, 297
Experiential factors, object
     relations theory and, 36–37
Eye-to-eye relationship
maternal–infant relationship
     and, 45
self within object and, 17
Ezriel, H., 59

Fairbairn, W. R. D., 12, 14, 15,
    23, 24, 29, 30–37, 137,
    161–162, 175, 234, 237,
    240, 267
False self. *See* True and false
    self
Family. *See also* Fathering;
    Mothering; Parenting
    object relations, dream as
        communication, 164–165
    Oedipus situation and, 235.
        See also Oedipus
        situation
Family role relationships,
    263–293
    child and adult differences,
        272–274
    child and adult differences
        in internal family,
        290–291
    child and adult similarities,
        271–272
    child as container instead of
        contained, 274–276
    child as incomplete entity,
        269–270
    family case example
        described, 277–286
        differentiating elements,
            288–290
        reparation leading to
            growth and
            differentiation,
            286–288
    overview of, 263–267
    parent as leader, 270–271
    partners-of-the-moment
        dynamics, 267–269
    therapist's role and
        emotional position,
        291–293

Family therapy, dream
    analysis, 207–229. *See also*
    Dream analysis (in family
    therapy with adolescents);
    Marital therapy
Fathering. *See also* Mothering;
    Parenting
    family role relationships
        and, 266. *See also* Family
        role relationships
    homosexual etiology and,
        139–140
    internal object relations and,
        109–112
Focused transference,
    described, 54–57
Freud, S., 10, 11, 12, 14, 17,
    30, 35, 41, 50–51, 56, 123,
    132, 161, 175, 176,
    181–182, 233, 234

Gaze interactions, self within
    object and, 17
Gill, M., 12, 56
Greenberg, J. R., 34
Group therapy, dream as
    communication, 176–180
Guntrip, H., 12, 15, 35, 37,
    162, 175, 216

Hamilton, N. G., 12, 34
Heimann, P., 51
Hill, J. M. M., 296, 299
Homosexuality
    case example, self recovery
        (in therapy), 138–152
    family role relationships
        and, 276–277
    object relations theory and,
        34
    Oedipus situation and, 238

therapeutic relationship and,
4, 5, 7
transference and, 62–64
Hughes, J. M., 162
Hysteria
object relations theory and,
35
transference and, 50

Infancy
family role relationships
and, 265–266. *See also*
Family role relationships
focused transferences and,
56
object relations theory and,
9–10, 15, 36
Oedipus situation and,
234–238
paranoid/schizoid and
depressive positions
(Klein), 38–39
self within object and, 16–17
Institutional settings, dream as
communication, 176–180
Internal object relations,
95–119
course of adolescent
treatment, 102–109
dream as communication,
164–165
mother's relationship,
112–116
prior childhood treatment,
96–102
refinding father, 109–112
termination, 116–119
Interpersonal relationships
development and, 14
dream as communication,
163–164

object relations theory and,
10, 13
Intimacy
adolescent echoes of
parental blocked
development, 305–306
life development perspective
and, 297–298
sexuality and, 139
Introjective identification
family role relationships,
295–296
self recovery (in therapy),
136
transference and
countertransference,
39–44, 53–54
Inventiveness concept,
developmental factors
and, 234
I-to-I relationship. *See*
Eye-to-eye relationship

Jacobs, T. J., 52
Jacques, E., 299
Jessner, L., 6, 7
Jones, E., 14
Joseph, B., 52, 53

Keith, D. V., 275
Kernberg, O., 12, 34, 56
Khan, M. D., 297
Khan, M. M. R., 12
Klein, M., 12, 15, 26, 29,
37–44, 56, 165, 237, 267
Klinnert, M. D., 270
Kohut, H., 12, 13, 15, 24, 35,
53

Lachmann, F. M., 12
Levenson, E., 52

Levinson, D. J., 299
Libido, object relations theory
    and, 32–34
Lichtenberg, J., 12, 265
Lichtenstein, H., 43, 58
Life development perspective,
    295–306
    adolescent echoes of
        parental blocked
        development, 305–306
    case example of family,
        299–305
    case example of individual,
        298–299
    overview of, 295–298
Loewald, H. W., 12, 42

Mann, Thomas, 4,7
Marital therapy, dream
    analysis in, 183–206. See
    also Dream analysis (in
    marital therapy); Family
    therapy
Maternal–infant relationship
    focused transference and,
        56
    transference and
        countertransference,
        44–45
McDougall, J., 52, 138
Meltzer, D., 39
Memory, 121–133
    adolescent memory, 129–130
    adult memory, 130–133
    childhood memory, 127–129
    earliest memory, 123–127
    overview of, 121–122
Mitchell, S. A., 12, 13, 15, 34,
    49
Modell, A., 12
Money-Kyrle, R., 12, 51

Mothering. See also Fathering;
    Parenting
    family role relationships,
        264–265. See also Family
        role relationships
    internal object relations,
        112–116
    Oedipus situation and,
        234–238
Muir, R., 275
Muslin, H., 56

Narcissism, Oedipus and, 246,
    247

Object and self. See Self and
    object intertwined
Object relations
    adolescence and, 207–208
    within family, dream as
        communication, 164–165
    infancy and, 9–10
    self recovery (in therapy),
        136
    of therapist, 309–318. See also
        Therapist's object
        relations
Object relations theory
    dream as communication
        and, 161–162
    interpersonal relationships,
        10
    psychoanalysis contrasted,
        11
    therapist's growth in
        therapeutic relationship
        and, 337–339
    transference and
        countertransference,
        30–37
Oedipus situation, 233–262

dramatic description,
239–248
family case example, 249–262
infant's invention of family,
234–238
discovery, 234–235
growth, 235
new ways of seeing,
236–238
regressive invention,
235–236
internal couple, 238–239
overview of, 233–234
Ogden, T. H., 12, 24, 34, 35,
39, 41, 43, 52, 137, 162,
164, 267, 296

Palombo, S. R., 161
Paranoid/schizoid positions,
transference and
countertransference, 37–39
Parenting. See also Fathering;
Mothering
family role relationships
and, 265–266. See also
Family role relationships
focused transference and, 56
homosexual etiology and,
138, 139
maternal–infant relationship,
transference and
countertransference,
44–45
object relations theory and,
36–37
paranoid/schizoid and
depressive positions
(Klein), 38–39
self within object and, 16–17
therapeutic relationship
compared, 18

Patient–therapist relationship.
See Therapeutic
relationship
Perversions, object relations
theory and, 34
Projective identification
dream as communication,
165
self recovery (in therapy),
136
transference and
countertransference,
39–44, 53–54
Psychoanalysis
development of, 12–13
dream analysis and, 181–182
life development perspective
and, 296
memory and, 123
origins of, 10–11
Psychosomatic partnership,
maternal–infant
relationship and, 44

Racker, H., 51, 52, 58
Regressive invention, Oedipus
situation, infant's
invention of family,
235–236
Reiss, D., 132
Repression, memory and,
123–124
Reverie, projective
identification and, 41
Role relationships. See Family
role relationships

Sameroff, A. J., 265
Sandler, J., 52

Scharff, D. E., 17, 31, 34, 53, 54, 56, 58, 184, 234, 249, 277, 295, 296, 299

Scharff, J. S., 17, 30, 31, 34, 43, 48, 53, 54, 56, 58, 69, 70, 71, 184, 234, 239, 249, 277, 295

Schizophrenia, developmental factors and, 24

Screen memory. *See* Memory

Searles, H. F., 12, 24, 52, 168, 329

Segal, H., 39, 41, 53, 165

Self
  adolescence, changing internal object relations in, 95
  ego contrasted, 35

Self and object intertwined, 9–27
  case example from couple therapy, 19–23
  inextricability of relationship, 14–16
  life development perspective, 295–306. *See also* Life development perspective
  object within self, 25–26
  Oedipus situation and, 233–234
  psychoanalytic framework and, 9–14
  self and object, 23–25
  self and object mutually held, 26–27
  self within object, 16–18
  therapeutic implications
    case example, 319–328
    termination of therapy and, 329–336
    therapeutic goals and, 328–329

Self psychology, term usage, 26

Self recovery (in therapy), 135–153
  case example, 137–150
  overview of, 135–137
  resilient self construction, 149–152
  therapist's self and, 152–153

Separation–individuation, adolescence and, 207–208

Sexual abuse
  memory and, 123–124
  Oedipus and, 242

Sexuality
  adolescent echoes of parental blocked development, 305–306
  intimacy and, 139
  Oedipus situation and, 237–238
  transference and counter-transference use, 84–93

Shapiro, R. L., 12, 165

Siblings, life development perspective and, 297

Slipp, S., 34

Socarides, C. W., 34

Sociocultural communication, dream as communication, 180–182

Sorce, J. F., 270

Steiner, J., 39, 328

Stenberg, C., 270

Stern, D., 12, 15, 265, 266

Stolorow, R. D., 12, 13, 53

Sullivan, H. S., 12

Supervision, therapist's object relations and, 309–310. *See also* Therapist's object relations

Sutherland, J. D., 12, 15, 24,
    25, 27, 31, 32, 35, 37

Terr, L. C., 124
Therapeutic alliance,
    contextual and focused
    transference, 55
Therapeutic relationship
    contextual and focused
        transference, 54-57
    dream as communication,
        166-172
    family role relationships
        and, 291-293
    parenting compared, 18
    self recovery (in therapy),
        152-153
    self within object and, 18
    therapist's growth and,
        337-339
    transference and
        countertransference in,
        30, 49-50, 57-58
Therapist's object relations,
    309-318
    family case histories
        illustrating, 310-314
    overview of, 309-310
    personal life history of
        therapist, 314-317
    vulnerability and learning,
        317-318
Tower, L., 51
Transference. See also
    Countertransference;
    Transference and
    countertransference
    dream analysis and, 4-5
    dream as communication,
        166

Transference and
    countertransference, 29-65
    case example, 59-65
    conjoint therapy and,
        58-59
    contextual and focused
        transference, 54-57
    current view of, 53-54
    maternal-infant relationship
        (Winnicott), 44-45
    object relations theory
        (Fairbairn), 30-37
    paranoid/schizoid and
        depressive positions
        (Klein), 37-39
    projective and introjective
        identification (Klein),
        39-44
    therapeutic process and,
        49-50
    therapeutic relationship and,
        57-58
    true and false self
        (Winnicott), 45-47
Transference and
    countertransference use,
    69-94
    case example, self recovery
        (in therapy), 140
    clarifications of envy and
        sexuality, 84-93
    co-therapy and
        countertransference,
        93-94
    enacting co-therapy
        countertransference,
        75-78
    initial stages in, 71-75
    self recovery (in therapy),
        136
    working through, 78-84

Transitional space
  container/contained
    phenomena reconciled
    with, 47–49
  maternal–infant relationship
    and, 45
Tronick, E., 267
True and false self,
  transference and
  countertransference, 45–47
Tustin, F., 35, 39

Unconscious
  dream as communication,
    165
  projective and introjective
    identification and, 42,
    53–54

VanDeusen, J. M., 53
Virag, R., 141
Volkan, V. D., 34

Whitaker, C. A., 275
Williams, A. H., 53
Winnicott, D. W., 12, 15, 17, 24,
    25, 29, 30, 36, 44–49, 51,
    54, 56, 136, 147, 234, 267
Wittig, B., 269
Working alliance, contextual
    and focused transference,
    55
Wright, K., 15, 24

Zetzel, E., 47, 55
Zinner, J., 12, 165